# LABOUR AND POLITICAL TRANSFORMATION IN RUSSIA AND UKRAINE

*To the memory of my father, Helmut Erwin Simon*

# Labour and Political Transformation in Russia and Ukraine

RICK SIMON
*The Nottingham Trent University*

Routledge
Taylor & Francis Group
LONDON AND NEW YORK

First published 2000 by Ashgate Publishing

Reissued 2019 by Routledge
2 Park Square, Milton Park, Abingdon, Oxon, OX14 4RN
52 Vanderbilt Avenue, New York, NY 10017

*Routledge is an imprint of the Taylor & Francis Group, an informa business*



A Library of Congress record exists under LC control number:

ISBN 13: 978-1-138-73216-2 (hbk)
ISBN 13: 978-1-138-73214-8 (pbk)
ISBN 13: 978-1-315-18860-7 (ebk)

# Contents

# List of Tables

# Preface

This book began life in 1990 as a doctoral dissertation at the University of Birmingham's Centre for Russian and East European Studies (CREES). The PhD was originally envisaged as a comparison of the emerging workers' movements in the Kuzbass and Donbass regions of the Soviet Union. However, before I had done little more than some background research on the relationship between workers and the Soviet state, the latter had disintegrated and the objects of my research were now located in two, newly-independent states. I had also become increasingly dissatisfied with the focus of mainstream democratisation literature on the role of elites and domestic factors in promoting political transformation and felt that this underplayed the interrelationship of domestic and global processes, as well as denigrating the role played by popular forces in undermining authoritarian regimes and promoting a democratic alternative. My thesis, therefore, transmuted into a more synthetic approach to the question of the labour's role in democratisation processes, utilising the collapse of the USSR and the subsequent evolution of Russia and Ukraine as case studies. The originality of both the Phd and this book lies, I hope, in the discussion of the global context of political change and of the role played by workers in the transformation of the Soviet Union.

I have used the transliteration system usually applied in the United Kingdom with the exception of names that have become accepted under a certain spelling, for example Trotsky and Yeltsin. To avoid any confusion, all Ukrainian place names have been transliterated from the Ukrainian versions operative since independence even when this applies to the Soviet period.

I would like to acknowledge the help of the following people in the writing of this book (with the usual caveat that they bear no responsibility whatsoever for its final form): Judy Batt, Vadim Borisov, Kirill Buketov, Simon Clarke, Boris Kagarlitsky, Arfon Rees, Sheffield Trades Council, Serge and Larissa, and my colleagues in the department of Economics and Politics at Nottingham Trent University, especially my great friend, Larry Wilde, who has provided unstinting support and encouragement throughout my academic career. I would also like to thank Sandra Odell for her administrative assistance. I am grateful to Nottingham Trent University for providing funds for me to travel to Russia and Ukraine to undertake research.

I would finally like to dedicate this book to my dad, for introducing me to the joys of the Eastern bloc, to my partner Tina, for introducing me to many other joys of life, and to our daughter, Dora, for being a joy and a barmy distraction from the pressures of academic work.

# 1 Labour and Political Change in the Global Political Economy

## Introduction

The final quarter of the twentieth century was characterised by fundamental changes in the global political landscape. On one hand, an unprecedented shift occurred from authoritarian regimes to forms of liberal democracy in various regions of the world. Perhaps of greatest significance, the so-called 'communist' regimes of the USSR and Eastern Europe collapsed, ending the Cold War and seemingly putting an end to communism as an ideological force. The scale of this transformation was sufficient for it to be called a 'global democratic revolution' (Diamond 1993) or, in Samuel Huntington's phrase, the 'third wave' of democratisation, the first two 'waves' having occurred in the late 19th and early 20th centuries and after World War II (Huntington 1991).

Such dramatic changes of course present a challenge to political scientists in terms of analysing their causes, the social forces behind them and their future prospects. As a consequence, studies of democratisation have constituted perhaps the most extensive literature in political science over the past 15 years. Geoffrey Pridham argues that two basic approaches to the analysis of democratic transitions have developed: the 'functionalist' or 'macro-oriented' school and the 'genetic' or 'micro-oriented' school (Pridham 1994, p.16). The former approach is undoubtedly linked to 'modernisation' theory, which states basically that all societies undergo a process of development, following the lead established by the more advanced capitalist states, and that as a result of attaining a more complex industrial society the prerequisites emerge for the establishment of liberal democracy. Thus, democratisation is linked fundamentally to long-term processes of capitalist development. The latter perspective, on the other hand, can be said to possess the following basic features: first, 'the reasons for launching a transition can be found predominantly in domestic, internal factors' (O'Donnell 1986, p.18); second, the motor force behind these transitions has, in almost all cases, been ascribed to elites of one kind or another rather than to popular action: 'elite dispositions, calculations and pacts' '*largely determine* whether or not an opening [to democracy] will occur *at all*' (O'Donnell & Schmitter, pp.19, 48); finally, the assumption is made, sometimes explicitly, sometimes implicitly, that pressure for radical social change to accompany democratisation endangers the whole transition project and threatens a resumption of authoritarian rule, thus creating a particularly narrow vision of what constitutes democracy. Whereas modernisation theory was very influential in the late 1950s and early 1960s, and gained fresh impetus in the 1980s, the pendulum among analysts has swung over the past ten years away from modernisation theorists, with their emphasis on the prerequisites of democracy, to those who concentrate on the *process* and *techniques* of democratisation itself (Shin).

Even critics of O'Donnell and Schmitter, the foremost proponents of the 'genetic' approach, have agreed with these emphases. Daniel Levine has argued that 'elements such as effective leadership, organizational strength, deliberate consensus building, and close attention to institutionalization' have been central to democratic transition and consolidation. He suggests, moreover, that 'creative and committed political actors have repeatedly underscored the centrality of national-level politics, countering deterministic expectations according to which national patterns are ineluctably set by the play of global or regional forces' (Levine, pp.377-8).

In an effort to steer a middle course between the 'functionalist' and 'genetic' approaches, Samuel Huntington argues on the one hand, in classical modernisationist fashion, that democratisation is promoted by the complex society produced by a broad-based industrial development (Bernhard, p.52), and that '[a]n overall correlation exists between economic development and democracy' (Huntington 1991, p.59). But, on the other hand, he qualifies this position by suggesting that 'no level or pattern of economic development is in itself either necessary or sufficient to bring about democracy' (ibid). Huntington then attempts to blend this view with some of the more recent arguments advanced by analysts of democratisation, which view democracy 'more as a product of strategic interactions and arrangements among political elites, conscious choices among various types of democratic constitutions, and electoral and party systems' (Shin, p.139). Gerardo Munck suggests that this amalgam is unsatisfactory and theoretically eclectic, making too clean a separation between the economic, social and cultural factors creating the breakdown of regimes and the role of actors in the transition process itself (p.357).

The emphasis on the positive role of actors in the transition process does have its attractions, including for those on the left, for whom to paraphrase Marx, 'men and women make their own history'. It is also claimed both by supporters and detractors of this approach that the perspective highlighting 'voluntarist' as opposed to 'deterministic' features of transition has emerged from the critical theory tradition. Whereas Marx did say that 'men make their own history', he also added the rider that they do so 'not under circumstances they themselves have chosen but under the given and inherited circumstances with which they are directly confronted' (Marx 1973 [1852], p.146). This does not mean that outcomes are predetermined but that there exist certain constraints, differing between societies and over time, on the range of alternative outcomes. Analysing outcomes thus depends on an investigation of how global and local processes interact to produce the *specific* circumstances in which change takes place. The false counterposition of national to international, political to economic, elite to masses produces an outcome which is both ideological (while claiming to be objective) and profoundly conservative (while claiming to be radical). As Ellen Wood has argued, the analytical distinction between economics and politics is the natural outcome of the seeming division in capitalist society between an economic sphere (the 'economy') and a political sphere (the 'state') which disguises the fact that both spheres are aspects of the social relations of production (Wood, pp.19-36). Furthermore, Karen Remmer contends that, by emphasising the autonomous role of leadership and the national basis of change, the voluntarist approach 'comes perilously close to the rejection of all theory in the conventional social science sense of the word.' By focusing on short-term processes of regime transition, she suggests that:

> the past and future of competitive institutions ... are not linked to shifts in the international economy, class structure, social institutions, or political attitudes and consciousness. Rather, democratic political outcomes are seen to depend upon the choices of particular political elites and specific historical conjunctures. In short, politics is stripped from its social moorings and explained principally in terms of *virtù* and *fortuna* (1991, p.483).

Over the past 10 years, the collapse of communism has presented democratisation theory with new opportunities to expand the scope of its analysis, leading to the emergence of a new sub-discipline, 'transitology', to replace the redundant Sovietology (Markwick). For some political scientists the changes in Eastern Europe 'offer a tempting opportunity to incorporate (at long last) the study of these countries within the general corpus of comparative analysis' (Schmitter & Karl, p.177). For Russell Bova they hold out the promise of a 'generalized theory of postauthoritarian transitions' (Bova 1991a, pp.136-7). In promoting an alternative perspective to that of mainstream democratisation theory, I argue that the application of democratisation theory to Eastern Europe and the USSR fails to provide an adequate framework for the analysis of these momentous changes. This is not to say that comparisons cannot be made but that both strands of democratisation theory fail to see the whole picture. In this chapter I will outline an alternative method, the starting point of which is a state's relationship to the global political economy which is crucial to an understanding of both the origins and breakdown of authoritarian regimes; second, I argue that, as a consequence of the contradictions of authoritarianism, civil society in general and labour in particular can play a significant role in the transition to democracy. In pursuing this argument I will first examine the emergence of authoritarian regimes in the promotion of industrialisation strategies and the general factors behind the crisis of authoritarianism after 1974. I will then discuss the historical relationship between labour and democratisation and the conditions under which labour can contribute to the establishment of democratic political systems. Finally, I will discuss the ways in which these two elements have interacted to produce specific transitions to democracy in Southern Europe and Latin America. This analysis will be extended in subsequent chapters to the specific conditions of the Soviet Union, and then to the processes of political transformation in post-communist Russia and Ukraine. In a concluding chapter I will discuss the collapse of communism in general, the applicability of democratisation theory, and some scenarios of potential development.

## Structural Power and Dependent Industrialisation

The global economy is characterised by extreme inequality, not simply of natural resource endowments, but also of productive capacity and financial resources. To use the terminology of world systems theory, the world economy is divided into a 'core' of capitalist states, comprising most of Western Europe, North America and Japan, in which economic power is concentrated, a 'periphery' of underdeveloped states (conventionally referred to as the Third World), and a 'semi-periphery'. Both periphery and semi-periphery display varying degrees of *combined and uneven development* in which the most advanced features of capitalism are intertwined with pre-capitalist and outmoded capitalist forms of production (Trotsky 1977; Löwy) so that the 'national peculiarities' of each state 'represent an original combination of the basic features of the world process' (Trotsky 1969, p.147). Because of this imbalance, relationships between states are highly structured, the power lying with those who 'shape and determine the structures of the global political economy within which other states, their political institutions, their economic enterprises and (not least) their scientists and other professional people have to operate' (Strange, pp.24-5).

This power structure originated with the development of colonial domination during the eighteenth and nineteenth centuries, a process which enabled core states to industrialise rapidly and reinforce their position within the global political economy. Decolonisation, particularly after World War II, has not fundamentally altered this picture but shifted the exercise of power from a relational to a structural pattern. This structure has been dominated by the United States, which emerged from the war as the hegemonic power in the international capitalist economy. Under its aegis, an unprecedented expansion of the global economy occurred, institutionally underpinned by arrangements made in 1944 at Bretton Woods, through which fixed exchange rates were set between the US dollar and other currencies, and the International Monetary Fund (IMF), World Bank and subsequently GATT were established. The long post-war boom provided the basis for the liberalisation of markets, the funding of domestic welfare states, and the space and opportunity for some Third World industrialisation (Mandel, E. 1975; Armstrong, Glyn et al.; Keohane; Cox; Martin).

Peripheral and semi-peripheral states have pursued a variety of strategies to try and overcome these structural disadvantages and achieve the levels of development associated with the core states. At their most basic level these strategies have either been a variant of the Soviet model, in which the state strictly controls relations with the global capitalist system and pursues a non-capitalist path, or they have pursued a capitalist path with varying mixes of state, domestic and foreign capital. The capitalist path has itself divided into two further orientations: either import-substituting industrialisation (ISI) or export-oriented industrialisation (EOI), although it would be erroneous to view these strategies as mutually exclusive, some states utilising one or other at different stages of development.

In line with these postulates I will argue in this chapter that it is not coincidental that the current 'wave' of breakdowns of authoritarian regimes began with the end of the postwar boom and consequent crisis of international capitalism, which was accentuated by massive increases in oil prices in the mid-1970s. The end of the favourable economic conditions of the post-war period threw into crisis the industrialisation strategies pursued by Third World states, while the billions of surplus dollars generated in the oil-producing states and lodged with Western banks seemed to offer an opportunity to renew industrialisation through massive borrowing. Unfortunately for the many states who borrowed money in the late 1970s the crisis in the West meant that the terms of trade had turned against them, while interest rates determined by the US Federal Reserve rose rapidly, provoking an unprecedented global debt crisis.

The crisis of global capitalism also resulted in the collapse of the Keynesian consensus, which had underpinned postwar political and economic arrangements, prompting the search for renewed stability. The United States was striving to reestablish its hegemony through new mechanisms of control in the global economy, prompting an ideological shift in advanced Western states towards neo-liberalism (Gowan). Promoted in particular by the Reagan administration and Thatcher governments, this orientation had two prime components: first, to establish the dominance of US financial institutions and the dollar (what Gowan terms the 'Dollar-Wall Street Regime') by opening up domestic markets to US penetration and the increased use of flexible production; second, to make the US dominant in military / security terms following the debacle of the Vietnam War by undertaking a major ideological and military offensive against the USSR and the concept of 'socialism'. This strategy had profound political ramifications. In order to establish regimes susceptible to external as well as internal influence and capable of carrying through programmes of structural adjustment, that is economic liberalisation, 'democracy' (i.e. liberal democracy) was increasingly advocated as the most desirable political form of the state.

In Latin America ISI became the dominant model employed to try and break the cycle of dependency. It was facilitated by the greater autonomy afforded the new regimes in pursuing an industrialisation strategy because of the economic crisis and world war which engulfed the advanced capitalist world in the 1930s and early 1940s. Malloy argues that the 'Great Depression [of the 1930s] was a watershed ... that shaped a number of key and recurring problems in the region's political economy' (p.238). These problems were essentially the need to establish a model of successful economic development, replacing the previously predominant export model; the need to establish viable institutions, incorporating new social actors, especially labour, into the political process; and, finally, the formation of viable ruling coalitions to accomplish the first two elements (ibid). In pursuance of these goals most Latin American countries 'experienced demonstrable cyclical shifts between authoritarian and democratic modes of government' usually because of the failure of the previous regime (pp.238-9). The ability of any regime to solve these problems was severely constrained, however, 'by the region's dependent position in the international capitalist system' (p.239).

An earlier phase of industrial development had advanced urbanisation and the development of an urban working class which shifted the political landscape in favour of a populist coalition promoting industrialisation and an expansion of the domestic market (O'Donnell 1979, p.54). Labour was integrated in a corporatist fashion into a 'clientilistic bureaucratic framework' in which, Malloy argues, political power was traded for 'particularistic economic benefits' and broad-based participation was subordinated to 'access to the central mechanisms that control the flow of particular benefits and privileges'. Consequently, labour leaders were frequently less predisposed to promote democratic institutions and the strategy of organised labour was not one of revolutionary opposition to the regime but 'one demanding an entree into the existing political game' (pp.240-1). Korzeniewicz suggests, however, that populist reforms were not just about incorporation but redistributed power in favour of organised labour, strengthening its ability to make effective demands (p.216). This point is reinforced by O'Donnell's comment that despite, or perhaps because of, their incorporation, union organisations grew in strength, increasing their influence (1979, p.56). As a consequence of this influence Collier and Collier argue that 'genuine populism ... was not a static or equilibrium condition but contained within it a political dynamic and contradiction that made it unstable' (p.197).

From the outset the ISI model was beset by contradictions: labour was integrated but the traditionally dominant export sector was pushed to one side while high tariff barriers were erected. Nevertheless, the export sector had to be kept sweet and continued to exert a disproportionate influence as the sole source of the foreign currency earnings crucial for the implementation of populist policies (O'Donnell 1979, p.55). Another problem of Latin American industrialisation was that it relied on extensive rather than intensive growth, was very expensive, and dependent on continued imports of intermediate and capital goods as well as technology to foster domestic industry. While the export sector continued to provide currency, and domestic industry continued to expand, the populist coalition could hold together (ibid, p.56). The euphoria of escaping from dependent development was, however, short-lived. The limits of extensive growth were soon reached and '[i]mport substitution proved to be an import-intensive activity', resulting in a chronic shortage of foreign exchange which 'has been at the core of many of the [Latin American] countries' economic problems' (ibid, p.58).

The shift to intensive growth could not be achieved by domestic efforts alone, raising the spectre of lowering tariff barriers and allowing an influx of foreign companies, thus increasing dependence and driving domestic, labour-intensive industries out of business, creating mass unemployment (ibid, pp.60-66). As austerity measures were implemented to cope with rising inflation, the popular sector became increasingly detached from the regime, producing demands for a more radical transformation of society. This, in turn, generated demands from industrial sectors for the exclusion of the popular sector. These factors coupled with the recent experience of the Cuban Revolution and US preparedness to support regimes against 'subversion' precipitated military coups in Brazil in 1964 and Argentina in 1966 (ibid, pp.67-70). 'Bureaucratic-authoritarian' regimes in Brazil, Uruguay, Argentina and Chile, 'from the outset follow[ed] antipopulist development strategies' designed 'to break the power of organized labor and push it out of the political process' (Malloy, p.245). In Ecuador, Peru and Bolivia, the new authoritarian regimes began with a populist phase but ended up in an antipopulist mode (ibid). While initially supported by all sectors of the economic elite, the military regimes became increasingly alienated from their original base and dependent on civilian technocrats, foreign capital and export-oriented sectors (Rueschemeyer, et al., pp.211-212). This dependence on foreign capital did, however, facilitate the regimes' access to loans with which to bolster economic performance and enhance regime legitimacy.

The origins of the Portuguese and Spanish authoritarian regimes bear some resemblance to those of populist regimes in Latin America in the 1930s and 1940s. While both were historically long-standing imperialist powers, their heyday predated the development of industrial capitalism. Consequently, the Portuguese and Spanish economies in the twentieth century can at best be described as examples of *semiperipheral* development, faced with many of the problems associated with late industrialisation. As in Latin America the insecurity fostered by economic crisis and unemployment in the 1930s generated a climate conducive to protectionism and isolationism, which assisted the regimes in resisting international economic pressures and promoting a strategy of slow but steady economic growth (Diamandouros, pp.145-6).

Under Franco, Spain attempted to overcome dependent development by following a 'Prussian' economic model in which banks and finance capital predominated over industrial capital, and capital formation was promoted through the state holding company, the National Industrial Institute (INI) (Maravall). By the late 1950s, however, the original Francoist model of development was in crisis, demanding the adoption of a new economic model. The result was the implementation of an ISI strategy requiring greater economic integration into the global capitalist economy via involvement in the IMF, World Bank, and OECD (Lopez, p.29). Foreign capital was imported, and the problem of increasing unemployment was 'solved' by exporting workers to the EEC and Switzerland whence their remittances proved a valuable source of finance for further development (Story & Pollack, p.129). As a consequence, Spain's predominantly rural and agricultural economy and associated social structure were rapidly transformed into a primarily industrial and urban society, experiencing growth rates of seven percent per annum during the 1960s (Maravall & Santamaria, p.74).

In Greece, the development of capitalism was conditioned by Greece's peripheral relationship to Europe. The Greek diaspora bourgeoisie, rather than the weak indigenous bourgeoisie, played a crucial role as intermediary between core and periphery, channelling resources into the mainland and funding the development of a top-heavy state and mercantile and financial sectors (Mouzelis, p.62). Increasing social unrest, resulting from growing economic difficulties, prompted the Colonels to seize power in 1967 in order to bring the situation under control (Mouzelis, p.70; Diamandouros, p.149).

## The End of the Postwar Boom, Debt Crisis and Neoliberalism

By the late 1960s, global capitalism was losing its dynamism and heading for recession and the United States, cornerstone of the postwar system, was tied up in the Vietnam War, a venture costly in both economic and political terms. The collapse of the post-war order was signalled by the US's decision to suspend dollar/gold convertibility in 1971 and the move to floating exchange rates with other currencies by 1973 (Armstrong, Glyn et al. 1984, pp.291-294). The other institutions established at Bretton Woods remained but with no clearly defined role. The end of the postwar boom signified not only the crisis of Keynesian growth and welfare strategies in advanced capitalist countries, but also the crisis of industrialisation strategies in many Third World states.

The collapse of the global economic order was then exacerbated by an energy crisis caused by the decision of oil-rich states grouped in the OPEC cartel to utilise their oligopolistic position to raise oil prices. The fourfold oil price rises between 1974-75 had a differential impact on developing countries. Small oil-producing states benefitted most, obtaining revenues beyond the capacity of the state to utilise them efficiently, creating small groups of extremely wealthy people; larger oil states such as Nigeria and Indonesia were not so lucky, remaining dependent on core states to promote industrialisation (Cammack, et al., p.302); some OPEC revenues were recycled in the form of aid to non-oil producing Arab states, or took the form of receipts repatriated by migrant workers brought in by smaller states because of the shortage of domestic labour (ibid, p.301). The most significant consequence, however, was that the import capacity of most Third World states was dramatically reduced, creating a demand for substantial loans to keep development projects going. The result was that the Third World itself became increasingly divided and differentiated between those experiencing strong economic growth and thus able to defend basic living standards and those subjected to the full force of adjustment (Walton & Seddon, pp.10-11). As 'luck' would have it private Western banks were becoming awash with money derived from the massive revenues being generated by OPEC states and were only too willing to loan it to governments in the Third World and Eastern Europe. In a period of high inflation, the banks ensured that they gained advantage from these loans through the use of variable interest rates, and by spreading the risks through syndication (O'Brien, p.88). O'Brien suggests that '[i]n retrospect the real origins of the debt problem probably lie in the decision to recycle the OPEC surpluses through private banks' (ibid).

Third World debt multiplied during the 1970s: borrowing was undertaken at a level far higher than earning capacity on the understanding that 'governments don't go bankrupt' so that servicing the debt required new borrowing (Cammack, et al., p.304). By the late 1970s, however, the banks were becoming wary of lending to potentially bad risks; loans were therefore made over a shorter period and were increasingly trade-related (Corbridge 1993a, p.36). The level of debt was accentuated by two other factors: first, US interest rates, which had averaged 6.7 percent between 1970 and 1973, averaged 15.5 percent between 1979 and 1982 after Paul Volcker became Chairman of the Federal Reserve Board and began to implement monetarist policies, tightening the money supply (ibid, pp.37-

38); second, the terms of trade for non-oil primary products took a sharp downturn worsening the terms of trade by 35 percent between 1980 and 1982. This was accentuated by increases in the cost of oil and decreased demand for exports due to protectionist measures. According to the World Bank '[f]rom 1970 to 1984, the total external indebtedness of developing countries rose from $64 billion to $686 billion, with the proportion of that debt owing to private banks rising from one-third to over one-half'(Walton & Seddon, p.14).

The debt crisis surfaced in 1982 when Mexico threatened to default and suddenly private lending dried up. Walton and Seddon suggest that 'the international debt crisis signaled a watershed in relations between the developed and developing countries: western banks now became less concerned with pouring capital into developing countries than with recovering their existing debts' (p.16). In the first 6 months of the debt crisis a powerful creditors' cartel was created which comprised private banks, creditor governments, IMF, and the formal machinery of the Paris Club within which government-government credits are negotiated. Each debt was dealt with on a strictly case-by-case basis so that each debtor was on its own faced by a powerful cartel of creditors (O'Brien, p.94). The hardening attitude towards Third World debt was a consequence of the shift in US thinking in the direction of neo-liberalism in the late 1970s. The US now pursued a two-pronged strategy, designed to re-establish its hegemony, following both the end of the postwar boom and the military debacle in Vietnam.

Reagan tripled US foreign debt in an economic offensive designed to transfer the costs of recovery onto the USSR and developing countries, and to revitalise the Bretton Woods institutions - the International Monetary Fund (IMF) and World Bank - as instruments with which to discipline debtor states by adopting austerity measures and implementing policies to liberalise and privatise their economies. While the IMF itself does not command huge financial resources its role became 'that of messenger, watchdog, international alibi and *gendarme* for those who do hold financial power' (George, p.47). Its policing was done in the name of the need for efficiency and economic growth barely disguising the ideological content of the message which viewed neo-liberal solutions as the only viable ones. The strategy of the IMF and World Bank, whose roles became increasingly intertwined, changed to one of 'structural adjustment'. The rationale of this strategy is simple, if not simplistic:

The system is stable and when left to itself tends towards dynamic equilibrium

> and growth. For states or international organisations to intervene in the system is to risk outcomes which are third-best and worse. The correct course of action is for the creditor powers to advise or pressure debtor nations to adjust their economies to a changing open market economy (that is, to cut public spending and boost exports), and to trust to the markets to make appropriate judgements about the value of debts outstanding (in the secondary markets, by debt-equity swaps and through case-by-case writedowns). In due course a resumption of voluntary bank lending to debtor nations can be expected. The ex-debtor nations will then resume their ascent of the ladder of development, taking their place in a new world economy in transition (Corbridge 1993b, pp.33-34).

'Structural adjustment loans' (SALs) were made available to those states 'prepared to undertake a programme of adjustment to meet an existing or to avoid an impending balance of payments crisis' and became increasingly employed as a means of manipulating the economic policies of recipient states. Conditionality was imposed to enable the borrower to remove what the lender saw as fundamental policy-induced obstacles to economic recovery and growth rather than to maximize the probability of repayment of the loan (Walton & Seddon, pp.17-18). As IMF and World Bank policies became more co-ordinated in the late 1980s, borrowing from one institution increasingly required lending from the other creating a cross-conditionality. Other external financial institutions would then fall in line with those conditions creating a straitjacket on the borrowing state, which had a major impact on savings and investment, and government budgets (O'Brien, p.95). As Walton and Seddon correctly point out this is not simply an economic question but one which has 'direct political implications ... not only restricting the room for maneuver for governments but giving explicit support to those within the country whose interests coincide with those of the IMF and the Bank' (p.19). It would thus be an error to see 'structural adjustment' as a purely one-way imposition of policies on a dependent state; significant sectors of Third World capitalism benefit from austerity and the worsening of workers' living standards.

The United States devised two 'plans' for dealing with the debt crisis. The first of these, the Baker Plan, was formulated in 1985. This aimed to secure 'adjustment with growth' by channelling extra credit to a small number of highly indebted states mainly in Latin America. The 'Baker Plan' was not however a success 'principally because of the reluctance of the commercial bankers to lend more to the indebted countries' (Riley, p.12). The second, the Brady Plan, or 'suggestions' as it was subsequently referred to by the US administration, was announced on 11 March 1989 after widespread riots in Venezuela, triggered by the government's proposal to lift subsidies on a number of basic goods to win the IMF's agreement to a US$4.8 billion loan, resulted in the deaths of 246 people (O'Brien, pp.85-6). The Plan sought to reduce the debt burden of middle income debtors by making available additional credit in the period to 1992. Assistance was provided in return for an IMF / World Bank adjustment programme (Riley, p.13).

The polarisation of the postwar world into two basic blocs had led the US to support regimes which defended its interests in the name of anti-communism, regardless of their democratic credentials and human rights' records. Jimmy Carter introduced the concept of human rights into the bargaining with the USSR during the period of detente but this was transcended in the early 1980s by the Reagan administration. In a speech to the British Parliament, Reagan announced a 'Crusade for Democracy' designed to promote democratic institutions in other states. A National Endowment for Democracy was subsequently established to pursue this aim on a permanent basis (Huntington 1984, p.193). This did not represent a fundamental reassessment of the moral worth of repressive regimes, but was part of an aggressive foreign policy against revolution (particularly in respect of Cuba, Nicaragua and Grenada) and designed to undermine the USSR economically (Gills, et al., p.9). The establishment of liberal democracies would facilitate the liberalisation of the global economy and create regimes receptive to US influence, while being only nominally accountable to their own electorates.

## Labour and Democratisation

The emphasis of much of the current democratisation literature on elites has led to a downplaying if not outright ignoring of the contribution made by non-elite actors, especially organised labour. According to Adler and Webster, 'transition writers neglect the role of labor movements as important actors in transitions' and that 'by undervaluing the capacity for innovation and the strategic use of power by social movements, the literature overlooks actors with extremely important influence over the transition' (p.76). Valenzuela reinforces this point, albeit from a position which tends to view labour as subordinate to elite actors, by arguing that 'labor movements and other popular sectors can unwittingly either facilitate or impede change towards democracy by helping to tip the political scales within the ruling circles one way or the other' (p.446).

Labour, however, 'occupies a special place among the forces of civil society ... [and] should not be discussed simply on the same plane with other segments of society' (ibid, p.447).

The current preoccupation with the interplay between different elements of the elite is at odds with the centrality of social class to the analysis of democratisation in earlier periods. Stephens notes that there have been two fundamentally different views of the driving force behind this process: the first, associated with Marx and subsequent Marxist writers, argues that the working class has been key (see Therborn for example). From this point of view, the proletariat represents an historic class, the bearers of a new mode of production, which must be established in order to end capitalist exploitation. While the achievement of socialism requires that the working class becomes conscious of its historical role, the nature of capitalist exploitation forces workers to organise and act collectively even if the demands they pursue centre around the betterment of their conditions rather than their overthrow. Moreover, the working class has not confined itself to economic demands but, as it has grown and become organised it has sought to promote the democratisation of society, thereby achieving its inclusion in the political process. The second view accords primacy to the bourgeoisie; as Barrington Moore famously expressed it: 'no bourgeois, no democracy' (p.418). Moore's argument revolved around the need for the rising bourgeoisie to assert its political power against the remnants of the feudal aristocracy. Stephens concedes that under certain conditions, for example the proletariat's lack of political organisation especially in Britain and France, the bourgeoisie could promote greater suffrage for its own advantage. Across western Europe, however, organised labour played a much more significant role than Moore's argument suggests. Stephens notes that by 1914, 'European labor movements, all members of the Second International, had converged on an ideology that placed the achievement of universal suffrage and parliamentary government at the center of their immediate program' (pp.421-2). Furthermore, between the wars, the bourgeoisie, in conjunction with other social groups, was a major force for the restoration or installation of authoritarian regimes in the face of working-class opposition (for example, in Italy, Austria, Germany, Spain). In the first wave of capitalist industrialisation, therefore, organised labour represented a rapidly growing and sizeable part of society able to exercise considerable influence over the democratisation of political institutions.

When examining the capacity for the working class in societies of dependent industrialisation to promote democratisation it is important not to assume a simple repetition of the experiences of the late nineteenth and early twentieth centuries. As we have already discussed, these societies are not following the path already pioneered by advanced capitalism, but have had to try and develop strategies for capital accumulation in a structurally subordinate position. This has had inevitable consequences for labour: in particular, industrial workers might not constitute a majority of society, they might not be well-organised, they might be dependent on the state or severely repressed. How workers are organised and their relationship to the state appear to be crucial to the capacity of labour to pursue a strategy of democratisation. Eva Bellin argues that the role played by the state in dependent industrialisation, potentially supporting both private capital and unions (through corporatist arrangements), can lead to a situation where neither labour nor the bourgeoisie need necessarily favour the introduction of democracy for fear of undermining their perceived interests. Support for democratisation thus becomes contingent on the degree to which the material interests of either or both parties are met.

Valenzuela has identified four factors affecting the potential influence of labour in democratisation processes:

- the strength or weakness of the labour movement and the economic context of the transition;
- the centralisation or decentralisation of the labour movement and its unity or division;
- the authoritarian regime's treatment of labour and its political allies prior to redemocratisation;
- the modalities of the transition to democracy and the relationship between the labour movement and the elites guiding the transition (p.452).

The strength or weakness of organised labour during transition depends primarily on the density of union affiliation, especially in key areas of economic activity, and the level of unemployment. Whereas in earlier cases of labour's influence on democratisation the working class constituted a substantial proportion of society, was well-organised in trade unions, had its own political party, and was an element of a rapidly expanding economy, such has not always been the case more recently. Union density, for example, has been low to medium: in Argentina comparatively high at more than 30 percent, but low in the Philippines at 10 percent. In some cases, however, for example Chilean copper miners, high union density in an economically vital sector has compensated for low membership elsewhere (ibid p.453). In all recent cases of democratisation, with one or two partial exceptions, for example South Korea, the economy has been in crisis, provoking unemployment and undermining the strength of organised labour (ibid).

In analysing the role of labour in processes of democratisation, Ruth Collier argues that it is not a question of a minimum percentage of workers being involved but 'whether a group of workers became part of the democratization process as a self-conscious collectivity and played an active role that affected the democratic outcome' (p.15). The degree to which labour played a significant role depends on it being 'engaged in activity that was pro-democratic, that is if it had a democratic agenda' rather than simply protesting around economic conditions (ibid p.16).

## Transitions to Democracy

I have argued that transitions to democracy have occurred in the last quarter of the twentieth century as a consequence of dramatic changes in the global political economy coupled with the activation of sectors of civil society, especially labour. In itself, however, these factors do not provide sufficient explanation as to why transitions occurred how they did, when they did. O'Donnell and Schmitter argue that 'there is no transition whose beginning is not the consequence - direct or indirect - of important divisions within the authoritarian regime itself, principally along the fluctuating cleavage between hard-liners and soft-liners' (O'Donnell & Schmitter, p.19). This assertion is not fundamentally in dispute but it leaves open the question, which Diamond correctly recognises, as to why the split occurs in the first place (Diamond 1993, p.43). Diamond's response is to argue that the regime must first suffer a decline in legitimacy and/or a decline in access to its coercive or material resources (ibid). The loss of legitimacy derives, according to Diamond, either from the regime's success in achieving its goals or from failure to achieve them (ibid). This would seem to leave little room for any alternative thus presumably making a legitimation crisis inevitable. Diamond also argues that O'Donnell and Schmitter underestimate the impact of changes in civil society. By concentrating on its resurrection and resurgence they miss 'the process of development and change that transforms many societies, creating organizations and capacities that never existed before' (ibid, p.45). In addition, splits in the regime also occur out of an anticipation of opposition not simply as a result of it (ibid, p.46). The problem with Diamond's analysis is its underlying assumption, deriving from modernisation theory, which asserts the existence of 'a positive causal relationship between economic development and democracy' (ibid, p.36). According to this schema all states must undertake a similar path of development, ignoring their structural subordination within the global political economy. The specificities of socioeconomic development are subsumed within broad ontological categories such as civil society. As Diamond himself admits, modernisation theory is not a useful framework, even within its own terms, for analysing comparatively short-term changes.

Apart from his accent on general long-term trends, Diamond's discussion of external factors is limited to those encouraging or discouraging democratic development: US / Western support for democratic movements, international diffusion effects and the impact of various international bodies promoting democracy. The contradictions of Diamond's analysis emerge in his conclusion in which he suggests that consolidating democracy may not be easy because of 'intense economic problems and social conflicts' (p.60), which will require 'economic assistance, access to Western markets and debt relief' (p.61). While economic difficulties appeared to play little part in the downfall of the regime, presumably because of the crucial role of economic development, they suddenly represent a source of instability in the consolidation phase.

I will now turn to the transitions to democracy in Southern Europe and Latin America. In each case I will outline the relationship to the global political economy, its impact on social structure and the forces involved in the actual transition process.

## *Southern Europe*

Analysis of democratic transition in Southern Europe has followed the modal pattern of explaining change 'largely ... in terms of national forces and calculations' (Schmitter, p.5), which is subsequently narrowed down specifically to 'conflicts within the dominant group and among its privileged supporters / beneficiaries' (ibid, p.7), that is struggles within the *elite*. In a review of Schmitter and O'Donnell's work, Robert Fishman also argues that there is an 'absence of any strong evidence for a parsimonious, largely class-based or internationally focused macro-level explanation' for the transition but that '[t]his is not to argue that class forces or the international context are irrelevant; rather, the point is that these forces are not the *sole* determinants of political developments and actions' (p.425, emphasis in the original). The latter point is not in dispute but the subsequent ignoring of such factors in Fishman's discussion of the relationship between state and regime in Southern Europe is. The thrust of both Schmitter's and Fishman's argument is at variance with that of Geoffrey Pridham who in suggesting that the international context 'is the forgotten dimension in the study of democratic transition', argues that the examples of democratisation in Southern Europe in the 1970s reveal 'the direct impact or indirect influence on democratisation of international organisations, of one or other superpower or other states in the same region and of non-governmental organisations' (1991, p.1). Pridham's emphasis on the role of international *organisations* is, however, still in line with the analytical approach developed in *Transitions from Authoritarian Rule*, Laurence Whitehead arguing essentially the same point. Pridham subsequently takes a step further than Whitehead, however, bemoaning the lack of attention paid to linkages between the international economy and domestic politics. 'The state of the international economy is' he argues, 'especially pertinent to the transitions to democracy in the mid-1970s, since they occurred at the time of the recession following the oil crisis' (1991, p.16). This is precisely the point. Fishman's argument is that the Greek and Portuguese dictatorships collapsed as a result of crises of failure resulting from external military catastrophes (for Greece in Cyprus, and for Portugal in its African colonies) which delegitimated the regimes while, in Spain, the regime collapsed as a result of a crisis of historical obsolescence, presumably of its industrialisation strategy (p.435). This would suggest that the failure of these regimes was intimately connected to the international dimension and should be analysed as a process which must be explained in terms of shifting relationships between domestic social forces and between domestic and international factors.

Poulantzas argues that, in the phase of Spain's development after 1959, the Francoist state was undermined by an emerging contradiction between fractions of the capitalist class which had differing orientations either to the United States or to the EEC (pp.26-40). According to this perspective, power in the ruling bloc shifted in favour of the latter fraction centred around the Catalan and Basque bourgeoisies and elements of state capital controlled by INI (Lopez, p.21). Maravall suggests, however, that it was not a question of a split between 'domestic' and 'foreign' capital, which Poulantzas emphasises, but of the emergence of a proletariat and an industrial bourgeoisie, which increasingly looked beyond the confines of Spanish capitalism to the expanding EEC (Maravall; Maravall & Santamaria, p.76). Indeed, Poulantzas, despite his Marxist credentials, can be criticised for his exaggeration of divisions within the regime and his underestimation of the role played by popular forces in bringing about its demise. In the early 1970s Spanish capitalism was further opened up to the influence of the global economy as Spain became 'an export platform for the multinationals [eg. Ford, General Motors] into the EC markets' (Story & Pollack, p.130).

The role of labour movement activity in bringing down the Francoist state is rarely emphasised but difficult to exaggerate. From the 1950s the state-controlled works committees were the target of militants affiliated to the tolerated workers' commissions which in 1966 emerged as a national movement (CCOO) promoting political as well as traditional economic demands (Foweraker, pp.63-64). Despite being made illegal the workers' commissions promoted direct action and bargaining (Roca, p.247) and 'prepared the conditions for a transition to democracy by schooling the working class in "free" collective bargaining and in a sense of its democratic rights', which resulted in a massive increase in strikes in the twilight years of the regime, culminating in the 'day of peaceful struggle' in November 1976 in which two million workers participated, making 'a simple continuation of the regime impossible' (Foweraker, p.65). Such was the extent of labour movement mobilisation, and its lack of subordination to any political party, with the partial exception of the Spanish Communist Party (PCE), during the downfall of Francoism that a major element of the 'pacted' character of the transition was the promotion of a social-democratic alternative to the CCOO in the shape of the General Workers' Union (UGT) and the incorporation of labour into the new democratic regime, specifically through the 1977 Moncloa Pact (Foweraker, p.66; Perez-Diaz, p.228; Roca, pp.252-3).

The degree of Portugal's economic integration into the global economy, the extent of changes in social structure and the impact of the international environment are difficult to ascertain as they are all but ignored in much of the transition literature. Nevertheless, what is clear is that, as Collier argues, 'the working class was centrally involved in the Portuguese transition' (p.161). The activity of multinationals in Portugal created new working-class strata, employed at significantly higher wages and in better conditions than workers in traditional industries (Logan, pp.136-139). From the mid-1960s, strikes became a pervasive feature of life and an initial liberalisation allowed workers to form autonomous trades unions (Collier, p.162). By 1974 Portugal was suffering the highest inflation rate in Europe, resulting in widespread labour unrest (Maxwell, p.114). Labour unrest combined with discontent among the army's officer corps, prompted primarily by the struggle against popular liberation movements in Portugal's African colonies, to produce the radical Armed Forces Movement (MFA) which seized power in the coup of April 1974. The international dimension was, therefore, more influential than in any other South European transition. The labour movement also played its most influential role in Portugal, contributing not just to the downfall of the dictatorship, but also pursuing a radical democratic agenda, which 'pushed the army's "revolution" to the left' (Drake, p.64).

In Greece, the Colonels' regime, from the outset, suffered from a major legitimacy deficit: the international and particularly European environment was hostile to such authoritarian rule and, like Spain, the EC offered a powerful pole of attraction to sections of the bourgeoisie. The ability of the junta to generate legitimacy through economic development was also severely affected by the end of the post-war boom. Mouzelis suggests that Greece was the 'first victim of the world recession' (Mouzelis, p.76) and the economy was badly hit by the oil embargo following the 1973 Arab-Israeli war (Verney & Couloumbis, p.110). The proximate cause of the regime's collapse lay very much in the international sphere, however, with the Turkish invasion of Cyprus in July 1974. Diamandouros criticises Schmitter for suggesting that relations *within* the Greek regime were the critical factor in its collapse, arguing instead that relations between regime and civil society were crucial: the 1973 rising of Athens Polytechnic students inflicting 'irreparable damage' on the regime (Diamandouros, p.153).

The collapse of all three authoritarian regimes in 1974-75 was made possible by the increasing integration of these countries' economies into the world economy and the penetration of their domestic economies by international capital, which meant that they were not cushioned from the impact of the deteriorating international situation. In addition, the social structure in all three countries had radically changed over a short period of time, bringing into existence social forces which did not identify themselves with the authoritarian regimes but saw, in the case of commercial and industrial capital, their interests being best served by membership of the European Community, a prospect which was specifically excluded by the continued existence of authoritarianism. In the cases of Spain and Portugal in particular, the EC actively promoted a democratic alternative to the existing regimes and powerful political organisations such as the German SPD provided financial support to nascent social-democratic parties with the aims both of replacing the authoritarian regime and, at the same time, preventing the emergence of a popular alternative further to the left.

*Latin America*

After a period during the 1950s and 1960s when United States' aid to developing countries was provided through so-called Official Development Assistance (ODA), the relationship between core and peripheral states in Latin America became more firmly structured when, in response to the Cuban revolution, US President John F. Kennedy initiated the Alliance for Progress which loaned a total of $10.69 billion between 1961 and 1969. The impact of this aid was diminished, however, as repatriation of profits of US companies operating in Latin America exceeded net direct investment in the same period by $5.74 billion, thus reducing the net flow of finance (O'Brien, p.87). By the beginning of the 1970s Latin America was already facing a worsening debt situation, total external debt having risen during the 1960s from $7.2 billion to $12.8 billion (ibid, p.88). This debt was overwhelmingly owed to Western governments.

The level of Latin American debt steadily increased during the 1970s, reaching $58.4 billion in 1974, tripling to $181.9 billion in 1979, the year of the second major oil price rise, and reaching a massive $315.3 billion by 1982 when the debt crisis broke (O'Brien, pp.88-89). Latin American debt was also highly concentrated, 86 percent of total regional debt in 1984 being owed by just six countries, and almost 55 percent being owed by just two countries: Brazil ($101.8 billion) and Mexico ($95.9 billion) (ibid, p.90). Foreign loans had no preconditions attached to them and, as a result, the link between borrowing and productive investment was broken. In Venezuela and Chile most of the imports went to satisfy the demands of the wealthy for consumer goods; in Argentina it was used for armaments and tourist trips abroad (ibid). In general, O'Brien suggests, 'foreign loans seem to have been a substitute for domestic savings' (ibid, p.91). In addition, Dornbusch argues that external borrowing helped to finance capital flight, in Argentina's case amounting to more than 50 percent of its accumulated debt in 1982 (p.8). The debt crisis reached such a level throughout the 1980s that Latin America transferred a staggering $200 billion to the industrialised nations, resulting in a decline in real GDP per capita of 5-10 percent (Smith 1991, p.613). The consequence of debt for ordinary people has been one of declining living standards and austerity, whereas domestic elites have benefitted from the debt, making them reluctant to campaign against the banks and forcing a reorientation of the economies towards liberalisation and international or regional trading organisations such as GATT or NAFTA (Cammack, et al., pp.305-307).

The overall consequences of the debt crisis were, however, even more marked. Remmer argues that these changes in the international environment intersected with a variety of domestic factors to produce the downfall of the Latin American military regimes (1993, p.96). The argument of O'Donnell et al, in their major work on democratisation, that transitions to democracy have been the 'result of ideological aspiration and political leadership, not because of economic contradictions' (quoted in Smith 1991, p.618) would seem, in the circumstances, impossible to sustain.

In Brazil, the increasing problems of the populist model of ISI, particularly the demands voiced by the popular sector, provoked a reversion to authoritarianism in 1964. A new exclusionary model was instigated based on coercion and repression of traditional labour organisations. Unlike the general model of military regime, however, the Brazilian model of authoritarianism consisted of a broader civilian-military coalition. Possibly as a result of this its economic strategy was also different from that of most other Latin American regimes. A greater proportion of its loans were utilised for the purchase of capital and intermediate goods and for large infrastructural investments which made a contribution to rapid industrialisation amd more sustained growth (Gillespie, p.49). Between 1967 and 1970, GDP grew by an average annual rate of 9.3 percent and in the early 1970s by an average of more than 10 percent per annum (Stepan, p.331). During this period the regime was also concerned to crush armed subversion, thus balancing its economic project with one of internal security. Success in the latter ironically undermined the regime's already fragile legitimacy at a time when the economic strategy was also experiencing difficulties as a result of the oil crisis. The regime responded to the crisis by centralising decision-making even further in the state and emphasising grandiose development projects.

In 1974, having defeated the left-wing insurgents, the regime initiated a process of liberalisation (*abertura*), designed gradually to reintroduce civilian rule, thus commencing the longest transition to democracy of any Latin American state. This strategy failed to revive economic growth, fuelled inflation, and increased indebtedness from $12 billion in 1973 to more than $70 billion in 1982, thus alienating part of the coalition based on private enterprise (Stepan, pp.335-6). Discontent with increasing interventionism and frustration at the lack of access to decision-making provoked the so-called 'anti-statism' campaign and increased calls from business sectors for an orderly return to democracy (Gillespie, p.50).

Industrialisation also led to a tremendous growth in the size and concentration of the working class during the 1960s and 1970s. The number of workers in industry grew between 1960 and 1970 by 52 percent and then by a further 38 percent between 1970 and 1974. Moreover, as a result of unimpeded activity by multinational corporations (MNCs), the working class became especially concentrated around São Paulo (Stepan, p.333). This concentration facilitated the emergence of the 'new unionism', which strove to negotiate directly with employers, bypassing the state's industrial relations procedures, a fact welcomed by some sections of the bourgeoisie as a weapon against the existing system of labour relations (Baretta & Markoff, p.59). Increased worker militancy combined with the struggle within the business elite over strategies to combat the economic crisis to create space for the emergence of mass movements, demanding workers' rights and a redistribution of wealth. These in turn increased the pressure for liberalisation and democratisation and forced the regime to make concessions, thus accelerating the transition (Harding & Petras, pp.9-10; Rueschemeyer, et al., p.213). While the labour movement did not initiate the transition to democracy, the upsurge in worker militancy in 1978-79 was 'a direct challenge to the regime and can be seen as expanding the scope of the transition both by extending the pro-democracy struggle beyond the electoral arena and by challenging the government's mechanisms of corporatist control' (Collier, p.136).

The Brazilian transition thus represents a case of a gradual worsening of the economic situation coupled with the dynamic emergence of civil society which, despite its activism, proved incapable of imposing a solution on the regime. Nevertheless, O'Donnell's contention that the Brazilian popular sector was 'weakly organized and scarcely activated politically' does not seem credible given the weight of evidence (1986, p.9). By continuing to liberalise the regime rather than resorting to repression the military retained much tighter control of the process and meant that they continued to exert considerable influence after the instauration of a civilian regime, meeting the threat of a general strike in November 1986, and planned stoppages in the ports and oil refineries in March 1987 'with shows of military might' (Hagopian, p.156).

Argentina was beset by economic and political upheavals throughout the postwar period. The postwar integrationist regime of Juan Peron was overthrown in 1955 by a front of bourgeois and 'democratic' military elements, which in turn was replaced in 1966 by a purely military, technocratic administration. The harsher line taken against both political parties and the Peronist-dominated unions provoked considerable instability leading to a period of liberalisation in the early 1970s. The reactivation of civil society helped bring the ageing Peron back to power in 1973.

Peron attempted to recapitulate his earlier regime, creating a corporatist framework for industrial relations, reactivating parliament and subordinating the military to the state (Cavarozzi, pp.39-40). Unfortunately for Peron the global economic framework had changed considerably rendering such a project unworkable. Peron died in July 1974 leaving his widow, Isobel, to try and continue the tradition in rapidly deteriorating circumstances. The economic chaos which ensued was met by yet another coup in 1976 this time with an overtly liberal project to restore order both economically and socially. The regime's focus was on eradicating inflation, subversion, economic inefficiency and an 'undisciplined' working class (ibid, p.44). Stepan suggests that, while maintaining a strong coercive capacity, the junta began to decline after 1980-81 as a result of 'the growth of contradictions within the state, more precisely between the military as an institution and the military as government' (Stepan, p.329). The regime's policies created an economic disaster of devaluations, capital flight and indebtedness. Between 1981 and 1983 GDP fell by 13 percent (Gillespie, p.49). The failure of the regime to advance industrialisation in the 1970s was paralleled, however, by the fragmentation of the Peronist movement, of which the unions were a vital element, and the failure to emerge of a coherent opposition. Stepan argues that although the power of the state declined in this period so did that of civil society (Stepan, p.330). As a result, the 'transition to democracy ... was less the result of growing pressures from civil society than self-destruction of the military regime', primarily through the debacle of the Falklands/Malvinas war (Rueschemeyer, et al., p.214). This is contested by Ronaldo Munck who argues that 'it was the constant level of working-class resistance since 1976, which was moving from a defensive to an offensive phase by 1982, which alone explains [the] bizarre political gamble by the armed forces' (p.78).

In other Latin American states the labour movement has proved influential at times in undermining authoritarianism. In Peru, in 1976 and 1977, general strikes against austerity programmes and repression of labour movement leaders (more than 2000 lost their jobs in this period) forced the regime into preparing a definite timetable for its withdrawal from the political scene (Abugattas, p.132). In Haggard and Kaufman's opinion, the July 1977 general strike was 'the pivotal event in pushing a wavering military establishment to hold elections for a Constitutional Assembly' (p.63). In Bolivia, a hunger strike by miners' wives in December 1977 resulted in an unrestricted amnesty, the re-emergence of an independent labour movement and the crumbling of the regime (Whitehead 1986a, p.59). In Chile, the 'protesta' movement of the early 1980s was initiated and led by the Comando Nacional de Trabajadores (CNT), created by the militant Copper Workers' Confederation. The regime was able to survive, however, through a combination of widescale repression of the labour movement, and high levels of unemployment resulting from the depth of the economic crisis (Garreton).

In the Latin American context, therefore, the changing social structure resulting from dependent industrialisation and the deteriorating economic situation, which led to increasing attacks on the working class, prompted the labour movement to oppose the military regimes in a number of countries even before processes of liberalisation had been instigated. The ability of the working class to influence democratisation in Latin America has, however, been limited. With one or two exceptions, the working class has remained weak despite, in some cases, spectacular growth as a consequence of industrialisation. As a result it has tended to play a subordinate role to middle class strata in democratic transitions. Rueschemeyer, Stephens and Stephens have argued that 'parties led and supported by members of the middle classes were the decisive forces behind democratization [in Latin America] more often than in advanced capitalist societies' but this was not due to a 'natural' middle class propensity to democracy as they frequently supported authoritarian governments (p.222). The degree to which the middle class promoted democracy was affected by the strength of the working class movement: 'Only under the influence of a significant working-class presence did they fight for and defend full democracy' (ibid).

## Dependent Democratisation

Most analyses of democratisation are flawed by failure either to situate democratic transitions in a global context or to ascribe a sufficent role to civil society and organised labour in particular. I have demonstrated that the recent 'wave' of democratisation was intimately connected to the end of the postwar boom, oil price increases, and consequent crisis of international capitalism, which also threw the industrialisation strategies pursued by Third World states into a crisis from which a majority have still not recovered. The establishment of liberal democratic regimes would not have been possible on such a wide scale, however, without the reorientation of the United States in an effort to reestablish its economic and military hegemony through new mechanisms of control in the global economy which prompted an ideological shift towards neo-liberalism. This strategy had profound political ramifications. In order to establish regimes susceptible to external as well as internal influence and capable of carrying through programmes of structural adjustment (economic liberalisation), 'democracy' (that is liberal democracy) was increasingly advocated as the most desirable political form of the state.

The West's promotion of economic and political liberalisation has, however, been a double-edged sword. On the one hand, it has assisted elite currents in the liberalisation of authoritarian regimes, thereby facilitating the penetration of previously protected economies but, on the other hand, it has also encouraged the emergence of popular currents and prompted increased activism in pursuit of democratic goals. While it is true that elites usually initiate change, they do so by virtue of their control of key power centres in the state or economy, and frequently under pressure from a confluence of changing economic circumstances and the emergence of radical political movements. Nevertheless, the 'third wave' can be characterised as a process of *dependent democratisation* in which democratising states are subordinated both politically and economically to the interests of western capital in most cases through very high levels of indebtedness, the 'relief' of which involves imbibing the structural adjustment medicine of the IMF and World Bank, and 'democratic' regimes dominated by the executive, overseeing growing extremes of wealth and poverty, and minimising the participation of the mass of people in the political process. While the orthodoxy of democratisation literature is that elite domination of the transition is desirable if it is not to be destabilised by too radical demands emanating from civil society, it provides no guarantee of genuine democratisation, interpreted as the growing influence of the mass of people over the decision-making process, but results in what Gills et al call 'low intensity democracy' or Diamond has referred to as 'hollowed-out' democracy, that is the retention of the institutional form of democracy deprived of its content (Gills, et al.; Diamond 1996). In such conditions the chances for consolidating democracy depend on breaking the cycle of dependence, and on shifting the balance of power away from elites through the emergence of a vibrant civil society in which trades unions and political parties, linked to organised labour, play a major role.

# 2 Labour and the Soviet State

To determine the potential of labour as a political actor in the Soviet Union, our starting point must be how Soviet society has evolved, what social forces have emerged, and what the dynamics of their relationships are to one another. As I argued in the previous chapter, this is not an exclusively domestic process so the interrelationship between internal and external processes must be emphasised. Having established the basic characteristics of Soviet society, I will discuss the relationship of workers to the state, focussing especially on the notion of 'social contract' and on the role played by trades unions.

## Soviet Industrialisation

The small size of the Russian working class at the time of the 1917 October revolution compared to the overwhelming preponderence of the peasantry is, of course, well-known and a fact which has been repeatedly used (and abused) since 1917 to show that the Bolsheviks had abandoned the Marxist theory that socialism could only be achieved in advanced capitalist countries in which the working class had already become the majority. The Bolsheviks themselves never claimed that they could build a socialist society in 'backward' Russia but argued that, because of its combined and uneven development, the Russian social formation possessed certain features which together with its relationship to the global political economy made the revolutionary overthrow of capitalism possible. This contradictory character of the Russian state was most eloquently advanced by Trotsky who asserted that while 'peasant land-cultivation as a whole remained, right up to the revolution, at the level of the seventeenth century, Russian industry in its technique and capitalist structure stood at the level of the advanced countries, and in certain respects even outstripped them' (Trotsky 1977, p.31).

From its very inception, therefore, the Soviet state had to confront and take account of the specificity of its position in the global political economy. First, Russia's comparatively backward economy meant that the

October revolution was undertaken on the premise of the spread of revolution to the advanced capitalist countries, particularly Germany; second, the Civil War pitched the Bolshevik regime not just against internal forces wishing to restore the *ancien regime* but against the interventionist armies of twenty other states; and, third, following the defeat of revolutions in Europe, the debate within the Russian Communist Party (RCP) centred on how an isolated Soviet Union could continue to exist in a predominantly hostile environment.

The New Economic Policy (NEP) with its uneasy compromise between proletarian state and mass peasantry also left open the future direction of economic development: those around Trotsky argued for greater Soviet integration into the world economy and increased tempos of industrialisation, while the Stalin-Bukharin leadership favoured economic autarky. The Soviet economy made a partial recovery under NEP but the apparent stabilisation of world capitalism necessitated a reorientation of relations with major capitalist states and diplomatic initiatives were undertaken to increase co-operation and attract investment (Reiman, p.9).

It was the collapse of this orientation which ultimately provoked the turn to rapid industrialisation and collectivisation. In 1927, the debacle of the Chinese Communist Party's alliance with the nationalist Kuomintang provoked a crisis of relations with Great Britain, which at the time was the USSR's biggest trading partner. This had a knock-on effect on developing relations with other capitalist states. The collapse of the RCP's foreign policy orientation was then exacerbated by rumours of imminent war, which provoked generalised hoarding among the population and, despite its groundlessness, pushed the leadership into a reorientation of economic policy towards intensive industrialisation (Fitzpatrick, pp.110-11; Reiman, pp.11-13). The imaginary threat of war permitted the Stalin faction to pillory Trotsky and the Left Opposition, accusing them of treason in the face of imminent attack, and almost certainly hastening their defeat. The war scare was also used to keep party cadres in a state of constant vigilance and mobilisation against potential enemies, leading to trials against alleged 'bourgeois saboteurs' most notably in the so-called Shakhty trial of March 1928, an incident in which internal and external threats were linked (Fitzpatrick, pp.111-12), and which 'marked the turning-point from the class-conciliatory NEP to the class-war policy of 1928-31' (Kuromiya, p.15).

These international factors interacted with domestic factors to produce the crisis of NEP and the drive for collectivisation and industrialisation which occurred after 1928. Nove suggests that among the major internal factors was the exhaustion of the first 'reconstruction' phase of NEP, necessitating the extraction of resources for any subsequent development, at least in part, from the peasantry (Nove, pp.138-140). In addition, the maintenance of artificially low prices on consumer and industrial goods prompted speculation and shortages especially in the countryside away from where the goods were actually produced. The latter policy was very much the product of the internal political conflict in the RCP, the forces around both Trotsky and Bukharin advocating higher prices (ibid, pp.140-2).

Industrialisation itself was a haphazard process driven primarily by political considerations. In order to maintain his alliance with Bukharin, Stalin had reviled the programme promoted by the Left Opposition until such time as Trotsky was defeated. With the latter exiled to Alma Ata, Stalin was able to utilise the situation to turn against Bukharin. Planning and industrialisation had been on the agenda since 1925, co-ordination of state industry having become an urgent priority, and was the subject of a fascinating debate between economists of varying political orientations (see Erlich).. Implementation of any plans had been resisted, however, because they were a fundamental element of the Left's alternative. With the Left in retreat, a first Five-Year Plan was instituted in late 1928 and became the framework for rapid industrialisation. The highest tempos of development were adopted but only after the plan had already been initiated. By promoting industrialisation in this way Stalin attracted support from many former Left Oppositionists who failed to appreciate the danger he represented and still viewed Bukharin as the main opponent of socialist development. In reality, the programmes promoted by Bukharin and Trotsky became increasingly similar, decrying the forced character of collectivisation and calling for more realistic plan targets.

Collectivisation of agriculture was itself a pragmatic and violent response to the problems of grain collection from the villages. It was begun as a return to forcible requisitioning (the so-called 'Urals-Siberian method') and was then extended to 'liquidating the kulaks as a class'. The consequences for Soviet agriculture in terms of loss of life, loss of livestock and crops, and loss of motivation were incalculable.

Planning was undermined by persistent changes in plan targets, creating imbalances and bottlenecks within and between different economic sectors while the balance between heavy and light industry was decisively shifted in favour of the former (Nove, p.188). Overfulfillment of plan targets became the watchword so that the first Five-Year Plan was declared fulfilled in four years, although subsequent plans became rather more modest. Nevertheless, despite its chaotic nature, Soviet industrialisation forged ahead at an unprecedented tempo at a time when the capitalist world was enduring a severe crisis.

A consequence of the period of industrialisation was that the Soviet economy became almost closed to the operations of the world capitalist economy. Initially, part of the financing of industrialisation was obtained through Western loans, amounting in 1931 to $721 million, but every effort was made to repay them quickly and the amounts rapidly diminished through the decade (Nove, p.211). In addition, industrialisation created the capacity for the Soviet Union to produce its own goods: in 1932, 78 percent of installed machine tools were imported; by 1936 this had fallen to only 10 percent (ibid, p.229). Rights which had existed to direct producers under NEP to engage in foreign economic activity were removed during this period and all such relations became concentrated in the hands of specialised foreign trade organisations supervised by the Ministry of Foreign Trade (Shmelev & Popov, p.221). Shmelev and Popov argue that there were international reasons for this, in particular, the crisis of 1929 which provoked a wave of protectionism throughout the capitalist world, but that the prime reason was the character of the Soviet economy which 'did not facilitate the growth of export potential - instead it smothered it' (ibid, p.222). The state monopoly of foreign trade coupled with centralised planning created no incentives to export because all prices within the Soviet economy were administratively determined, acting as accounting devices rather than signals for the allocation of resources, and enterprises received the state price for an export item even if its price on the world market was higher. A further disincentive was that export goods had to be of higher quality than for domestic consumers with lower expectations (Evangelista, pp.166-7). A consequence of this system was that '[i]n 1988 - at the high point of its international economic activity - the USSR's foreign trade represented a mere 1.7 percent of total world trade, even though, as the world's second or third largest economy, it produced 13.6 percent of world Gross National Product' (ibid, p.159).

## The Impact of Industrialisation on Social Structure

Not surprisingly, the profound political and economic changes of the 1920s and 1930s had a massive impact on the social structure of the USSR. In its analysis of these changes Soviet social science was straitjacketed, however, by the official ideology. Thus, in line with the 1936 Constitution, the Soviet Union was considered to be made up of two classes, the working class and the collective farm peasantry, and a social stratum, the intelligentsia which, according to Stalin, 'recruits its members from among the classes of society' (quoted in Unger, p.84). These social categories enjoyed a 'non-antagonistic' and non-exploitative relationship towards one another although, within this framework, the working class constituted 'the leading productive and socio-political force of the society of developed socialism' (Chulanov, p.10). Until the late *perestroika* period any challenge to this conception of Soviet society, any notion of a ruling elite or bureaucracy, or of antagonistic relations, was considered heretical.

Despite their ideological constraints and preconceptions, Soviet sociologists did, however, provide a picture of the dynamic growth of the working class over the past sixty years. In 1928 the size of the working class in the Soviet Union was 8.5 million. By 1940 this had undergone a 270 percent increase to 22.8 million primarily as a result of the influx of former peasants into the cities and newly-created industries. As a proportion of the working population, industrial workers had increased from a tenth to one third but, at the same time, the working class suffered a 'dilution' in terms of a decreased percentage cultured in working class ways and mores. In Gordon and Nazimova's opinion, former peasants were characterised by:

> insufficiently durable and settled habits in respect of machine technology; a comparatively low general culture and even elementary literacy; skills drawn from experience, example, unique talent but not from mass stereotyped knowledge based on uniform instruction; a labour discipline strongly influenced by patriarchal peasant traditions; an insufficiently developed ability to subordinate themselves consciously to expedient organisation and simultaneously to display initiative, collectivism and a capacity for self-organisation. It is natural that the productive potential of a working class, seemingly experiencing a second period of formation, is lower than that of a working class linked to heavy industry for many generations (Gordon & Nazimova, p.40).

Thus the peasant influx had a dual effect. Despite the massive scale of the migration into the urban areas, the peasants did not immediately adopt urban norms of living but brought their own traditions and habits, and frequently maintained links with their old rural area. This rendered the working class less proletarian, a factor that contributed to the deformations in the political system in the 1930s, and created a lag in the level of skill in the working class behind the rapid industrial growth (Gordon, et al., p.60).

Filtzer argues that the dilution of the working class and differentiation between 'shock workers' and the rank-and-file were essential to the victory of the Stalinist elite, enabling it to prevent the working class acting as a cohesive force, while mobilising workers behind regime goals (1986, pp.254-7).

During the Second World War, the number of workers fell to 19.7 million as a natural consequence of conscription and the ravages of wartime conditions, but rose swiftly in the post-war reconstruction period to 44.7 million by 1960, an increase of 230 percent. Workers now constituted one half of the working population. The final spurt of working class growth came in the period to 1975 when there was a 160 percent increase to 72.3 million or roughly two-thirds of the working population. The changing proportions between the different classes and groups can be seen in the table 2.1.

**Table 2.1 Changing proportions between groups and classes (figures in percent)**

| *Year* | *1939* | *1959* | *1970* | *1979* | *1984* |
|---|---|---|---|---|---|
| Workers | 32 | 48 | 57 | 60 | 62 |
| Employees | 18 | 20 | 23 | 25 | 26 |
| Kolkhozniki | 47 | 31 | 20 | 15 | 12 |
| Individual peasants | 3 | - | - | - | - |

*Source*: Gordon & Nazimova, p.30

Thus, '[f]rom a minority, concentrated in a limited number of major industrial centres, the working class grew into a majority of Soviet society and became the predominant group of working people in city and countryside in all regions of the country' (Gordon, et al., p.59).

While unable to challenge the basic image of Soviet society as fundamentally harmonious, distinctions were made in Soviet analysis between different categories of worker. These generally related to 'the level of professional and skill training, education, experience, craftsmanship, the level of productive and socio-political activity etc' (Chulanov, p.13). The general mass of workers, other than the collective farm peasantry, were referred to as 'working people' (*trudyashchiesya*), which included both industrial workers and white-collar employees (*sluzhashchie*). The definition of *sluzhashchie* as white-collar workers is slightly misleading as they are generally clerks on the bottom rung of the social ladder, rather than skilled, technical workers who are generally referred to as *inzhenerno-tekhnicheskie rabochie* or 'ITR'. Industrial workers (*industrial'nyi otryad trudyashchikhsya*) have been defined as

> workers [*rabotnikov*] in industry, construction, transport and communications, whose community has been conditioned by relations of productive-technical and social co-operation. The characteristics of the internal unity of this section of working people [*trudyashchikhsya*] are: hired labour in enterprises (associations) and institutions in the state sector of the economy; professional occupation with industrial and scientific- industrial forms of labour; receipt of basic income in the form of wages (Igitkhanyan, et al., p.4).

Excluded from this definition would be workers on state farms engaged in forms of labour analogous to those performed by the collective farm peasantry but not those engaged in labour in the so-called 'agro-industrial complex'.

Official ideology declared on numerous occasions that, having achieved a socialist society in the 1930s and having progressed by the 1970s to a higher stage, variously referred to as 'developed' or 'mature' socialism, there was a tendency inherent in travelling the path to full communism for society and its working class to become more homogeneous. This derived from Marx and Engels' notion that, under communism, class society would be completely eradicated, the distinction between urban and rural life would disappear and people would simply labour for the benefit of society as a whole.

Placing their analysis of current trends in the working class within the framework of a process of homogenisation proved extremely difficult for social scientists to achieve given the rapid development of the working class, its increasing differentiation according to skill, and the uneven introduction of more and more advanced techniques into production. Chulanov, displaying an idealistic attitude to the working class characteristic of the Brezhnev era, argued that this differentiation had a 'political' character with 'advanced strata', who formed the kernel of the working class, aspiring to the ideals of communism, providing an example to less-advanced sectors and enhancing the movement towards homogeneity (pp.10-13).

Together with the process of proletarianisation, urbanisation also proceeded apace. The urban population became predominant over the rural and the rural population gained urban norms of living. By 1981, 72 percent of urban-dwellers lived in cities with a population in excess of one hundred thousand; small towns, especially in central Russia, were in decline (Kagarlitsky 1990, pp.285-6).

Western analysts of Soviet class structure were confronted with fewer ideological constraints but depended for much of their work on the published data and interpretations of their Soviet colleagues. Much Western writing has been general sociological analysis of class and group composition, social and occupational mobility, education etc., but there has also been interesting discussion of the extent to which a working class existed in the Soviet Union. According to Lane and O'Dell, the Soviet working class comprised 'all manual and non-manual labour occupied in publicly owned institutions concerned with production, distribution and exchange' (Lane & O'Dell, p.3). This definition is so all-embracing that it excludes only the collective farm peasantry and is reinforced in their conclusion by their statement that 'the economic class structure is a unitary one' (ibid, p.132). As Arnot points out, 'the only conclusion that can be drawn from this is that they view the Soviet Union as a classless society' (Arnot, p.28). Littlejohn echoes Arnot's criticism of Lane and O'Dell's approach, arguing that class is defined by differential access to the means of production. Thus, if a unitary class structure exists, in which no section of society has gained privileged access to the means of production, then, by definition, it must be a classless society (Littlejohn, p.230).

Furthermore, Littlejohn and Arnot would also agree that Lane and O'Dell's concentration on the stratification created by technology leads them to a form of 'technological determinism' and a thesis that 'convergence is taking place between East and West, driven by the imperatives of a neutral technology' (Arnot, p.28). For Lane and O'Dell, 'the [Soviet] occupational structure has evolved in a way not unlike that of capitalist societies' (Lane & O'Dell, p.18). This is questioned by Littlejohn who argues that the preponderance of the machine-building and metal-working branch of the economy, which accounted in 1975 for 40 percent of total employment, 'is clearly a result of state economic policy, as are many other features of the Soviet occupational structure, whether directly or indirectly' (Littlejohn, p.236).

In an analysis which parallels that of Lane and O'Dell, Alex Pravda argues that the concept of a working 'class' is a myth generated in order to sustain the regime. He claims that, in fact, the working class has a heterogeneity rooted in the division of labour, the differences across class divisions being more important than the class divisions themselves (Pravda 1982). This conclusion is possible because Pravda, and Lane and O'Dell, confuse the technical division of labour, which arises at the level of the enterprise, with the social division of labour. Arnot argues that classes derive from the social division of labour which arises from the production and expropriation of the surplus product. He, therefore, concludes that a distinct working class did exist in the Soviet Union because it did not control the social surplus. Littlejohn is much more hesitant, however, arguing that no single social group had privileged access to the means of production to the permanent detriment of another. The sole exception was the collective farm peasantry which did, therefore, constitute a distinct class (Littlejohn).

Other analysts have also argued that Soviet workers do not constitute a class by virtue of their atomisation and fluidity (see eg. Zaslavsky; Connor 1988, pp.70-1; Ticktin). Zaslavsky identifies social atomisation with the division of the working class into skilled and unskilled strata. Certainly this schism prevented or at least severely hindered opportunities for united action by workers but it does not mean that a degree of social integration did not exist within each of the two strata Zaslavsky identifies. In workers' day-to-day lives, a privatised existence was the norm in which such individualistic actions as changing one's job to better one's conditions were of paramount importance. Nevertheless, if Soviet workers were so atomised it would be difficult to explain the degree of cohesion displayed when they decided to take collective action, for example in Novocherkassk in 1962 or during the 1989 miners' strike. Such action was usually taken against decisions upon which individual sanctions could have no effect and the central authorities' usual response to such manifestations of collective strength was an extremely rapid attempt to defuse the situation by, first, returning the workers to a privatised existence through increased supplies of food and consumer goods or by rescinding price rises, and then punishing the strike leaders. Such an approach does demonstrate that the regime itself saw collective opposition, even on a comparatively small scale, as a severe threat to their vital interests. Nevertheless, it is clear that Soviet workers were never able to display such cohesive activity across industries and on a more widespread basis. The experience of Solidarity in Poland is an instructive one: it took several waves of strikes over a comparatively short period of time (1970, 1976, 1980), rapidly deteriorating economic conditions and repeated attempts by the regime to impose austerity, and the emergence of an alternative ideological focus in the form of a substantial dissident intelligentsia and the Catholic Church (both in Poland and in the shape of a Polish Pope), for Polish workers to achieve genuine class consciousness. Claudio Katz is quite correct to argue that objective conditions in themselves are insufficient for an adequate definition of class and that class consciousness is itself a fundamental component. A serious question mark is, therefore, raised about the degree to which Soviet workers constituted a distinct class until they began to develop their own independent class organisations expressing their own specific interests.

## The Character of the Soviet State

Despite the central role claimed by official ideologists for the working class in the Soviet Union's political processes, western analysts of Soviet politics have tended to concentrate on the upper echelons of decision-making. This approach has reflected a preoccupation, common in the West, that politics is solely about policy-making and the institutions which determine policy outcomes. This has generally been the case both for those writers influenced by the notion of the USSR as a form of totalitarianism, in which attention was naturally focused on the top leadership of the Soviet Communist Party (CPSU) as the source of all power, and for those writers who, in comprehending some of the failings of totalitarian theory, developed a more nuanced approach based on the concept of interest groups. While the latter acknowledged a greater dispersal of power within the Soviet system, power was still seen to reside, in the main, at its apex. This approach was coupled with the problems of empirically verifying the influence that amorphous social categories, such as classes or strata, rather than well-structured, homogeneous groups could have on the decision-making machinery.

Unsurprisingly, Western analysts of the Soviet social system were rather more critical than their Soviet counterparts, usually discerning fundamental differences of interest between social classes or strata. There were, however, a number of different interpretations. Analysts of the USSR as a form of capitalism argued that the social structure was fundamentally similar to that pertaining in Western capitalist societies (see Cliff for example). Those arguing that the Soviet Union represented a new form of society promoted the idea of a new ruling class (see for example Djilas, and theorists of bureaucratic collectivism), whereas theorists of the USSR as a transitional society argued that the political power of the working class had been usurped by a bureaucratic stratum (for example Mandel 1968, Trotsky 1972[1937]); a similar position was argued by theorists of the Soviet Union as an historical detour (for example Füredi, Ticktin).

Ticktin and others have suggested that the elite was economically irrational and unable to promote the Soviet Union's development except through extensive methods. The elite exercised control over the centralised planning process because of its monopoly of political power but this control was imperfect because different sections of the bureaucracy pursued different priorities. The bureaucracy below the central level came into conflict with the centre and, as a result, bargaining over the distribution of resources became more the norm than genuine planning. The whole process was underpinned by the provision of false information to the centre. This resulted from the endemic requirement of the enterprise to hoard labour in a situation where neither the supply of vital components, nor their quality, could be guaranteed, resulting in 'storming' in order to meet plan targets at the end of each plan period.

This mode of operation is at variance with the notion that the USSR represented some form of capitalism. As Cliff himself admits, the distribution of resources through market mechanisms (in Marxist terms through the law of value) was subordinated to their political allocation via the plan (Cliff, pp.208-9). To extricate himself from this position, Cliff argues that the Soviet economy as a whole operated in relation to the world economy in precisely the same way as any capitalist firm, and it was this which determined its capitalist character. As we have noted above, however, the Soviet Union's integration into the world economy was negligible and far from determining the character of the Soviet system.

At the heart of the Soviet system was the CPSU which allocated appropriate people to all levels of the state and party hierarchy through the so-called *nomenklatura* mechanism. At the apex of the pyramid, the CPSU Politburo and Central Committee took all fundamental political decisions as well as determining the composition of the government, the leading personnel in the central ministries, planning apparatus, military and security organs, trades unions and social organisations. The 'elite' or 'bureaucracy' was not synonymous, however, with the *nomenklatura*, which included technical positions at comparatively low levels of the political and economic structure. It does include, however, those at the higher levels of the *nomenklatura* associated with making fundamental political and economic decisions. The Soviet elite was, therefore, politically appointed and promotion up the hierarchy depended on personal contacts and qualities rather than any independent source of power. To argue that the *nomenklatura* represented a new ruling class is difficult to maintain. The social 'glue' binding the *nomenklatura* together was the possession of political power and its attendant privileges rather than ownership of the means of production. Crucially, no economic mechanism existed for extracting the social surplus product and developing the forces of production. Overt coercion and ideological mobilisation were employed to construct the Soviet Union's industrial base but once the limits of that industrialisation were reached it became increasingly difficult for the *nomenklatura* to rationalise the production process. Instead, more and more of the social surplus was devoted to defending the elite's political power through the 'social contract', which will be discussed in the next section, and military expenditure.

The party, organised on the so-called 'territorial-production principle', ensured that its influence permeated to the lowest levels of society and was particularly felt in the workplace. All enterprises had their own party committee, which together with management and the trade union committee, formed the so-called 'troika' through which relations with outside bodies were maintained and plan targets achieved. The party committee did not play simply a directive role but was also of crucial importance as a feedback mechanism through which workers' grievances could be communicated to higher levels. The party was a mass organisation, with a membership at its peak of around 19 million, which sought to incorporate the most active workers into its ranks 'to retain some credibility as a "proletarian" party' (Rigby, p.5). Indeed, workers in key industries, such as coalmining, were targetted thus producing a higher level of membership than in society at large.

Nor did the party's functions cease there. As the sole legal political organisation, the party determined the ideological orthodoxy, not just within the USSR, but also within the wider communist movement. This latter function was to be severely undermined during the 1960s by the rise of China as an independent communist state, highly critical of the Soviet Union's 'leading role', and by the regeneration of critical Marxist currents in both Eastern Europe and the West.

## Social Contract

In the few Western studies of the Soviet working class produced, particularly in the last thirty years, the prime aim was generally to demonstrate that the Soviet working class enjoyed no democratic rights, poor working conditions and had no independent trade union organisation to defend its interests. If this had been the case the Soviet economy would have been much more globally competitive and would scarcely have needed to restructure. The clear implication is that Soviet workers had no power, a capacity seen purely in terms of visible relationships of compulsion with empirically verifiable outcomes. As Steven Lukes has pointed out, this may constitute one dimension of power but it does not and can not explain negative influences, the setting of the agenda for policy-making, and the overall social constraints within which power is exercised. Despite the denial of many formal rights workers potentially wielded considerable power. For Lane 'the working class acted as an effective "veto group" on the political elite and those who seek to increase the extraction of surplus by increasing workers' productivity' (Lane, p.136).

The question of legitimacy - whether a regime's right to rule is acknowledged (at least tacitly) by those with the power to affect that right, and legitimation, the process and mechanisms through which a regime maintains its rule, have been major themes of Western political science. These concepts are, however, problematic in that the class character of the state is conjured out of existence by the use of 'objective' criteria. Max Weber's categorisation of 'charismatic', 'traditional' and 'legal-rational' modes of legitimation is ahistorical and provides no clues as to the class relationship which might obtain in each mode. The 'legal-rational' mode of legitimation refers to the complex of institutions, particularly involving electoral and law-governed processes obtaining in modern capitalist states, which makes the domination of a bourgeois class seem 'natural' and accepted by all in society. It has clear parallels with the procedural model of democracy which emphasises the role of institutions rather than the social forces exercising political power.

In counterposition to the concepts of legitimacy and legitimation, the Italian Marxist Antonio Gramsci developed the concept of 'hegemony'. Gramsci used 'hegemony' in two related senses: as 'the consensual basis of an existing political system within civil society' in contrast to domination, the state's monopoly and employment of coercive power; and secondly as the achievement of class consciousness 'where class is understood not only economically but also in terms of a common intellectual and moral awareness, a common culture' (Adamson, pp.170-1). The question of dominating and dominated classes, and the class character of a particular state, are thus promoted to the foreground. In Western capitalist states hegemony has been achieved in both senses by the bourgeoisie whose ideology liberalism, in one variant or another, permeates all sectors of society. The key concept in the achievement of hegemony is that of 'civil society'. Civil society is the medium through which the ideology of the dominant class is disseminated and its rule legitimated. Gramsci famously referred to the state in capitalist society as being protected by civil society, a fact that necessitated a complex and subtle strategy ('war of manoeuvre') if the state was to be overthrown in a socialist revolution. This contrasted with Russia where civil society was 'primordial and gelatinous' and left the state open to direct assault (the so-called 'war of position').

If we return our attention to the Soviet Union it is clear that the bourgeoisie had been eliminated and with it any vestige of liberalism. In its place the USSR was declared a socialist society in which the working class was the dominant force and Marxism the dominant ideology. As we have seen this picture served to draw a veil over the existence of an elite with distinct interests from those of the working class. Nevertheless, the Soviet elite was in a weak position: it did not constitute a separate class and was unable to develop an independent ideology, distorting Marxism to serve its own interests. Furthermore, civil society in the form of autonomous organisations and economic activity was strictly subordinated to the CPSU and the state. The elite could not, therefore, establish its hegemony in either of the forms analysed by Gramsci. Even comparatively trivial disputes could quickly assume a political character, rendering the state vulnerable to assault. The frequent use of coercion to quell opposition engendered instability both within the state and within the elite itself. Consequently, the elite sought to develop consensual mechanisms and the establishment of a specific arrangement, commonly referred to as the 'social contract'.

Little attention was paid to the question of legitimacy in the Soviet Union and the analogous societies of Eastern Europe despite the fairly clear ideological motivations for doing so. Given the body of work that exists on legitimacy and legitimation in the West, lack of a theoretical framework would not appear to have been an obstacle. However, theorists addressing the question of legitimacy in Soviet-type societies were confonted with the problem that the existing framework, derived in particular from Weber's categorisation, was inadequate or inappropriate for a thorough understanding of the processes at work in these societies. As a result, novel extensions of existing theories were developed to accomodate phenomena absent from either democratic or authoritarian Western societies. In a seminal discussion of Weber's modes of legitimation and their applicability to Soviet-type societies, Stephen White argues that communist regimes are legitimated primarily through socioeconomic performance or what he refers to as 'social eudaemonic' legitimation, a formula which 'may be described as a "social contract", "social compact" or "social compromise"'. While providing few civil liberties 'communist regimes do generally provide a high level of social welfare' (White 1986, p.463).

The usage of the concept of 'social contract' has become the most commonly-accepted framework for examining regime-society relations in Soviet-type societies. Although other frameworks have been elaborated, for example Ferenc Feher's notion of a 'paternalistic mode of legitimation', I will argue that the notion of a social contract is the best way of understanding relations between the Soviet bureaucratic regime and the wider society, but that much Western writing on this subject has been inadequate because of a lack of theory concerning the character of the Soviet state.

The concept of 'social contract' originated in the middle ages and achieved its 'classical' exposition in the works of Hobbes, Locke and Rousseau. Few authors employing the notion of a social contract in the Soviet context have attempted, however, to relate it to its origins in political theory. The chief exceptions to this are Janine Ludlam and Zbigniew Rau (1987 & 1991). Ludlam, for example, argues that the Stalin period involved the 'perpetuation of the uncertainty and arbitrary state of nature described by Hobbes' and that the post-Stalin social contract was Hobbesian in character because of the continued dominance of the state over civil society (p.289).

There appears, however, to be a fundamental flaw in Ludlam's attempt to create this lineage. In 'classical' theory, the contract was an individual one established between the members of society, although its existence benefitted all society, and not a collective one between society and government. In contrast, the Soviet contract can be seen as an implicit arrangement between regime and a major section of society (industrial workers); it was a zero-sum game in the sense of there being 'winners' and 'losers', rather than the positive-sum game envisaged by Hobbes and Locke; and there was no independent arbiter to determine when the contract had been broken. In addition, the contract was perceived by Locke and Rousseau to be a voluntary agreement, although there is some ambiguity in their writings as to how far an individual could opt out. It is certainly true that, for Hobbes, the social contract was a more coercive arrangement, imposed by the monarch on society in order to end 'the war of all against all'. The idea that Stalin imposed order in a quasi-monarchical fashion does not, however, bear scrutiny. The 'terror', despite its apparent similarity to the 'state of nature's' unpredictable and lawless character, was itself the product of governmental action and was directed at specific sectors of society. Other sectors of society benefitted from the 'terror', although not necessarily from direct participation in it. The application of the concept of 'social contract' as formulated in the writings of the classical theorists cannot, therefore, be justified in the Soviet context.

This does not mean, however, that the concept of 'contract' is inappropriate. While Hauslohner notes that it may never have been a genuine contract because it was 'negotiated' by only one of the parties to it, 'the historical evidence suggests that one side's welshing has prompted the other side also to renege; this implies the presence of something of a quid pro quo element which perhaps makes contract a not entirely inappropriate label' (p.58).

Alex Pravda, in a survey of the East European social contract which is equally applicable to the Soviet Union, argues that the contract was a product of a stage of development characterised by 'social upheaval, political mobilization, and extensive economic growth', i.e. the period of rapid industrialisation of the 1950s (Pravda 1981, p.163). Pravda does not explicitly link the origins of the East European social contract to developments in the Soviet Union after the death of Stalin, leaving unclear the imperatives for the contract. Nor is he specific about when the contract was initiated in Eastern Europe. In this regard, Connor suggests that it was first implemented in Czechoslovakia with its large working class and comparatively developed economy, and was part of Gomulka's post-1956 settlement in Poland (Connor 1981). The inference would seem to be therefore that, allowing for certain national peculiarities, broadly similar 'contracts' were implemented in countries with analogous social systems to the Soviet Union at a particular stage of their economic development.

Arguing that the social contract was 'based on the fulfillment of mutual expectations' between regime and society, Pravda delineates three basic spheres in which the contract was operative: production, consumption and citizenship (1981, p.163). The production sphere comprised a range of job rights including full employment, job security, slack labour discipline and an egalitarian wage distribution. The consumption sphere included the ready availability of, and improvement in the range of, basic consumer goods and stable prices, while the sphere of citizenship demanded a 'high level of formal compliance [to the regime] but minimal commitment of any real significance' (ibid). The 'bottom line' of the social contract was, therefore, the regime's satisfaction of what were 'largely economic welfare expectations' (ibid), although Connor adds that the regime also undertook 'to avoid broadscale terror or coercion in everyday administration' (1981, p.165). It thus served as a 'mechanism for staving off widespread social and political unrest', i.e. it 'bought' legitimacy (Gilbert, p.182). The *quid pro quo*, Connor argues, was that '[t]he "people", but workers most specifically, [would] foreswear political challenge and organized expression of discontent, [would] work (regularly if not always well), and generally remain quiet' (1981, p.165).

In a similar vein, Peter Hauslohner identifies four basic elements: steadily improving consumption; high job security and stable prices; an egalitarian wages policy; and a degree of personal freedom to citizens as workers and consumers which could and, indeed, did co-exist with government repression of political dissent (p.58). Furthermore, because the benefits of the social contract were not evenly targetted at all groups in society, but were biased towards the manual working class, the regime gained its positive support and willingness to preserve any marginal advantages derived therefrom (ibid, pp.58-60).

The question of how the contract was implemented is of crucial significance, particularly with regard to what would happen if it broke down. Hauslohner argues that the contract was also based on norms accepted by both the public and the regime as the rules of the game, which were institutionalised particularly through the State Committee of Labour (*Goskomtrud*) (ibid). On a daily basis and at a level which constantly affected workers' lives, the social contract was administered through the medium of the enterprise, the trade unions acting as both defender and overseer of social policy, and agent of its implementation. Certain elements of the contract, for example the character of the work regime, were solely down to relations within the enterprise. Not surprisingly, while the Soviet economy allowed the regime to meet its basic commitments, labour disputes tended to concentrate on control over production, frequently at the level of just one shop, although the provisions of labour legislation could be enlisted to promote the interests of management or workers. Other material benefits necessitated the provision by the state of sufficient investment and resources to ensure that the enterprise could meet workers' expectations. There were, however, mechanisms through which enterprises could obtain benefits for their workforce without recourse to petitioning the state. Falsification of production figures was a major means of maximising bonuses, but also the development of informal 'horizontal' links with other enterprises allowed scarce components and goods to be obtained through the medium of barter exchange. The enterprise could, thus, cushion the worker from emerging economic difficulties, reinforcing an identity between workers and 'their' enterprise, which cut across any potential development of class consciousness.

An exception to this situation was the question of prices. The difference between the cost of production and the price in the shops was maintained through ever increasing subsidies from the state. It was the breakdown of this direct relationship between the state and all workers, who would be affected by price rises regardless of where they worked, that the regime viewed with the utmost apprehension. It was reneging on this provision of the social contract, which the regime had learnt produced the most immediate and wideranging response from workers. This was the lesson of Novocherkassk in 1962, when Khrushchev tried to raise basic food prices, and of *Solidarnosc* in Poland.

Much emphasis has been placed on the contract as an object of deliberate policy to maintain social stability. The question of evidence has been redressed somewhat by Linda Cook in her book on the Soviet social contract in which she analyses key pressure points when the regime was confronted with policy choices which could either reinforce or undermine the social contract. She argues that, when it came to the crunch, the Soviet leadership was constrained to maintain the social contract (1993 especially chapters 3 and 5). The problem with Cook's approach and that of other supporters of the social contract thesis is that they have been unable to provide an adequate explanation as to why the contract, as opposed to other forms of legitimation, was employed with certain national variations in all Soviet-type societies. The role of ideology is crucial in this context. The elite could not develop a distinctive ideology with which to justify its existence but instead employed a bowdlerised version of Marxism, which allotted a leading role to the proletariat, albeit mediated through the vehicle of the CPSU. The elite was thus constrained to adhere to some of the goals it proclaimed including egalitarian social relations, the right to a job, and steadily increasing living standards. In return, workers expected the regime to deliver on these promises made in its name.

The emergence of the social contract is linked to the stabilisation of the ruling bureaucracy in the USSR in the post-Stalin period, the elimination of terror within the bureaucracy as a pre-condition of its effective functioning and the extension of less coercive arrangements to society as a whole. It is also crucially connected to the development of Soviet society from a predominantly rural to an urban society and from a working class, which had emerged from the peasantry, with all the baggage that entailed about individualistic attitudes, level of literacy and cultural values, to the appearance of a stable, settled and increasingly hereditary working class employed in big enterprises, whose links to the countryside, while still extant, were being gradually eroded. On this basis, Breslauer argues that the social contract, or what he refers to as 'welfare-state authoritarianism', did not emerge until the Brezhnev era (pp.222-3).

Zaslavsky does not explicitly use the term 'social contract', preferring to talk of the emergence of a consensus between workers and the Party apparatus during the Brezhnev period. Consensus implies a rather stronger notion of identity between the goals of the regime and the working class than does the concept of social contract, which implies rights and obligations on the parties to the contract. Zaslavsky discerns the origins of the social consensus in a combination of objective and conjunctural factors. Among the former are the social atomisation of the working class as a result of intra-class differences deriving from the division between basically unskilled and skilled workers; the right enjoyed by workers to change their jobs; the failure of the economic reforms of the 1960s; the crucial role of vodka in private consumption; and decreased structural mobility affecting skilled workers in particular. Conjuncturally, the pivotal moment is the defeat of the economic reforms of the 1960s. Declining economic performance had opened up divisions within the bureaucracy, which began to manifest themselves as alternative solutions to arrest the decline. The 1965 economic reform, initiated by Premier Kosygin, sought to give enterprises greater autonomy and introduce indicators of quality to replace those of quantity which had marked the traditional planning system. The emphasis shifted away from the bureaucracy in the ministeries and away from the semi-skilled working class in the factories towards enterprise management and technical and specialist employees. Semi-skilled workers became increasingly threatened by the spectre of unemployment as superfluous labour was 'shaken out'. An informal alliance was entered into between the bureaucracy and working class, which successfully defeated the reforms, greatly enhancing the legitimacy of the Brezhnev regime. Thus, 'to some workers the regime actually emerged as a defender against the arbitrariness of local managers, the danger of new technology, and the threat of a reorganization of the production process, which meant unemployment and tiresome retraining' (Zaslavsky, p.51). This does not signify simply an accidental confluence of interests but of an acknowledgement on the part of a significant section of the elite that the greater good of the preservation of its power depended on a retention of the workers' allegiance and a recognition of the potential social turmoil should their social benefits be fundamentally challenged.

Fulfilling the social contract's requirements demanded more and more resources to increase wages, maintain full employment and hold down the prices on basic goods, a feat was possible while the economy was growing at a respectable rate but from the 1960s onwards, Soviet economic performance began to show a steady decline, making a reform of the system imperative.

Apart from the 'social contract' two other frameworks for understanding state / society relations have been suggested: corporatism and paternalism. In the early 1980s, the popularity of the concept of 'corporatism' led some Western analysts to apply the label 'state corporatist' (as opposed to 'liberal corporatist') to the Soviet Union (see Bunce & Echols III; Bunce 1983; Ruble 1983). To an extent, Bunce uses the expression 'corporatism' in much the same way as other people use 'social contract'. 'Corporatism' gives a sense of negotiation between different interests rather than simple imposition but it is possible to argue that the two concepts operated at different levels. The 'social contract' established general norms applicable to the entire working class, but interest articulation via the trade unions at the level of the state fine-tuned the contract and brought potential problems to the attention of the regime. The difference between the role of the state as the guarantor of the social contract and the role of the trade unions can be seen in the practical distinction made by workers on the rare occasions when they engaged in large-scale action. In Novocherkassk in 1962, and in the 1989 miners' strike, workers by-passed their union organisations and addressed their demands directly to the regime.

While the concept of 'corporatism' implies the possession of certain resources and power by the parties to the arrangement, Lane and O'Dell have posited the notion of the 'incorporated' as distinct from 'alienated' worker and of 'a more effectively socialised and incorporated working class' (p.41). The basic characteristics of this incorporation are that:

> ... groups of workers may influence and even seek to change the pattern of exchange between themselves and the political elite, but the working class has little independent class power to resist government action. Much more important are differences of interest and attitudes between various strata of workers within the enterprise; such interests should be seen as stemming from their place in the division of labour; and ... some workers are more effectively 'incorporated' than others (ibid, pp.41-2).

'Incorporation' was reinforced by 'cooling out' working class ambition through socialisation at factory level, declining differentials between workers and by placing the onus of educational achievement on individual endeavour. What distinguishes Lane and O'Dell's notion of the 'incorporated' worker from concepts of 'corporatism' is that the working class *qua* class was incorporated rather than there being a distinct arrangement between the state and the workers' organisations and, in particular, the trade unions. They reject both Ticktin's claim that, despite being atomised at a societal level, workers were able to exert some autonomous power over the production process and Conquest's assertion that workers had no influence at all. Nevertheless, they consider that '...the effects of socialisation and the institutional structure of the Soviet industrial enterprise will ... be sufficient to accomodate the kinds of economistic demands likely to be articulated by the contemporary Soviet worker' (ibid, p.38).

It would, of course, have taken a very brave or foolhardy writer in the seemingly stable years of the Brezhnev era to predict the social turmoil of the late 1980s. Nevertheless, the decline in Soviet economic growth and productivity was becoming sufficiently apparent to have envisaged a possible conflict between the regime's efforts to reestablish an upward trend in economic growth and the bases, even within Lane and O'Dell's own terms, of working-class 'incorporation'.

The concept of paternalism can also be used to nuance the concept of social contract rather than in counterposition to it. Ferenc Feher, for example, periodises the emergence of a paternalistic system in the USSR in a similar way to the one suggested for the emergence of the social contract. He argues that full-blown paternalism was only embedded under Brezhnev as such a mode of legitimation had proved incompatible with Khrushchev's accrual of power and proclivity for experimentation which ran counter to the continued security and interests of the elite (Feher, p.69). Feher does, however, identify paternalism as a purely top-down process, the fundamental features of which are the conscious rejection of revolutions from above, the obtaining of certain benefits on the part of the population, and the security obtained by the elite itself (ibid, pp.69-72). The stabilisation of the post-Stalin elite and their motivations are certainly important factors to consider for any model of regime-mass relations. His model assumes, however, that the elite acted *only* in the interests of an easy life for itself and says nothing about the ideological dimension or the perceived threat posed by a disgruntled working class, presumably because these are thought to be irrelevant. The paternalism model is therefore one-sided and inadequate.

While Feher's paternalism centred on state-society relations, another form of paternalism has been promoted by Sarah Ashwin. This focuses more plausibly on the role of the enterprise. Ashwin argues that the enterprise collective 'was the concrete expression of the common interests of its members, and constituted the basic unit of Soviet society' (p.10). By providing a whole range of benefits and services, to which there was no alternative source of supply, Soviet workers were subjected to a form of coercive paternalism, at once integrated collectively and atomised by the imposition of strict limits on autonomous activity (ibid, pp.11-15). This is an important corrective to state-centred studies, but in focussing on the enterprise, Ashwin leaves unclear the relationship between regime and workers at a society-wide level.

**The Role of Trades Unions**

The role of trade unions within the Soviet system was always an ambiguous one. If the state was a workers' state controlled by the workers and in which the capitalist class had been eliminated, then trade unions would appear to have been redundant as their functions derive from the conflict between labour and capital.

Indeed, the precise role of trade unions was raised soon after the October Revolution and became the subject of a famous debate among the Bolsheviks in 1920. On one side, Trotsky and Bukharin maintained that the trade unions' prime function was to mobilise and discipline workers during the reconstruction period following the Civil War; on the other side, Kollontai and Shlyapnikov, leaders of the Workers' Opposition faction, argued that the trade unions should be the mechanism for the exercise of workers' control over the economy; in the middle, as he often was, Lenin developed a hybrid position which eventually became Soviet orthodoxy: the trade unions should have dual functions - on the one hand, mobilisation of the workforce to attain production targets, but also the defence of workers' interests against management and even their own state (see Daniels, pp.119-136). The latter element acknowledged that the interests of workers and management, although consonant in the long term, could be conflictual in the short term (Kuromiya, p. 65). During the period of the New Economic Policy (NEP), enterprise unions could exercise some control functions over management via the so-called 'troika' comprising management, party committee and trade union committee. Kuromiya argues, however, that this arrangement was unstable, the unions and party tending 'to become either "adjuncts to management" or control organizations usurping managerial functions' (ibid.). With the introduction of the first Five-Year Plan, however, the troika was abolished and the emphasis in enterprise management was placed entirely on the principle of *edinonachalie* (one-person management).

Blair Ruble suggests that in the notion of the 'dual functioning' of Soviet trade unions 'a factory union leader in the Soviet Union must both mobilize workers behind production goals and defend those same workers against unscrupulous administrators' (1981, p.9). This principle is not, however, governed by a balance between its two parts:

> ... factory trade union committees play an instrumental role in protecting a worker's right to a labor contract and in protecting a worker's right to a proper wage. However, when juridical rights come into conflict with other desired ends, such as increased industrial production, a significant number of factory union and management officials tend to overlook the juridical rights (Ruble 1979, p.79).

According to Ruble this orientation was reinforced during the latter part of the Brezhnev period such that 'Party and union resolutions have come slowly but perceptively to favor a production orientation in the execution of union duties' (1981, p.42). There was, therefore, a marked shift in the dual functions model away from trades unions as defenders of workers' interests to the role of mobilising the workforce.

Ruble's thesis of dual-functioning trade unions has been cogently criticised by Simon Clarke and Peter Fairbrother as being too focussed on their constitutional and juridical status rather than on actual practice in the enterprise (1993, pp.92-4). Their argument is essentially that the duality was not between management and workers but between management and the party, to which the union was subordinated. They argue that 'from this point of view the 'dual functions' of the trade union were their functions for the enterprise administration, on the one hand, and their functions for the party-state, on the other, and the tension was between these two roles' (ibid, p.93). Soviet trade unions were thus, at best, ineffective defenders of workers in the workplace.

The subordination of the trades unions to the party was an essential component of Stalin's triumph. As early as 1926 he had suggested that unions and other 'mass organisations' should be 'transmission belts' conveying the party's will to the rank-and-file worker (Conquest, p.151). At a national level unions were organised according to the following principles: first, all unions were industrial unions organising all the workers in a single industrial sector irrespective of their job or position within the hierarchy; even enterprise directors belonged to the relevant union. Second, the unions' internal structure increasingly came to be modelled on the party itself: i.e the hierarchical subordination of lower to higher levels and operation according to the bureaucratic interpretation of the concept of democratic centralism in which the democratic involvement of the rank-and-file in decision making was eliminated in favour of centralism, the implementation of the leadership's will. All unions were grouped into a single confederation, the All-Union Central Council of Trade Unions (AUCCTU). In keeping with the general subordination of interest groups to the party-state, no independent unions were permitted to exist and attempts to establish them were ruthlessly suppressed. The dependence of the unions on the party was demonstrated by the fact that leadership positions were filled by party appointees through the *nomenklatura* system. Tomsky, the only national union leader to have had genuine union experience, was removed in 1929 as he attempted to promote trades union autonomy from the party and state bureaucracies. Subsequent leaders were party-appointed figures from diverse backgrounds in the party-state apparatus: in the late 1960s and 1970s, AUCCTU chair Aleksandr Shelepin had even been head of the KGB.

It seems clear that trades unions played no real role as defenders of workers' interests in the Soviet system. But, if the social contract is a viable explanation of the relationship between workers and the state, did trades unions play a role in mediating this relationship? As we noted above, the enterprise played a key role in the Soviet system as a focus for the disbursement of a whole range of welfare benefits: enterprises recruited workers and could not reliably meet plan targets without a pool of surplus labour, thus maintaining the policy of full employment; housing, social and pre-school childcare facilities were provided by enterprises; pensions were through enterprises. Within this framework the enterprise's trades union committee was the body responsible for allocating benefits to workers. Consequently, the trades union committee had considerable power in maintaining discipline: poor work meant no priority for certain benefits.

The concrete operation of the welfare systems permits a more nuanced understanding of the social contract. At one level, as well as trying to satisfy its own material interests, the *nomenklatura* had an ideological commitment to the raising and maintenance of workers' living standards coupled with a fear of what could happen should workers organise and act collectively and autonomously from the party. At another level, the actual mechanism for the disbursement of welfare benefits sought both to fulfill the ideological commitment and to ensure that workers would not have the incentive or the capacity to act collectively and autonomously. The prioritisation of individual workers or groups of workers was an effective mechanism for divide and rule. It is significant that a majority of disputes in Soviet industry occurred in just one section of an enterprise and that it was exceptional for disputes to spread to an enterprise level, let alone beyond the confines of a single enterprise (Alekseeva).

The major exception to this is the workers' uprising in Novocherkassk in southern Russia in 1962. Here the trigger for action concerned an infringement of the social contract: a rise in food prices. This combined with specific grievances at the major locomotive factory to produce a city wide protest that was only finally suppressed through the use of KGB troops and the arrival of a delegation from the Politburo itself. Despite the use of repression, the regime rescinded the price rises, thereby acknowledging that it had unjustifiably breached unwritten norms.

## Conclusion

Soviet industrialisation in the specific circumstances of economic isolation produced a very specific set of social relations. by virtue of the elimination of the bourgeoisie and the nationalisation of the means of production, but political power was not directly exercised by the working class but by an elite. That elite was, however, a political creation, heterogeneous, ideologically tied to the working class and dependent for its reproduction on the party drawing cadre primarily from amongst industrial workers; it proved incapable both of developing a mechanism for expropriating the social surplus product and of securing its own hegemony in society. To maintain its rule, therefore, the elite had to come to an arrangement with the working class, the social contract, which made certain concessions to notions of social justice and equality. Maintaining the social contract demanded the expenditure of ever greater resources in conditions of declining economic performance, while the elite sought to create conditions through which it could extract the social surplus and also realise its hegemony, that is through its transformation into a (capitalist) class. The problems the regime faced in juggling these conflicting tendencies will be examined in the next chapter.

# 3 *Perestroika* and Labour's Response

I have argued in the previous chapters that an understanding of political change requires an analysis of the interrelationship between domestic and global factors. This chapter will examine the specific factors that led to the promotion of economic and political liberalisation (*perestroika*) in the USSR. In this context I will examine the impact on the social contract and the origins and consequences of the 1989 miners' strike, an event that represented a fundamental break between a core section of Soviet workers and the regime.

## The Looming Crisis of the Soviet System

### *Deteriorating economic performance*

The aims of Soviet policy during the 1960s and 1970s can be outlined as follows: domestically, the desire was to maintain social peace through the 'social contract' and elite unity through the so-called 'stability of cadres'; externally, the goal was to keep Eastern Europe tied to the Soviet Union through the 'Brezhnev Doctrine' and to achieve parity in nuclear weapons with the United States. These disparate aims could only be realised if economic growth were maintained. By 1980, Brezhnev and the Soviet Union appeared to be at the height of their powers but apparent success in all these cases disguised the depth of the emerging problems, postponed the search for viable solutions and exacerbated the crisis when it finally appeared in the mid-1980s.

The steady decline of the Soviet economy can be seen from the data contained in Table 3.1. Officially, Soviet national income grew ninetyfold between 1928 and 1985 but, in a re-examination of the figures and a questioning of the methodology, Selyunin and Khanin argued that growth in the region of six or sevenfold was nearer the mark, although still 'an outstanding success by any measure' (p.192). According to their figures key indices were beginning to decline even in the early 1960s (ibid, p.194).

Whatever the statistical truth, and regardless of the indicators employed, Soviet economic performance was deteriorating.

**Table 3.1 Soviet economic growth, 1951-85 (average annual rates of growth, official data, percent)**

| | National Income Produced | Gross Industrial Production | Gross Agricultural Production | Labour Productivity in Industry |
|---|---|---|---|---|
| 1951-55 | 11.4 | 13.2 | 4.2 | 8.2 |
| 1956-60 | 9.2 | 10.4 | 6.0 | 6.5 |
| 1961-65 | 6.5 | 8.6 | 7.2 | 4.6 |
| 1966-70 | 7.8 | 8.5 | 3.9 | 5.8 |
| 1971-75 | 5.7 | 7.4 | 2.5 | 6.8 |
| 1976-80 | 4.3 | 4.4 | 1.7 | 4.4 |
| 1981-85 | 3.6 | 3.7 | 1.0 | 3.4 |

*Source*: White 1990, p.85

Soviet economic growth was achieved through 'extensive' methods of mobilising more and more factors of production, particularly labour. This method could be utilised during industrialisation because of the enormous reserves of labour in agriculture. By the 1980s, however, labour was becoming an increasingly scarce resource, the main growth area being Central Asia, far from the industrial heartlands of the Soviet west. The Soviet population was also becoming proportionately older, placing an increasing burden on the state at the same time as large numbers were becoming comparatively inactive economically. People's growing awareness during the 1970s of increasing economic difficulties translated itself into a dramatic rise in alcoholism, and a 'motivational crisis' which jeopardised the legitimacy of the regime, without necessarily threatening its downfall.

As well as labour becoming a scarce resource, many basic raw materials, particularly in the energy sector, were also becoming more difficult to exploit because of their increasingly remote geographical location and lack of infrastructure. Agriculture, long the Achilles heel of the Soviet system, was also in crisis with a decreasing workforce and lack of basic storage facilities and communications; from being the world's greatest exporter of grain in the early twentieth century, the Soviet Union had become its greatest importer. The one bright spot on the economic front was that big rises in oil prices during the 1970s brought the Soviet Union an unexpected windfall. This was somewhat offset, however, by the declining performance and increasing indebtedness of East European states. The Soviet Union's economic relationship to Eastern Europe had become one of increasing subsidisation. Soviet oil and gas was exported to Eastern Europe at below world market prices. In return, Eastern Europe exported goods of decidedly unsatisfactory quality to the USSR, while higher quality produce was exported to the West for hard currency with which to pay off accumulated debts.

*Military competition*

The Soviet Union's relationship to the capitalist world was mediated primarily through military competition. During the 1970s, Brezhnev shifted Soviet policy from 'minimum deterrence' to one of seeking parity in nuclear weapons with the United States (Halliday, pp.148-151). The emergence in the West of a neo-liberal axis centred on the Reagan and Thatcher administrations threatened to change the global balance of forces completely. In its efforts to recapture its pre-Vietnam preeminence, the Reagan administration stationed Cruise and Pershing missiles in Western Europe and attempted to enforce sanctions against Poland, following the imposition of martial law in December 1981, and against the USSR for the invasion of Afghanistan in December 1979. A major feature of this policy was its attempt to 'decouple' the USSR from West Germany, the former's main source of high technology (Johnstone, pp.187-91). While Cruise and Pershing were only a temporary measure, a longer-term, more strategic, development was taking place in the form of the Strategic Defense Initiative (SDI), commonly referred to as 'Star Wars'. While different classes of missile could be roughly matched at the current Soviet level of technology, SDI was altogether different. The promotion of SDI was intended to have a two-fold effect: first, to cripple the Soviet economy by greatly expanding the proportion of GDP devoted to military expenditure making it more vulnerable to capitalist penetration and, second, to utilise military research in the West to accelerate technological development, thus aiding recovery from recession. From a Soviet point of view, the technology to be employed in Star Wars, which depended increasingly on newly-invented microprocessors, was beyond the capacity of its industry at its current level of development. The Soviet Union was thus threatened with a fundamental shift in the balance of military power and its ability to engage in the next phase of the technological revolution was brought into question. The level of spending devoted to arms by the regime at a time when economic performance was declining could not fail to have a serious impact on the resources provided for other areas of social provision. Health Minister, Evgenii Chazov, suggested at the 1988 Party Conference that arms spending had had a disastrous effect on healthcare (Trehub, p.213).

Ultimately, the Soviet economy did not run into difficulties simply as a result of conjuctural factors, but also as a consequence of accumulated contradictions which derived from the nature of the Soviet system itself. In addition to the emerging technology gap, Ticktin argues that the roots of the burgeoning crisis derived from first, the end of the growth of the absolute surplus, which resulted from an incapacity to replenish the workforce and intolerable pressure on the provision of raw materials; second, the increasingly urbanised and integrated character of the economy in which shortcomings in the supply system were becoming intolerable; and, third, the increased strength of the workforce (pp.139-144). For Lewin, economic organisation, manifested in 'departmentalism' (*vedomstvennost'*), particularly in respect of the ministries and large enterprises, and their accompanying centralism and vertical links, was 'at the heart of the malfunctions in the economy' (p.104).

*The crisis of leadership*

Brezhnev's death in November 1982 added another element. Indeed, the leadership crisis had begun even earlier as Brezhnev had been seriously ill since the late 1970s, but his unassailable position at the apex of the Soviet system ensured that the struggle to succeed him had assumed a purely covert form. As the problems confronting the Soviet economy became more acute, potentially threatening the stability and viability of the system itself, this struggle began to emerge into the open. Brezhnev's immediate successor was Yurii Andropov, former head of the KGB and therefore as aware as anyone of the general problems confronting the Soviet system. Andropov's watchword was 'discipline': attempting to make the ailing economy work more efficiently. There was a brief upturn in the economy under Andropov but his own failing health cut short his tenure as General Secretary. Andropov's successor in February 1984 was Brezhnev's old crony, Konstantin Chernenko. While things did not quite stay at a standstill under Chernenko, the balance of forces inside the leadership prevented any moves toward a thoroughgoing economic reform. Chernenko was the last leader to come from the Brezhnevite 'gerontocracy' and he too soon succumbed, dying in March 1985. His successor, Mikhail Gorbachev, was appointed with unprecedented speed, suggesting that a reform coalition had been assembled. This reflected a high degree of consensus within the Politburo that the uncertainty of the past few years could not continue, and that a dynamic young leader was needed who could promote an appropriate strategy to tackle the Soviet Union's problems.

## Economic Reform

### *'Acceleration'*

The new leadership's strategy, while concentrated on reform of the economy, was also profoundly political in its striving to maintain the rule of the dominant elite. The elite's heterogeneity did mean, however, that different types of reform could infringe and damage the interests of its various elements. The trick was, therefore, to assemble a coalition in favour of a reform which would not threaten the interests of the key Soviet institutions, but which would inject some dynamism into the economy. The problems for Gorbachev were that the accumulating difficulties required a more radical approach than had previously been applied, which would inevitably affect some major interests, and that the leadership he inherited was put in place by his predecessors and would be difficult to change in the short-term. As various reform measures were outlined, however, the extent to which he possessed a coherent strategy became a prime focus of discussion almost up to the moment of the USSR's demise.

Gorbachev's initial strategy was premised on a belief in substantial hidden reserves in the economy which could be mobilised given the correct policies. This phase was referred to as 'acceleration' (*uskorenie*), an attempt to achieve substantial gains by boosting industrial production through improved productivity, and reorganising the bureaucracy to achieve greater coordination especially in machine-building and agriculture. The 12th Five Year Plan (1986-90) conservatively emphasised traditional Soviet methods - the prioritisation of the machine-building sector – while overambitiously demanding a 40 percent increase in that sector's output, which could only be attained through considerable investment and a substantial increase in rolled steel output, both of which had fallen in the previous plan period (Hanson). It was also assumed that the increase in output would come entirely from productivity gains, something never before achieved (Rumer, pp.27-8).

The value of imported Western technology, viewed as crucial to improved productivity, actually declined in 1985 and, most crucially, a fall in world oil prices and West European gas prices in early 1986 delivered a huge blow to Soviet hard currency earnings, the major source of which was energy. A drastic shift in Soviet foreign trade also occurred during this period. In 1984, the Soviet Union enjoyed a current trade surplus of $6.3 billion. In 1985, this fell to $1.5 billion. The current trade surplus with socialist and third world states also fell from 3.8 billion to 2.1 billion roubles over the same period. As a result, lending to socialist and third world countries was reduced, and borrowing from the West increased.

The reality of 'acceleration' was that Gorbachev undertook 'no radical steps to revive the economy' and was 'basically engaged in patching up and repairing - using old techniques inherited from his predecessors' (Rumer 1986, p.22). Hints in respect of future reform were, however, contained in the draft Party Programme published in October 1985, which mentioned enterprise autonomy, self-management, and marketisation in industry while remaining unspecific in terms of policies to realise these goals, thus leaving Gorbachev 'maximum room for maneuver' (Dyker, p.4).

### *Glasnost'*

It was apparent by early 1986 that 'acceleration' was not delivering the improvements required in a deteriorating international environment, but the majority of the reform coalition was too deeply wedded to the traditional system to move much beyond some tinkering with the economic mechanism and an emphasis on increased discipline. It was this climate which promoted the search for alternative solutions to the burgeoning crisis, to an alternative 'reform coalition', and however hesitatingly to the initiation of political liberalisation.

*Glasnost'* became the most potent symbol of political liberalisation under Gorbachev, but the nature of the concept changed over time and different versions were espoused by the emerging factions within the leadership. As a notion of giving people voice within the Soviet system, *glasnost'* was already being promoted in 1985 as an adjunct to 'acceleration', but its parameters were limited to combatting bureaucratism (*Pravda* 20 October 1985; 22 October 1985). Moreover, it was compatible with increased centralisation by promoting accountability of lower to higher party and state bodies. For Yegor Ligachev, who would soon emerge as the leading 'conservative' in the CPSU, *glasnost'* was a means of strengthening the social order, of raising discipline, and of criticising obsolescence, while leaving the fundamental structure of the system untouched (Remington, p.71). Within this restricted version of *glasnost'*, and to keep the original reform coalition together, the main target of attack was the stagnation (*zastoi*) of the Brezhnev period. This enabled Gorbachev to achieve comparatively sweeping changes in the leading bodies of the CPSU at the 27th Congress in February 1986, removing a number of Brezhnev-era figures. During 1985-6, editorial positions in the mass media were also affected by the leadership transformation. Remington suggests that the only explanation for the scale of the turnover in this period was 'to build a broad base of support for the new Gorbachev leadership's policy programme by disrupting existing political alliances and appointing new staff capable of enforcing the objectives of the *glasnost'* campaign' (ibid, p.69).

While the more conservative elements within the party leadership consistently adhered to a narrow vision of *glasnost'*, linked solely to a reform of the economic mechanism, Gorbachev's interpretation of this concept began to change decisively. Gill argues that 'developments seem to fit better with the view that Gorbachev's policy position became radicalised in the second half of 1986 by his realisation that the earlier measures were not working' (p.32). As Gorbachev made a conscious effort to win the support of the creative intelligentsia, the original reform coalition, restricted solely to the party leadership, began to unravel and be replaced by a much broader coalition, extending beyond the leadership's narrow confines. In capitalist states, this process is facilitated by the existence, however repressed, of some form of civil society. In the Soviet Union, however, the regime was all-pervasive, leaders of cultural and other organisations were usually members of the CPSU Central Committee, and no autonomous organisations were permitted to exist. The notion of reaching beyond the regime to some form of civil society was, therefore, nonsensical. Initially at least, Gorbachev was more interested in changing the balance of forces inside the party by transforming the bodies over which it had jurisdiction, rather than mobilising public opinion. But even this limited strategy did not have the desired impact: the Writers' Union, for example, remained under conservative control and resistant to reform (Woll, p.46). The radicalisation of *glasnost'* in mid-1986 thus had two main purposes: first, to build up a head of steam against bureaucratic obstruction through its exposure in the press and by encouraging ordinary people, as individuals, to complain; and, second, to encourage the cultural intelligentsia to support Gorbachev by creating a space for more critical artistic endeavour (Sakwa 1990, p.74). The latter function, which contained the essence of the political liberalisation, was the more important, because the possibilities for independent action outside the parameters of official organisations were expanded, creating the opportunity for the emergence of a civil society, and thus laying the foundations for a new 'reform coalition'.

## 'New Political Thinking'

A powerful additional factor in liberalising the regime was the realisation that the solution to certain problems was beyond purely domestic measures. The need to reduce Soviet military expenditure and gain greater access to Western technology necessitated negotiating with the West and especially the US. Gorbachev's project for ending the Soviet economic crisis depended on developing a strategic alliance with leading elements of the West's bourgeoisie. In a situation of declining American economic power, the US administration was keen to ensure that the USSR did not pursue this strategy solely with Western Europe and in particular West Germany. The price of such strategic co-operation was, however, pressure to embark upon a programme of economic and political liberalisation.

Under the aegis of new foreign minister, Eduard Shevardnadze, fundamental changes were initiated in Soviet foreign policy, summed up in the phrase 'new political thinking'. This emphasised the 'deideologisation' of international relations, through which common problems in an interdependent world, could be tackled regardless of the social character of the states involved. Among its main elements were 'the gradual liquidation of nuclear arms by the year 2000, the establishment of a system of comprehensive security, a doctrine of military sufficiency and non-aggression, and improvements in the world economy' (White 1993, p.196).

Throughout 1986 and 1987, Gorbachev pursued a strategic arms agreement with the US. Arms control had been the subject of ongoing negotiations between the superpowers since the early 1970s with, arguably, little real impact on nuclear arsenals. A series of summit meetings between Gorbachev and Reagan between 1985 and 1987 presaged the signing of the Treaty on Intermediate Nuclear Forces (INF), which abolished a small but significant class of land-based missiles, which had been the focus of the increased tension of the early 1980s. Despite being hailed as a 'victory for new political thinking', the Treaty affected the Soviet nuclear arsenal more than than the American and left SDI research untouched (ibid, p.203).

A general relaxation of tension was required to allow Eastern Europe to ease its economic problems and permit a withdrawal from Afghanistan without concerns for the security implications. Developing a new 'détente' also meant making concessions on human rights. In this respect, the release of Andrei Sakharov in December 1986, following a personal phone-call from Gorbachev, was highly significant. As well as producing a favourable response in the West, it sent a signal to the intelligentsia that dissident thought was no longer a punishable offence (Doder & Branson, pp.172-4).

## Deepening the Liberalisation Process

The dangers of liberalisation in conditions of deteriorating economic performance, declining ideological conviction and the rise of a dynamic ideology on a global scale promoted by the world's major power, are well illustrated by the progress of *glasnost'*. The increasing polarisation in the CPSU leadership became apparent in January 1987 at the Central Committee Plenum, which had been postponed three times because of failure to agree its agenda. A fundamental division became apparent in the CC between supporters and opponents of glasnost, among whom Ligachev emerged as the leading figure (Hazan, pp.16-17). Gorbachev repeated the need for glasnost and stated that '[f]urther democratization of Soviet society is becoming the party's urgent task' (ibid, p.16). Elections were to be employed increasingly as a weapon to dislodge conservatives and allow greater public participation. A special party conference was to be held in July 1988 which, while restricted in its capacity to change the composition of leadership bodies, could provide a platform for the legitimation of further reform measures. Steps were also taken to deepen economic reform by introducing a draft of the Law on the State Enterprise, the final version of which was to be agreed at the June 1987 CC Plenum.

Outside of the party the openings afforded by *glasnost'* resulted in the emergence of discussion groups and clubs ostensibly in support of *glasnost'* and *perestroika*. Although these groups were primarily composed of intellectuals, they also involved workers in some cities. In the past, such autonomous activity would have been swiftly suppressed, but now the energy and dynamism was harnessed to push forward *perestroika*. Sections of the intelligentsia seized on the opening to pursue an increasingly damning investigation of fundamental elements of the Soviet system itself. With some support of the party hierarchy, 'blank spots' in Soviet history were re-examined, victims of Stalin's purges (except Trotsky) rehabilitated, and even the October Revolution and Lenin's legacy, previously considered untouchable, came under fire, including from analysts within the CPSU itself. As this ideological assault on the bases of the regime progressed, many of the discussion groups began to promote much more radical variants of social, political and economic change. While the CPSU remained the only legal political party, many of the new organisations were patently embryonic political parties in an increasingly pluralised political spectrum. Liberalisation thus accelerated the process of institutional disintegration and ideological decay, evident since the death of Stalin.

Gorbachev was not, however, loosening ideological ties and activating dormant political forces for their own sake. His priority was always economic change; political liberalisation was simply about assembling the forces in order to enable economic liberalisation to proceed. The context of economic liberalisation both domestically and internationally was, however, changing rapidly, polarising political forces between those favouring a reassertion of control by the party and those favouring ever more radical political and economic liberalisation. Gorbachev was caught in the middle trying to ride two horses whose paths were swiftly diverging, throwing his weight first to one side and then to the other in an effort to rein them in.

## *Perestroika* and the Social Contract

It is possible to identify certain strategic objectives which Gorbachev wished to achieve: first, a shift in Soviet economic development from an extensive to an intensive pattern, promoting gains in productivity through rationalisation of the production process, enhancing its technological component over the still-dominant manual labour; and, second, a radical improvement in the quality of output, which as well as having an impact within the USSR would also make it competitive on the world market. The means of achieving both goals were, however, couched in such general terms - enterprise autonomy, workplace democratisation, more strategic planning, etc. - that translating them into workable legislation was an almost impossible undertaking. Gorbachev shuffled the coalition of interests required to progress the key pieces of legislation but in doing so had to make concessions to the very institutions that could hamper their implementation. The various laws and resolutions passed to transform the economic mechanism were thus profoundly influenced by the conflict and accomodation of different interests within the party-state. This imparted a contradictory character to much of the written form of the legislation which was then interpreted in a range of different ways by different ministries, in different regions and republics, to produce an utterly incoherent practice.

The June 1987 Central Committee Plenum approved a major document titled 'Basic Provisions for the Radical Restructuring of Economic Management' establishing the enterprise, which was promised more independence, as the primary economic actor, with central planning shifting from a directive to a more strategic role (Tedstrom 1987, pp.93-4). A few days later, the Supreme Soviet adopted the centrepiece of the legislation for economic reform, the Law on the State Enterprise, which came into force on 1 January 1988. The prospect of an enterprise law had been greeted by reformers as an 'attempt to cut the feet from the ministries and central economic bodies', but on publication even the Draft was considered a failure that ministries and central bodies 'had transformed ... to their liking' (Aslund 1989, p.32). As Tedstrom observed, the retention of the ministerial framework immediately placed obstacles in the path of enterprise autonomy, and the question of price reform proved 'so controversial that the June plenum could not arrive at any consensus' (1987, p.95). Leading reformer Boris Kurashvili argued that, while a step forward, the Enterprise Law and the Basic Provisions agreed at the June 1987 Central Committee Plenum were 'contradictory, half-hearted and intermediate' and 'the fruit of a temporary compromise between radical and conservative approaches, between the initiators of cardinal reform and the inert, bureaucratised apparatus of management, which resorts to the phraseology of *perestroika* in order to disguise its conservative positions and proposals' (p.10).

Irrespective of their actual outcome, it was clear that the objectives of the economic reforms conflicted with the social contract as it had operated under Brezhnev. Hauslohner observed that the social contract and economic modernisation were 'mutually constraining' in that economic reform was constrained by the social contract and the social contract by economic performance (p.54). While correctly noting that 'Gorbachev's ideas on economic reform [were] blocked by the social contract', Ludlam's suggestion that *perestroika* entailed just reform of the social contract fails to convey the extent to which the latter had to be dismantled (p.302).

From the perspective of the social contract, improving productivity meant widening wage differentials to 'reward' workers for greater effort, decreasing job security by creating the possibility of redundancy, and changing the situation on the shopfloor so that managers had much greater authority; second, enterprise autonomy could only be achieved if the 'social wage' was greatly reduced by allowing prices to be set by the market, eliminating subsidies, and introducing payment for formerly free services. This was clearly a massive undertaking which could not be introduced in one fell swoop, tackling the social contract head on, not least because, as well as undermining the regime's main legitimating mechanism, power had to be taken away from mainstays of the system: the party and planning and ministerial bureaucracies. Unsurprisingly, because of the threat posed to key institutions, no clearcut agreement could be achieved within the ruling stratum itself. Indeed, the ambivalence of the Soviet leadership can be seen in Gorbachev's defence of the USSR's social achievements in late 1987 (*Pravda* 2 December, 1987). The introduction of a new mode of legitimation thus required the careful implementation of a combination of carrot and stick policies relating to workplace democratisation, wages, prices and employment.

### *Workplace democratisation*

The proposal for workplace democratisation, Gorbachev argued, was a natural accompaniment to economic development, as 'the acceleration of society's development is inconceivable and impossible without a further development of all the aspects and manifestations of socialist democracy' (p.69). This was not, however, a philanthropic gesture of democracy after decades of repression; it was precipitated by the slowing of Soviet economic growth, and particularly declining rates of labour productivity. Joel Moses makes it clear that worker self-management had 'nothing to do with achieving Communism, democratizing Soviet society in a Western liberal sense, or abolishing single-party rule.' It was about reforming the economy (p.208).

The more farsighted reformers, increasingly aware of the Soviet economy's predicament, realised that the absence of private property in the means of production and the accumulation of capital deprived enterprise managers of the incentive to maximise their productive potential and increase labour productivity. While enterprise managers had an interest in the performance of the economy as a whole as this maximised their privileges, and helped maintain their position of power, they had no economic interest in the results of their own enterprise's production. The alternatives were, therefore, either to create private property in the means of production, which at that time was politically unacceptable, or to give workers an incentive to improve productivity.

Under the 1987 Law on the State Enterprise, the 1983 Law on Labour Collectives was extended to give the collective a wider range of issues on which its decision would be final, to enhance the role of general meetings, and to form a labour collective council (STK), composed of representatives of management, Party committee, trade union committee, Komsomol, brigade councils, rank-and-file workers and specialists, to act as an executive body between general meetings. Despite the democratic rhetoric the composition of the STK in practice reinforced the position of the traditional institutions of the Soviet enterprise and the principle of one-man management (*edinonachalie*). The weakening of links between enterprise and ministry and the introduction of contractual relations also made the enterprise workforce more responsible for its economic viability, making possible the phasing out of subsidies and, while encouraging a more collective approach to work at one level (for example, through the brigade system), serving to relate each employee's earnings directly to their input. Thus, the new mode of legitimation would no longer guarantee the social benefits of the old social contract but would ensure a degree of participation in workplace decision-making in return for stricter working conditions, the possibility of unemployment, and greater inequalities between social strata. To have gone beyond the enterprise level, through national co-ordination of STKs, at which there were subsequent efforts from the bottom up, would have challenged the prerogatives of the planning bureaucracy and, by extension, those of the ruling CPSU itself.

It was certainly the intention of the Soviet leadership that the reform legislation would lead to a major restructuring of employment. It was estimated that between 13 and 19 million jobs would be lost in manufacturing by the year 2000 if labour productivity could be sufficiently improved (Kostakov, p.80). Chapman suggests that the constitutionally guaranteed right to a job was being reinterpreted as 'a guarantee (promise?) that an appropriate job [would] be forthcoming' (p.29). In practice, although enterprises began to restructure their workforces as a result of the Law on the State Enterprise, most displaced workers were found jobs in other parts of the same enterprise. Clearly, the legislation was insufficient to reverse the imperatives of the Soviet production process and the social contract. Trehub's comment that the expanding job placement service, introduced to find redundant workers an appropriate job or retraining, would 'be getting a workout in the next few years' proved to be wide of the mark as unemployment rose only marginally (p.209).

The introduction of fees for previously free services, particularly in health, and the partial privatisation of the state housing sector also undermined the previous provisions of the social contract. A resolution on the improvement of the health service indicated a five-fold increase in paid medical services by the end of the century (*Pravda*, 27 November, 1987) and by the end of 1988 'there were hundreds of medical cooperatives in the Soviet Union' although many of these went bankrupt in a short space of time (Trehub p.215).

## Political Liberalisation

The deepening of differences within the CPSU leadership became apparent with the removal of Boris Yeltsin from the Politburo in November 1987 following an outspoken attack at the October 1987 Central Committee plenum 'upon Ligachev and the way the apparatus operated, upon the speed of reform and upon the increasing glorification of Gorbachev' (Gill, p.61). The removal of the most forthright proponent of radical reform forced Gorbachev into adopting a more cautious stance in order to maintain the facade of leadership consensus. The deadlock made the creation of pressure from outside the party more and more important although Gorbachev hoped that the party could continue to play its ascribed leading role. The development of *glasnost'*, the activation of the creative intelligentsia and the use of the media were weapons for taking the struggle back into the party to turn it into a force for radical change.

The 19th Conference of the CPSU in June 1988, the first such party forum since 1941 represented an opportunity for Gorbachev to appeal to the rank-and-file of the party, who were judged to be in favour of deepening the reform process and replacing dead wood with pro-reform elements. For more conservative elements, on the other hand, the conference represented an opportunity to rein in the reform process and place it firmly under party control. Despite manipulation of the election of delegates in favour of apparatchiki, the conference was notable for its departure from the stage-managed arenas of the past and, in many ways, represented a turning-point in the whole process of liberalisation. By undermining the *nomenklatura* appointments system through the introduction of competitive secret ballot elections, and by opening the party up to public scrutiny through an extension of *glasnost'*, '[t]he decisions of the Conference posed a direct challenge to the party and its established way of operating' (Gill, p.67). In addition, the decision to create a new legislative body, the Congress of People's Deputies (CPD), was a major step towards ending the fusion of party and state.

The CPD represented the furthest point of Gorbachev's liberalisation. It comprised 2250 deputies of which 750 were to be nominated by the party and associated social movements. The other 1500 deputies were to be elected through single-member constituencies on the basis of potentially competitive elections. Gorbachev's aim in creating this body was to maintain party domination of the system while creating a popular mandate for *perestroika*. The results of the election in March 1989 confirmed Gorbachev's hopes by increasing the number of deputies who were members of the CPSU, but it was a pyrrhic victory. The contradictory character of liberalisation was revealed by the fact that the Congress did not represent a straightforward strengthening of Communist rule. It initiated an end to the fusion of party and state that had been a core feature of the Soviet system and, for the first time, an opposition to the CPSU came into existence in the shape of the Inter-Regional Group of Deputies (IRGD). The emergence of the IRGD also reflected the increasing factionalisation of the CPSU as most of the opposition belonged to and retained their party membership.

## The 1989 Miners' Strike

The miners' strike of July 1989 is usually considered to have been an important event but of secondary significance to the struggle taking place within the elite. This is a totally inadequate view of the political processes underway in the Soviet Union. While the regime wished to undertake a transformation of the mode of legitimation by supplanting the old social contract, the miners' strike initiated a process of delegitimation from which the regime never recovered. From this point on, the workers' movement which emerged from the July strikes was the most organised proponent of the further democratisation of the Soviet system, and provided the foot soldiers for the liberal opposition, which would otherwise have remained an elite phenomenon. The strike resulted from a combination of domestic and global factors: a climate in which strikes could be seen as legitimate phenomena; the deterioration of living conditions in the coalfields as a result of the failure to orient away from oil and gas; the emergence of an opposition to the regime; and the perceived failures of *perestroika*.

### *Strikes before 1989*

The existence of strikes, a consequence of antagonistic relationships in the relations of production, was denied in pre-*glasnost'* official Soviet propaganda as it would have conflicted with the image of the USSR as a workers' state against which it would have been nonsensical for workers to rebel. Given that strikes did not officially exist, they were neither legal nor illegal. Nevertheless, they did take place, although they were usually small-scale actions, confined to a shop or section within an enterprise. Industrial disputes were normally settled very rapidly by conceding to the workers' demands, and then dealing with the ringleaders later. While this often entailed repression, it could also take the form of 'incorporation' of troublesome workers into the managerial hierarchy. Strikes on a larger scale were very uncommon and tended to be an extreme measure taken when there appeared to be no alternative. They thus represented, in the words of Lyudmila Alekseeva, 'an extraordinary occurrence'.

Glasnost and *perestroika* produced a gradual increase in strikes and other labour disputes and also more information about work stoppages. *Perestroika*'s activation of nationalist movements in some of the Union republics, particularly the Baltic States and Transcaucasia, was accompanied by the emergence of strike movements in their support, which were patently political from the outset and helped to promote the disintegration of the USSR. I would argue that it is not possible to talk about a workers' movement in the strict sense in these republics as the fundamental impetus for action derives from the workers' ethnicity rather than their position as workers (see Berezovskii et al., p.54). Although these movements were clearly significant in furthering political change in the Soviet Union, this analysis will concentrate on events in the two largest republics, Russia and Ukraine, where it is possible to speak of the emergence of a class-based workers' movement.

The strike movement in Russia and Ukraine began comparatively slowly in 1987-88 with the involvement of just a few thousand workers pushing almost exclusively economic demands (Kabalina, et al., p.75). These actions were generally 'spontaneous, uncoordinated, and localized' and directed mainly against reductions in pay, resulting from the new wage policy or *gospriemka* (the state quality control system), and occasionally against poor working conditions (Cook 1993, p.154). More than half the strikes in 1987-88 occurred in transport, especially affecting bus drivers (Monusova 1992a, p.21). Nevertheless, these strikes represented a valuable accumulation of experience, which was transmitted via the burgeoning 'informal' movement to other groups of workers. By 1989 workers were much more organised in their actions and usually led by elected strike committees (Kabalina et al., p.75).

*The decline of the Soviet coal industry*

The changing circumstances of the Soviet coal industry during the 1970s and 1980s provides an important backdrop to the 1989 miners' strike. The Soviet Union had estimated coal reserves of seven trillion tons - the largest in the world - with an energy potential many times greater than that of its oil and gas reserves (Tedstrom 1989, p.13). Nevertheless, the fortunes of the Soviet coal industry were inevitably intertwined with those of other abundant sources of energy in and which, as we have noted, provided the USSR with most of its hard currency. The Soviet leadership's attitude to the coal industry, in terms of level of investment and subsidy, was strongly influenced, therefore, by the state of the global markets for coal and other energy sources.

After the oil crisis of the mid-1970s, the Soviet leadership vacillated over which fuel source should be given priority in its energy policy. At the Twenty-Fifth Congress of the CPSU in 1976 a major turn was announced towards coal as the Soviet Union's main long-term energy source. Such a strategy would have entailed a major investment in the coal industry particularly in terms of new technology. In practice, the hard currency earned by the oil and gas sectors promoted a pragmatic reorientation to the development of oil and gas especially in Siberia to the detriment of the coal regions and other industrial sectors (Shabashev & Mishenin). Despite increased levels of investment during the Tenth Five-Year Plan, the coal industry received a declining share of investment compared to gas and oil. As a consequence, coal production for 1980 'came in a phenomenal 74 million tons short of the low end of the initial 10th Plan target' and enterprises tried to switch from coal to oil and gas as a source of energy (Gustafson 1982, p.123). In the Eleventh Five-Year Plan, coal production was 145 million tons short of its target, 1985 output representing a mere 1.7 percent increase on 1975 (Friedgut & Siegelbaum, p.7). Coal's share of total Soviet fuel production declined from 58 percent in 1960 to an estimated 19 percent in 1990.

Throughout the 1980s coal production stagnated at around 550 million tons per annum - about 2 per cent below plan target. Nevertheless, the Twelfth Five-Year Plan envisaged raising this figure by 1990 to 795 million tons annually, an increasing proportion of which would be gained by opencast methods (Gustafson 1989, p.52). This would have entailed higher levels of investment going to the more easterly coalfields, in particular to the Kuzbass, which predominantly utilised opencast and drift mining. Moreover, coal quality had been declining particularly in the

Donbas, the oldest coalfield in the Soviet Union and based mainly on deep mined coal, the Podmoskove region near Moscow and the Ekibastuz region in Kazakhstan.

Tedstrom points to four major problems contributing to the decline of the Soviet coal industry. First, deep mine coal was becoming ever more difficult to extract in the Donbas and Kuzbass; second, this was not being replaced by new capacity coming on stream; third, there was an acute shortage of manpower exacerbated by declining labour productivity and, finally, mines in the east were being developed too slowly (pp.13-14). These factors led, in turn, to increased strain on the amount of investment allocated to the already severely underfunded and underdeveloped social infrastructure of the mining regions.

*Origins of the strike*

The critical situation in the Kuzbass had been highlighted by the First Secretaries of the Kemerovo Oblast Party, Nikolai Ermakov at the 27th Congress of the CPSU in 1986 and Vadim Bakatin at the Nineteenth Conference in 1988 (Kostiukovskii, p.23). In the coal industry, tension was beginning to increase from late 1988. In October 1988 the Kemerovo Regional Party Committee submitted a statement to Gorbachev regarding the situation in Kuzbass. The centre's failure to address the accumulating problems helped in the defeat of party representatives in the March 1989 elections to the Congress of People's Deputies. In the immediate aftermath of this humiliation and four months prior to the strike, Prokopevsk was visited by Premier Nikolai Ryzhkov who, despite being presented with the facade of a Potemkin village, claimed that he had never seen a worse town and promised help for the Kuzbass. The promise was not kept, causing great resentment (Maksimova, p.66). A month later, regional party committee secretary and Ligachev protege, Mel'nikov, warned the Central Committee plenum that problems had reached crisis levels in the Kuzbass (Kostiukovskii, p.23).

Throughout the spring of 1989 a number of localized strikes occurred in the coal industry, the significance of which cannot be underestimated as they represented an escalation over earlier strikes. First, they were concentrated in one sector with similar demands; second, they had a strong anti-management bias; third, their resolution required central and not local intervention; finally, the workers had taken action after petitioning lower-level authorities (Cook 1993, pp.160-1). The motivation for these stoppages is to be found in a variety of unsatisfactory elements. The housing situation was 'most critical' and affected workers of all grades; wages were similar in all pits and were considered by an overwhelming majority to be too low; particular problems arose between ordinary-grade workers and engineering and technical staff (ITR), who were persistently better paid. The failure of the party and union organisations to protect workers also increased dissatisfaction (Mal'tseeva & Pulyaeva, pp.39-42). In addition, there were a number of factors specific to the coal industry, in particular, the large number of miners doing dangerous work, including a still very high proportion undertaking manual labour, and the low profitability of the coal industry as a result of continuing state price controls while international demand for coal was high (Cook 1993, p.157). As a consequence of declining investment in the coalfields, the standard of living and availability of basic commodities in the coal regions fell drastically during the late 1980s, creating the 'spark' which ignited the strike (Shabashev & Mishenin). According to official statistics only 50 out of 1200 goods were readily available (Cook 1993, p.158).

In other coal-producing regions, conditions were no better. In a survey conducted in the Donbas, 86 percent identified shortages of basic supplies, especially soap, as a major cause of the strike. Low wages were seen as the next major cause and indeed, all of the causes identified in the survey related to basic living and working conditions. Although miners' wages were comparatively high, the income per family member was comparatively low: 'almost 60 percent receive less than 130 rubles monthly per family member, and this, at a time of rising prices, hidden inflation, and black-market speculation for needed goods, is woefully insufficient' (Marples 1989, p.31).

In an analysis of the 1989 strike, Borys Kachura, a secretary of the Ukrainian Communist Party, noted that 'for more than a decade investment in the Ukrainian coal industry had been geared to raising coal output rather than to the social sphere' (Marples 1989, p.30). Money earmarked for social needs was not being spent and basic commodities were in short supply, forcing miners to resort to the black market and co-operatives, whose high prices and incomes were deeply resented. As in the Kuzbass, the increasing area of land given over to industrial development was affecting the volume of food production for the local population.

Housing was another area causing great disquiet. Most miners' accomodation was under the jurisdiction of the Ministry of Coal and yet the conditions were deplorable. According to A. V. Kasyanov, chair of Voroshilovgrad Oblast Executive Committee, 'at the start of 1989, 20 percent of the residences lacked a water supply, 26 percent were not connected to a sewage system, 28 percent did not have central heating, 63 percent lacked hot water, and 49 percent were without gas' (quoted in Marples, 1989, p.31).

The coal industry was restructured under *perestroika* but without the decentralisation intended by the 1987 Law on the State Enterprise. In January 1988 the industry had transferred to self-financing but a new tier of organisation, associations, was established which assumed the rights afforded by the 1987 Enterprise Law. Individual mines did not therefore have rights as enterprises, although this meant little while coal prices were fixed by the state and state orders comprised the bulk of the industry's output. The degree of continuing central control was indicated by the schedule of closures drawn up by the Coal Ministry for the Donbas which earmarked 21 pits in Donets'k province alone for failure to meet economic accountability criteria (*Pravda*, 8 July 1989, p.6).

Twelve days before the strike began the leadership of the miners' union presented an ultimatum to the Ministry of the Coal Industry with a list of demands to be satisfied. The main demands included permitting the pit labour collective to determine the regime of work and rest; the granting of a common day off on Sundays; night and evening shifts to be paid at a higher rate; payment for the time taken to travel from the pit shaft to the miner's place of work and back and for more investment to be devoted to miners' social needs (Maksimova, p.66). Coal Minister, Mikhail Shchadov, reappointed a mere four days before the strike, seems not to have acknowledged the ultimatum although he emphasised the problem of social conditions in mining areas (Clarke, et al. 1995, p.22).

Neither the ultimatum, nor a programme of demands drawn up by managers in Prokopevsk in an effort to derail the strike, met the demands of the miners in full. Both sets of proposals addressed themselves solely to the central authorities in Moscow whereas the miners were also concerned with local injustices and had little confidence in local leaders. It was this lack of attention to what was happening at the grassroots where 'as before, the leaders attempted to decide and think for the rank and file' which Maksimova suggests was a major factor precipitating the strike (Maksimova, p.67). In itself, this was insufficient but, coupled with the breakdown of other aspects of everyday life, produced 'a spontaneous explosion of anger with every aspect of the system and a rejection by the workers of all their self-appointed leaders' (Clarke, et al. 1995, p.27).

The strike began at the Shevyakova mine in Mezhdurechensk, which did not have its own coal association and therefore had no control over its own resources, which seemed to be siphoned off to Moscow via the regional centres of Kemerovo and Novokuznetsk (ibid, pp.28-9). By the end of the first day, 10 enterprises in Mezhdurechensk had stopped work and 15,900 people were on strike. The following day, workers were transported to the city square 'in a move which proved the decisive escalation of the strike' (ibid, p.32).

*Demands*

The significance of the 1989 miners' strike relates both to its scale, which is undisputed, and the more controversial issue of the degree to which its main demands represented agreement with *perestroika* or rejection of the Soviet system. Supporters of the former interpretation include, not surprisingly, Mikhail Gorbachev and the Soviet media. The apparent emphasis on mine autonomy permitted Gorbachev to claim that the miners were striking to promote *perestroika* 'from below' against bureaucratic resistance. An article in *Izvestiya* argued that 'an analysis of the demands made by the miners shows that they are in accord with *perestroika*' (*Izvestiya* July 15 1989, p.2). Some academic commentators concur with this. Theodore Friedgut and Lewis Siegelbaum argue that 'for many leaders of the strike committees the strike was a conscious effort to extricate *perestroika* from the clutches of their immediate bosses, who were widely perceived as having blocked or distorted its thrust ... [and] an attempt to attack the apparat at the grass-roots level and replace it with a truly representative and democratically elected local leadership' (Friedgut & Siegelbaum, p.12). The strike was, therefore, about implementing *perestroika* in the face of central and local bureaucratic intransigence. Paul Christensen also suggests that the 'essence of the demands was a call to implement Gorbachev's policy of industrial perestroika' (p.82).

At the heart of the debate is the question of the provenance of the demand for greater enterprise, or in this case mine, autonomy. In their analysis of the demands emerging from the strike, Clarke et al are unequivocal in maintaining that initial demands were parochial and directed at mine management, the demand for mine independence being a low priority at the outset, but that they were subsequently subverted by enterprise management and local authorities. In support of this, Mandel points out that enterprise autonomy had not been among the original demands of strikers in Mezhdurechensk, Donbas or Vorkuta, and in Kuzbass it was eighteenth out of 25 demands (Mandel 1990). The advantage of this demand for mine management was that it enabled them to deflect criticism away from the local level and highlight the obstruction of this demand at a ministerial level. In addition, it focused the miners' anger on a target consonant with *perestroika*: bloated bureaucracy; the call for mine autonomy was accompanied in most cases by the demand for the abolition of production associations, which were perceived to perform no other function than to siphon off much needed resources. In a survey carried out by Donets'k Scientific Centre, 73 percent of those interviewed favoured the dismantling of production associations, whereas only 16 percent favoured a transfer to full-cost accounting (mine autonomy) (Marples 1991, p.211). Clarke contends that 'in making the independence of the mines their central demand the Workers' Committees had allowed themselves to become embroiled in a spider's web of conflicts within the ruling stratum in which the interests of the miners were set aside' (Clarke & Fairbrother 1993b, pp.134-5).

Mandel considers the demand for regional self-financing, although related, to have a different character from that of enterprise autonomy as it placed the emphasis on local self-government against the unjust demands of the central authorities (Mandel 1990). This was a political demand which could not be ceded by the coal ministry alone but demanded a response from central government. In this respect it too was consonant with the interests of sections of the local elite.

The general theme of Clarke's discussion is that the miners were manipulated by bureaucratic forces into acting as a battering ram on their behalf. To an extent this is true and reveals the complete lack of an independent power base for the elite either at a regional or national level to pursue their own demands. There could be no capital flight or lockout, only control over a movement with real economic and ideological power. Clarke's focus on the issue of mine independence does, however, downplay certain other demands, both economic and political, which are arguably more the product of the workers' concerns and anxieties.

Other demands centred on the themes of the social contract and social justice. *Izvestiya*, for example, suggested that *perestroika* was violating the social contract: a Kuzbass miner told a reporter that:

> for years we were told: 'Produce more coal, and don't worry about a thing. We'll give you food, drink and clothing, we'll give you housing, kindergartens and palaces of culture and sports.' So we worked hard and produced coal, but now we hear: 'Don't just produce coal, provide everything else for yourselves.' How? We went everywhere and to everyone with our requests and complaints – It was no use, all we got were promises.' Other miners are saying the same thing...(*Izvestiya* July 14 1989, p.3).

Despite their basic argument that the miners went on strike because *perestroika* was passing them by, Friedgut and Siegelbaum note that, in Donbas, co-operatives were an important target of the strikers' demands (Friedgut & Siegelbaum, pp.21-22). The legalisation of co-operatives had, of course, been an important element of the reforms but they were often perceived to receive exorbitantly high incomes from charging excessive prices for basic goods, rather than offering greater variety. The demand for the closure of co-operatives thus reflected a notion of social justice which was being violated. This was also evidenced in the Kuzbass where two-thirds of workers favoured the elimination of official perks (Britvin, p.44).

The influence of local political and economic organs does not, however, explain the emergence of political demands which went rather further than the architect of *perestroika* intended. This applies in particular to the demand for the abrogation of Article 6 of the Soviet Constitution which assigned the leading role in society to the CPSU. This demand was very much in line with the thinking of the newly-emerged 'opposition', the IRGD, whose leading member, Sakharov, had argued for this at a recent session of the Congress of People's Deputies. The demand for early elections to the soviets can be seen as beneficial to local authorities wishing to escape the tutelage of the CPSU and enact a genuine separation of powers at a local level, but the same cannot be said about the demand for a new constitution, which emerged during discussions in Mezhdurechensk. The promotion of this type of demand represented a significant escalation in the process of democratization as it surpassed the current slogans and intentions of the CPSU leadership and accorded with the programmatic demands being formulated by the liberal / social-democratic opposition.

### *Organisation*

The strike was quite startling in terms of the high degree of mobilisation and participation by rank-and-file miners. The most graphic image of the strike was of miners, their faces black with coaldust, filling the squares of mining towns in continuous mass meetings. The problem from the miners' point of view was that a large number of demands emerged from such meetings which needed to be codified into a coherent set of positions to be advanced to the relevant authorities. There was an equivalent problem on the authorities' side: it was virtually impossible to negotiate in such an atmosphere. There was a pressure, therefore, on both sides to establish some form of smaller organisation. Soon after the beginning of the strike, a unified strike committee had been established in Prokopevsk, which handled negotiations with representatives of the central and regional authorities, and after only six days, Christensen suggests, the strike committees had established a pyramid of organisations 'parallel and analogous to those of the Party, state, and trade union apparatuses' (p.82). Kubas' suggests that, as well as for the pragmatic purpose of negotiation, the establishment of a regional Council of Workers' Committees secured it the legal status of a social organisation.

In the face of local authority disarray, committees helped maintain order in mining communities, preventing looting and stopping the consumption of alcohol. Kagarlitsky notes that, in some towns in Kuzbass, they even became active in the fight against corruption, particularly where this affected local union officials (1991, pp.179-80). More negatively, Clarke et al view the emergence of such committees as cutting against the miners' control of the strike and assisting in the regaining of the initiative by local and central bodies. They argue that it was this institutionalisation which allowed diverse demands to be replaced by the central demand for mine independence (Clarke et al. 1995, p.40). In addition, the committees' alienation from the workers was reinforced by increased reliance on the opinions of academic 'experts' in respect of complex economic questions (ibid, p.41), and the committees' monopolisation of the platform (Borisov 1993). The implication is that bureaucratisation was an inevitable consequence of organisation. This need not have been the outcome if the mass meetings had discussed the proposals as they emerged and had mandated those engaged in the negotiations to accept or reject them, i.e. that the strike committees were composed of recallable delegates, rather than representatives who acted according to their own instincts and were only held accountable *post facto*.

### *Impact*

The subsequent manipulation of the strikers' demands concealed the disarray among party and local officials when the strike commenced. The CPSU was naturally affected in different ways at different levels. In the new conditions of glasnost, overt repression of the strike was inconceivable, but in Kubas's opinion, 'party organs in practice co-ordinated the activities of all opponents of the strikes' (Kubas', p.52). Clarke et al suggest, however, that the party's role was not so overtly antagonistic, a party line being established early on which recognised the justice of the miners' demands, while trying to get the workers back to work as quickly as possible (Clarke et al. 1995, p.56). Friedgut comments that in Donets'k a high proportion of strike committee members were party members and that the 'Party played an active and influential role in the strike' (Friedgut & Siegelbaum, p.11). In the Kuzbass, party members who had participated in the actions which preceded the July strike were threatened with expulsion from the party. As part of the new line, local party organisations dropped these punitive measures and after the July strike the Oblast Party Committee acknowledged that participation by communists had been justified, although probably in the realisation that expulsion would have decimated party membership in the mines (Maksimova, p.66). In addition, the party provided facilities and refreshments to the strikers and assisted in the drawing up of demands (Clarke et al. 1995, p.56). In those regions without regional coal associations, party committees saw the strike committees as instruments for exerting influence on economic bodies with a view to solving the most pressing local problems.

The apparatus of production associations, as well as trying to influence the demands of the strikers, attempted to disrupt the unity of the strike movement by proposing that strike leaders assume leading positions in the associations, which the strikers had demanded should be reorganised. This was rejected as 'attempted bribery and the creation of a workers' aristocracy'(Kubas', p.51).

Trade unions, the organisations which should have defended workers' interests, were seriously affected by the strike. At an enterprise level, the unions were completely bypassed by spontaneous action and the formation of alternative modes of organisation. According to *Izvestiya*, local union officials 'appeared to be powerless' and their authority 'insignificant compared with that of the strike committees' (*Izvestiya*, 19 July 1989, p.6). In the Donets'k survey mentioned above, 91 percent of workers considered unions incapable of leading strikes and 60 percent considered them subordinated to the interests of mine management (Marples 1991, pp.210-11). A meeting in August of the Kuzbass regional trade union committee concluded that:

> During the course of the strike, some leaders of trade union organisations made no attempt to take charge of the situation and remained aloof from the workers' struggle for their rights. As a result, they lost authority and confidence within their own collectives (quoted in Kubas', p.52).

At this stage the question of founding alternative trade unions was not seriously posed. Friedgut and Siegelbaum observed shortly after the strike that 'the Donbas miners appear to have no intention of founding an alternative system of trade unions, but fully intend to purge and reactivate the existing system' (Friedgut & Siegelbaum, p.25).

As a rule, labour collective councils (STKs) also became inactive during the strike, many workers seeing little difference between them and other bodies, such as production conferences, established at an enterprise level during the Brezhnev era (Bova 1991b, p.34). STKs tended to be dominated by engineering and technical workers (ITR) who, rather than invoke the wrath of management by striking alongside their colleagues, went into the countryside to engage in agricultural labour. In Maksimova's judgement, 'the impotence of the 'office intelligentsia' [kontorskoi intelligentsii], the sham role of sanctioned and regulated self-management and the dependence of the trade unions became apparent during this time' (p.70).

*Government response*

The miners' movement had to be swiftly contained to prevent its overpoliticisation and to stop it spreading to other groups of workers. This was done through a more sophisticated version of the traditional strategy of concessions and repression. First, a commission was rapidly dispatched to the Kuzbass to negotiate with the strike leaders, reach a settlement and get the miners back to work. The commission was headed by Politburo member, Nikolai Slyunkov, and comprised First Deputy Prime Minister, Lev Voronin, and Chair of AUCCTU, Stepan Shalaev. The inclusion of the latter on the government's side was indicative of the role of the trade unions. Two days later it was announced that agreement had been reached on 35 of the miners' 42 demands and that a return to work had been advised by the strike committee. Teague noted shortly afterwards that '[n]othing was said about the miners' political demands, which, it seems likely, were not granted' (1989, p.18). It was certainly true that the government's concessions to end the strike were in respect of the economic demands but, over the next few months, a number of the political demands were also implemented, as the regime became increasingly factionalised.

The document which settled the strike was the USSR Council of Ministers' Resolution 608 which established a schedule for meeting the miners' demands. The most controversial element of the agreement was, however, the miners' insistence that the strike committees remain in existence to monitor its fulfillment. The regime wanted the miners to be pushed back into reliance on the bureaucratic union structures and not retain organisations which could provide an alternative autonomous focus. As it turned out, the regime's hostility was justified, the strike committees becoming the core of alternative political and trade union organisations in the coalfields.

## The Aftermath of the Miners' Strike

From the point of view of the regime, the miners' strike was undoubtedly a profoundly contradictory and disturbing phenomenon. On the one hand, the reform coalition around Gorbachev was able to utilise and manipulate the demands of the miners' strike to promote notions of a '*perestroika* from below' which coincided with the desire at the grassroots to remove obstructive and callous bureaucrats. as a result of which whole layers of 'conservative' apparatchiks were purged from mine management through the powers granted to STKs, whose membership in many pits was thoroughly transformed through the election of strike leaders (Friedgut & Siegelbaum, pp.27-8). On the other, Gorbachev concluded that economic reform should be more decisively enacted and that strikes would destroy the project of renewal (*Argumenty i Fakty* No.30, 1989). The swift passage of a restrictive strike law appeared to be the best way of reining in the strike movement by making concessions with one hand and taking them away with the other.

Yeltsin's position was in the process of transition. Unlike many of his more intellectual colleagues in the IRGD, who were frightened and resentful of 'coarse' industrial workers, Yeltsin professed an affinity with the 'common man' expressed through populist rhetoric. His response to the strike was to legitimate the miners' action by calling for the enactment of a law on social justice and the removal of elite benefits and privileges (*Argumenty i Fakty* No.30, 1989). Such a proposal was never to see the light of day.

AUCCTU was also disturbed by the miners' strike, particularly the way in which its monopoly of worker representation was threatened as enterprise trade union committees were bypassed and new organisations established. The re-establishment of the authority of the official trade unions, particularly at an enterprise level, was therefore crucial and took two different forms: first, the passage of legislation which reasserted the rights of the enterprise trade union committee and, second, a reorientation of the unions, at least verbally, to defend workers' rights in deteriorating economic circumstances.

The realisation of the first priority involved the passage of the first Soviet legislation concerning strikes. AUCCTU had introduced a draft law on trade union rights in late spring but the experience of the miners' strike helped concentrate the minds of Supreme Soviet deputies and expedited the passage of the law 'On the Procedures for Resolving Collective Labour Disputes (Conflicts)', which was signed into law by Gorbachev on 9 October 1989 (for text see Zabastovka). The law represented a step forward in the sense that, for the first time, Soviet workers were explicitly granted the right to strike (Article 6) and the potential role of strike committees was recognised although it also considered that 'a strike is an extreme measure for resolving a collective labour dispute (conflict)' (Article 7). Workers in a range of 'sensitive' industries, particularly transport, communications, energy, civil service, defence and internal security were, however, banned from taking strike action altogether (Article 11). During the parliamentary discussion of the law it was mooted that between 35 and 40 percent of workers would be affected in this way (Fedin, p.53). In addition, a number of procedures had to be gone through, including a so-called 'conciliation commission' and 'labour arbitration', before a strike could legally be undertaken (Articles 3-5). Even then the Supreme Soviet could suspend a strike for up to two months (Article 9). The penalty for participants in illegal strike action could involve loss of job or a fine equivalent to three months salary (Article 14).

In an interview concerning the strike law, AUCCTU leader Stepan Shalaev made clear why the trade unions supported its provisions: at its heart was the emphasis on the enterprise collective agreement, which was drawn up between enterprise management and the trade union committee (Zabastovka, pp.134, 139). Collective agreements have little to do with collective bargaining as it is understood in capitalist industrial relations but help to consolidate relations between management and the trade union committee. It appears to have been Shalaev's hope that the ambiguity concerning the role of trade union committees, which arose with the establishment of labour collective councils, was being resolved in favour of the former.

The reorientation of AUCCTU away from an emphasis on the fulfilment of production tasks to one of defence of workers' rights took place at the Sixth AUCCTU Plenum in September 1989. In an unprecedented display of self-criticism, Shalaev acknowledged that 'workers preferred to express their protest against flagrant violations of social justice through strike committees rather than their own trade union organisations' (*Trud* 6 September 1989). This resulted from the fact that the 'trade unions had been gradually incorporated into the administrative-economic system and alienated from their main function' (ibid). The resolution passed by AUCCTU was something of a turning-point in the organisation's development. The new orientation was to defend workers' rights, the major instrument for which being the collective agreement, and autonomy from state and other bodies (Zabastovka, pp.145-6). The principle of democratic centralism was also effectively dropped through an acknowledgement that primary and sectoral organisations should have the right to determine their own priorities (ibid, p.148). The increasing autonomy of republics was also acknowledged through the decision to hold a conference of Russian trade unions early in 1990 to create a distinctive Russian council of trade unions.

In Kuzbass, unions attempted after the miners' strike to create a counterweight to the workers' committees by organising a conference of city and regional councils of labour collectives. According to Kubas', however, the conference did not go according to the regional unions' plans and a split was averted.

The struggle for the support of the working class mirrored the emerging divisions within the elite. In July 1989 the United Front of Workers of the USSR (OFT) had been founded in Leningrad as a counter by the local party apparatus to the efforts of the radical intelligentsia to democratise the city's party apparatus (Clarke et al. 1994, p.57). OFT, while ostensibly in support of *perestroika*, promoted itself as a 'champion of the ideas of scientific communism and traditional Soviet values, as a representative and defender of the interests of all working people [trudyashchikhsya], particularly industrial workers [rabochikh], against the emerging Soviet "bourgeoisie", and against the restoration of the capitalist order in the USSR' (Berezovskii et al., p.57). In September 1989, OFT of Russia was founded which, with its liaison with organisations promoting the interests of Russophone workers in other republics (especially the Baltic States and Moldavia), confirmed its identification of the USSR with its Russian heartland (see *Sovetskaya Rossiya* 13 September 1989).

### *Continuing strikes and the demise of the strike law*

In the period after the miners' strike there was a mounting wave of strike action but the new strike law was tested and arguably rendered inoperable by the resumption of strike action in Vorkuta. The strike recommenced on 19 October at one mine and was subsequently joined by other pits in the

Vorkutaugol' coal association (*Izvestiya* 23 October 1989). The main grievance was that Resolution 608, which had brought the July strike to an end, was not being implemented. Workers in the Kuzbass and Donbas also discussed the possibility of action but an all-out strike was rejected in favour of more restricted protests. Despite appeals from Prime Minister Ryzhkov and Coal Minister Shchadov, the Vorkuta strike continued for some time. During this period the strike was declared illegal under the new legislation by both the Supreme Court of the Komi republic (27 October 1989) and the RSFSR Supreme Court (14 November 1989). As Fedin argues this was a retroactive and tendentious application of the new law given that this was a dispute whose origins were before the strike legislation was passed and this was a continuation of that dispute, a right specifically granted in Resolution 608 in the event of its non-fulfilment (Fedin, p.55).

The strike in Vorkuta graphically demonstrated the fragile alliance that existed between the liberal opposition and the emerging workers' movement. During the July strike Pavel Bunich, a leading figure in the IRGD, had dismissed such actions as 'extreme forms of protest, arguing that the strikers should put their faith in parliamentary solutions to the crisis' (Kagarlitsky 1991, p.189). Now that strikes were being renewed, another liberal, Anatolii Sobchak, mayor of Leningrad, displayed a tough stance, declaring that:

> We passed a law providing measures for dealing with strikes that are found to be illegal; close the enterprise and fire all those who took part in the illegal strike. Remember how Reagan stopped the air controllers' strike. If a strike harms the interests of the people, decisive action must be taken. Not by using the troops but by using the law (quoted in Bova 1991b, p.39).

Nevertheless, the law was made redundant by the Vorkuta miners' action, necessitating the enactment of another version in 1991, and despite some liberals' hostility to the emerging workers' movement, the latter's leadership became increasingly allied to the liberal opposition.

## Conclusion

It is clear that, in the Soviet context, political liberalisation was instigated by a section of the regime because of the failure of particular policies rather than as a result of popular pressure. In the language of democratic transition literature this process could be seen as the reformist wing ('blandos', or 'softliners') trying to overcome the resistance of the conservatives ('duros', 'hardliners' or, in Huntington's phrase 'standpatters') by reaching outside the institutions of the regime to involve other social strata.

As the process of economic and especially political liberalisation deepened, Soviet workers began to intervene into the political process. This initially involved the formation of small political clubs in the big industrial centres and a gradual increase in the number of small-scale industrial disputes. This low level activity was suddenly transformed into a powerful movement by the strikes of July 1989. When the miners struck it was out of a combination of ideological and economic disillusion. *Perestroika* had done nothing to maintain their vanguard position, instead their comparative earnings had deteriorated, there were no goods in the shops, and still nothing was being done about the basic conditions in mining settlements; mines did not have the same facilities as big factories, nor did they enjoy the same legal rights as other enterprises. The miners were undoubtedly influenced by the elections to the Congress of People's Deputies and the emergence for the first time since the 1920s of a distinct 'opposition' around Boris Yeltsin and Andrei Sakharov (Dunlop 1993, p.106). But while the liberal intelligentsia could talk, the miners could act.

The miners' primary demands were economic and directed at the cumulative effects of underinvestment in the social infrastructure of the coal-mining regions. Economic demands were, however, soon augmented by political demands which undoubtedly promoted the democratisation of the political system. They shattered the myth that the Soviet regime was the defender of workers' interests and brought into question its legitimacy as its control over the distribution of resources and hence over the implementation of the social contract diminished.

The miners' capacity to promote and develop an independent strategy was compromised, however, at an early stage. Gorbachev was able to utilise the strike to further his own strategy, harnessing the militancy of the miners to advance *perestroika* and defeat its conservative opponents. Gorbachev's hopes of preventing any further outbreaks of potentially ruinous industrial conflict were, however, deflated by the reduction to complete ineffectiveness of the anti-strike law.

The liberal opposition was the main beneficiary of the July strike, despite the fear and loathing of industrial workers expressed by some of its intellectual leaders. Ideologically adrift, the miners had lost all faith in the structures of the Soviet state and increasingly viewed the liberals as the only chance of a better future. This was a bitter irony given the regime's constant promise that the workers were building a better tomorrow in the shape of communism.

The workers' leaders, who emerged during the course of the strike, had by-passed the traditional union and party organisations, although many of them belonged to both. In addition, the strike had been conducted through the creation of entirely new organisations: strike committees, which the miners were very reluctant to see disappear. Over the next few months, the failure to implement Resolution 608, and the continued failure of *perestroika* to improve living standards or live up to its promise pushed the miners more and more towards advancing political demands. The miners were to prove a special case, however, in that no other major groups of Soviet workers were to engage in such extensive action, develop such a level of self-organisation, or promote such overtly political demands over the next two years.

# 4 Labour, Democratisation and the Collapse of the USSR

By the beginning of 1990 the Soviet state was entering a profound and ultimately terminal crisis. This crisis itself derived from the interaction of the following factors: first, the liberalisation of external relations which resulted in the overthrow of Eastern Europe's communist regimes in late 1989, fatally undermining the international prestige of the USSR and boosting the liberal alternative to Soviet-style communism; second, an economic crisis manifested in a drastic decline in output, which originated in *perestroika*'s rupturing of traditional relations between the centre and enterprises; third, domestic political liberalisation which allowed the CPSU's organisational monopoly to be irreversibly breached and its ideology challenged; fourth, a legitimation crisis resulting from the failure of the regime to maintain the social contract, evinced by the 1989 miners' strike and subsequent emergence of autonomous workers' organisations.

As the Soviet state became progressively weaker, different elements of the elite, no longer held together by the glue of a strong party and *nomenklatura* system, adopted conflicting strategies for survival and enhancement of their power. The fundamental bifurcation occurred along the faultline of centre / regional (or republican) orientations and overlaying this division, but by no means identical to it, was the split between conservatives and reformers. While some of the prerequisites for democratisation were in place, the polarisation of political currents and institutions meant that an authoritarian backlash was also a conceivable outcome.

In these circumstances a mass workers' movement had the potential to ensure that democratisation was successfully implemented, but had rather less interest in the transformation of production relations insofar as this would entail a further deterioration in living standards and a drastic decline in job security. In this chapter I will first examine the elements of the crisis indicated above. I will then discuss the development of the workers' movement and the problems it confonted both ideologically and organisationally and will assess its contribution to the process of democratisation.

## The Crisis of the Soviet State

### *Eastern Europe and the international situation*

It is difficult to overestimate the impact of events in Eastern Europe on the USSR itself for they severely damaged Gorbachev's strategy for revitalising the Soviet economy and society in a number of vital areas. First, CMEA, which was to have played a major role in promoting economic integration and access to high technology, was rendered redundant. Second, Gorbachev's vision of a Common European Home as a counterweight to the US was wrecked as the new non-communist governments saw their goal as integration into the European Community leaving the Soviet Union isolated. Third, the legitimacy of the Soviet state, of which Eastern Europe was considered an extension because of Soviet control of military affairs through the Warsaw Pact, suffered a crushing blow, even though troop withdrawals had begun prior to the collapse of the regimes. When combined with the widely-perceived notion of defeat in Afghanistan and the rising tide of independence in the Baltic States, Transcaucasia and Moldavia, the Soviet state appeared to be shrinking on all fronts, dealing a massive blow to the integrity of the armed forces. Fourth, and perhaps most crucially, the East European revolutions represented a popular rejection of Soviet-style socialism in favour of some notion of capitalism on the very borders of the USSR itself; in Poland, the influence of neo-liberalism was only too apparent in the adoption by the new Solidarity government of a strategy of 'shock therapy' (the so-called Balcerowicz Plan) which envisioned a rapid transition from state socialism to a full-blown capitalist economy. Even without these external shocks the state of the Soviet economy was undermining efforts to attract foreign capital and investment. In 1987, the state monopoly of foreign trade had been breached by allowing ministries, associations and enterprises to establish direct links with their customers and suppliers through the medium of joint ventures (Hoffmann, p.184). By early 1990, however, of the 1542 such ventures registered, only 200 were operational and most of these were 'small, seriously undercapitalized, and focused on supplying services rather than involved in manufacturing as the authorities had hoped' (ibid, p.187). Progress towards membership of IMF, World Bank and GATT had also been very limited and these institutions were now preoccupied with Eastern Europe.

The last six months of 1989 thus represent the turning-point in the fate of the Soviet Union. Both at home and abroad the traditional supports of the Soviet state were being kicked away and new ones could not be put in place. Even the backbone of the state, the CPSU, was losing members, riven by opposing factions, and increasingly reduced to a deadlocked inactivity.

*The decoupling of party and state*

The establishment of the Congress of People's Deputies in March 1989 and the election therefrom of a new Supreme Soviet fundamentally changed the character of state institutions. For the first time since the beginnings of the Soviet regime parliament became formally detached from the party and, constitutionally, the locus of decision-making in the state. In addition, the Council of Ministers and other state bodies became responsible to the Supreme Soviet. The status of the government was thereby enhanced and the profile of Nikolai Ryzhkov, appointed prime minister in June 1989, 'was raised sharply and in effect he became second only to Gorbachev himself' (Sakwa 1990, p.151). Gorbachev was elected unopposed by the Supreme Soviet to the position of executive President of the USSR, thus occupying the leading positions in both party and state. This was a situation that had often obtained before when the presidency was a virtually meaningless ceremonial post, but the new constitutional arrangements provided Gorbachev with an alternative institutional base through which to enact his proposals. This was now essential as, despite the large number of CPSU members in the Supreme Soviet, the growing divisions between different camps rendered the implementation of policy extremely difficult. Nevertheless, measures were passed which deepened the democratisation of the political system.

In December 1989, the Congress of People's Deputies abolished the quota system for election of deputies, whereby one-third of the Congress were nominated by the CPSU and other social organisations, and simplified the nomination process (Sakwa 1990, p.140). These rules were adopted and applied to the elections to most of the new republican parliaments, which were held between December 1989 and March 1990. As a result there was a substantial increase in the number of radical deputies elected at the various levels (ibid, p.141).

By early 1990, with the deterioration of the domestic and international environments, Gorbachev sought to establish a strong centre which could push through a programme to meet the crisis. The question of the presidency and the checks and balances on its power revealed tensions among those who supported the radicalisation of economic reform. In June

1989, Sakharov had proposed a Decree on Power, decrying the concentration of power in the hands of one man. Shortly after the miners' strike, two well-known radicals, Klyamkin and Migranyan argued for a firm hand and dictatorial powers to implement reforms in the face of conservative and bureaucratic opposition (*Literaturnaya gazeta* 16 August 1989). Clearly for some radicals the introduction of the market took precedence over the deepening of democracy.

Having been supported by the CPSU Central Committee at its plenum in February, Gorbachev gained the support of the Congress of People's Deputies in March 1990 to create an executive presidency with more sweeping powers to nominate key personnel in the state apparatus and to issue decrees. Gorbachev himself pointedly rejected the idea that he should put his candidature to a national vote and he was eventually elected by Congress deputies in an uncontested ballot, gaining 71 percent of the votes of those deputies who agreed to take part (Walker, p.134). In addition, two new bodies were created to strengthen the executive branch: the Council of the Federation and the Presidential Council. The latter body, appointed by Gorbachev and containing a wide spectrum of political opinion, appeared to be a means of centralising decision-making power away from the party. Its utility was limited, however, because of the increasing arrogation of power by republican leaderships and it was abolished in December 1990. The Council of the Federation proved more useful precisely because it brought together the leaders of the various republics and allowed Gorbachev, at least temporarily, to collaborate with Yeltsin around a programme of economic reform.

### *The factionalisation of the CPSU*

The CPSU was itself being severely affected by the disintegrative processes at work. Membership fell in 1989 for the first time since 1954 and during the course of 1990 a staggering three million members departed (White 1991, p.408). In December 1989, the Lithuanian party seceded and ultimately renamed itself, and, in March and April 1990, the party organisations in the other Baltic States split into pro-independence and pro-Moscow factions (ibid, p.409). In addition, for the first time since the 1920s, factions or 'platforms' began to organise openly to promote an alternative to the leadership's platform for the forthcoming 28th Congress of the CPSU, which had been brought forward from 1991 initially to October 1990 and then to July.

The main opposition faction was 'Democratic Platform' (DP), founded in January 1990 on the basis of party clubs created at the time of the Nineteenth Conference. DP brought together broadly social-democratic and liberal currents within the CPSU together with similar forces outside the party (Gladysh). DP adopted a programmatic document with the same title at its founding conference which argued for the repeal of the 1921 ban on factions, the abandonment of democratic centralism, multicandidate elections to all posts and the abolition of workplace party organisations. DP envisioned the development of parliamentary democracy in which the CPSU would compete for power electorally with other parties (see *Pravda* 3 March 1990). At a conference in June 1990 to discuss tactics at the forthcoming Congress a majority were in favour of arguing for their position but then leaving the CPSU should it be defeated, which was virtually a cast-iron certainty (Gill, p.123).

In February 1990 the Central Committee plenum met in Moscow to the accompaniment of an opposition demonstration of half a million people (Gill, pp.104-5). The plenum represented a watershed. Under pressure from the mass movement and in a situation where the party's status as the only legal political organisation was daily being challenged, the plenum discussed the abolition of Article 6 of the 1977 Soviet Constitution, which accorded the CPSU its leading role, but did not come to any definitive decision although its repudiation was inevitable. The plenum also adopted the Central Committee's draft platform for the 28th Congress, titled 'For an humane, democratic socialism' (*Pravda* 13 February 1990). The platform was inevitably a compromise between the reformists around Gorbachev and more conservative elements. It made appropriate noises concerning the further democratisation of society, the rights of individuals and political parties, the transition to a 'planned market economy' and a new union treaty guaranteeing the rights of republics within a renewed federation. In its affirmation of the territorial-production principle on which the CPSU was based, however, it rejected the model of a parliamentary party (Gill, p.106).

Barely a month later yet another plenum was held. The plenum finally agreed to the abolition of Article 6, a decision subsequently implemented by the Supreme Soviet, and brought forward the 28th Congress to 2 July 1990. The meeting did not, however, have the groundbreaking feel of its predecessor and was most remarkable for the depth of criticism to which the leadership was subjected. Gill notes that:

> The disunity in the party was more extensive than it had been before and more open to public view. The image of a party uncertain of what it was, what its

> role should be, and unclear about how to stop the process of disintegration was apparent (p.110).

The party's woe was compounded by a series of defeats in local and republican elections in the first quarter of 1990, which affected major urban areas, especially Moscow and Leningrad, rather more than outlying regions and republics. Indeed, leading opposition figure Sergei Stankevich suggested that the focus on the cities was in fact a conscious strategy:

> The city is the one level at which it is really possible to demonstrate a difference between the current and democratic forms of governance. It is still impossible at a regional level or at the level of the RSFSR ... But in Moscow, although we are not promising to create a paradise, it is possible to make Muscovites feel that there is already another power. Such a victory is possible in several major cities (quoted in Okulov, p.9).

The factionalisation and differentiation of the CPSU continued apace with the foundation of a distinctively Russian party organisation. The RSFSR alone among Union republics had not possessed its own party organisation since the 1920s as it would have been superfluous. In the new environment of growing regional and republican autonomy, and a desire by conservative forces to establish a powerbase which could challenge the Gorbachev leadership of the CPSU, moves were made to revise this practice. At the December 1989 Central Committee plenum a Russian Bureau was created, the main objective of which was to organise a meeting of Russian delegates prior to the 28th Congress. Gorbachev appreciated that the Bureau represented a first step towards the formation of a separate party and declared his opposition to any such move (Gill, pp.93-4).

Sensing the leadership's lack of enthusiasm for a Russian organisation, conservative elements pursued the holding of a founding congress from the bottom up, establishing the Russian Communist Party (RCP) in June 1990, and electing Ivan Polozkov as its first secretary. As a result, both the CPSU leadership and Yeltsin altered their stance towards the RCP, albeit for different reasons. For Gorbachev, the RCP's foundation redressed the communists' lack of organisation and influence in Russia's own newly-elected Congress of People's Deputies with Yeltsin as chair of its Supreme Soviet (Gill, pp.126-30). For Yeltsin, on the other hand, the defeat of his candidate, Ivan Silaev, for the post of first secretary wrote the RCP off as a potential counterweight to the CPSU and vehicle for radical change.

The 28th Congress itself represented another stage in the CPSU's disintegration rather than its renewal. Political liberalisation and economic crisis had undermined the party's control and ideological domination, allowing competing ideologies to clash openly for the first time in seventy years. As the party's economic and administrative functions also diminished many in positions of real power began to question the utility of membership. For those whose power derived from the central institutions of the state, particularly the military and security forces and related industries, it was a question of trying to reestablish the party's power, while for those who benefitted from increased enterprise autonomy, the legalisation of co-operatives and privileged access to import-export channels, opportunities were arising for self-enrichment beyond the merely comfortable existence afforded by the *nomenklatura* system. These differing social tendencies naturally gravitated towards different ideological and organisational positions in order to promote policies in their own interests.

The programme or 'platform' which emerged from the Congress was clearly a compromise, a highly demoralising fact for many members, as it was patently inadequate to deal with the crisis. It is difficult, however, to envisage the circumstances in which even the most coherent and forthright programme would have brought the Soviet people behind it. The comparison with both the 27th Congress and the Nineteenth Conference is striking; whereas these events raised such hopes and enthusiasm for the proposed changes, the 28th Congress was assailed on all sides with little confidence expressed in the party to resolve anything. Concretely, the changing balance between party and state was affirmed by the Congress: the Politburo was expanded to include all republican party first secretaries, while its leadership function was considerably reduced by the decision that it would meet on a monthly rather than a weekly basis; the status of the party secretariat was enhanced but real decision-making authority was removed from the party leadership and vested in the Presidential Council and the Council of the Federation.

Democratic Platform followed through its decision to leave the party should its policies not be adopted, paving the way for the foundation of an alternative reformist party, 'Democratic Russia'. Explaining Democratic Platform's departure, V. Lysenko argued that the 'CPSU ... in practice rejected the transfer of all power to the soviets, which had been demanded not only by Democratic Platform, but also by the First Congress of the country's miners, and by the Russian and other republican parliaments' as well as other demands relating to the separation of power between the CPSU and the state (*Argumenty i Fakty* No.35, 1990). Perhaps more fundamentally it represented the complete collapse of the reform coalition around Gorbachev, the desertion of much of the intelligentsia to the liberal camp and the increasing isolation of Gorbachev himself at the apex of the state apparatus.

### *Economic crisis and the radicalisation of economic reform*

The fragmentation of the party-state was completely intertwined with the collapse of the economy. Through a combination of errors in the implementation of policy and conscious (and unconscious) sabotage of the reform process by sections of the *nomenklatura*, *perestroika* in reality came to an end in 1989 (Khanin, pp.83-4). Nevertheless, significant shifts were taking place in Soviet property relations. The legislation passed under *perestroika* permitted an acceleration of the process of '*nomenklatura* privatisation', through which well-placed members of the old elite were able to transform their political position to their economic advantage. In June 1990, a new version of the law on the state enterprise was passed by the USSR Supreme Soviet. The difference with the rhetoric of democratisation associated with *perestroika* could not have been more stark. The major concession to the workers under the 1987 law, the capacity to elect enterprise management, was removed from the new version, eliminating an important constraint on managerial behaviour.

Throughout 1990 economic programmes were presented by different bodies within the increasingly complex and mutually conflicting institutional set-up of the fragmenting Soviet state, in an effort to bring the accelerating crisis to an end. Each succeeding programme sought to outdo its predecessor in terms of radicalism and the pace of the transition to a market economy. In each case the implementation of the measures was baulked by resolute opposition.

At the end of 1989 Leonid Abalkin, who had built a reputation as a reformist intellectual, prepared a programme of economic reform, adopted by the USSR Supreme Soviet in December 1989, which envisaged a two-stage transition, dismaying the more radical reformers of the IRGD. Abalkin was effectively proposing that reform be halted while the economy was stabilised, which would take about five years, after which the second stage of transition to a market economy could be undertaken (Rumer 1990). For Hewett and Zoteev, however, Abalkin's programme was important because it no longer spoke of creating a market economy through reform of the existing system, but of replacing the old system with an entirely new one (Hewett & Zoteev, pp.41-2).

'Radical economic reform', the coded expression for the introduction of a market economy, rather than *perestroika* was now the main item on the agenda, although its content varied between different political currents. After a hiatus in the first half of 1990 as Prime Minister Ryzhkov tried to implement a programme of stabilisation, Yeltsin's assumption of the chair of the Russian Supreme Soviet, making him de facto Russian president, gave fresh impetus to reform. Discussions began over what proved to be the most radical programme assembled within the Soviet Union before its complete disintegration - the so-called '500 Days'. Different teams of economists formulated their own strategies but what they all had in common was that they could 'see no way out of the emerging economic dead-end other than the transition to a market economy' (*Argumenty i Fakty* No.34, 1990, p.1). The '500 Days' programme, put together by a team of radical economists led by Stanislav Shatalin, was the product of a rare joint effort by Yeltsin and Gorbachev to develop a programme of transition common to both the USSR and the Russian republic, and was clearly influenced by the recent experience of the Balcerowicz Plan in Poland (Kolganov, p.42). The programme, published in September 1990, envisaged the achievement of the following goals: macroeconomic stabilisation, the creation of a regulated market, and the structural reorganisation of the economy, in 'four comparatively independent stages, each distinguished by its specific purpose and the scale of the changes' literally within the space of 500 days (*Argumenty i Fakty* No.33, 1990, p.4). At the heart of the programme was extensive privatisation, the removal of subsidies, the freeing of prices and the convertibility of the ruble.

The '500 days' programme was never implemented, however, as interests at the heart of the Soviet state pushed for a curtailment of reform. Within the Supreme Soviet Gorbachev came increasingly under attack from an organised conservative faction called *Soyuz* (Union), whose supporters were those institutions which stood to lose most from the transition to the market and the disintegration of the Soviet Union. Unfortunately for Gorbachev, these institutions also represented what was left of his executive power. Within a month, Gorbachev had backed away from the '500 Days', promoting a more moderate version, which still envisaged the transition to a market economy but over a longer timescale. In order to implement this programme Gorbachev requested and received from the Supreme Soviet special powers enabling him to issue decrees with the force of law without reference to parliament.

Emboldened by Gorbachev's concessions on economic reform, *Soyuz* stepped up its pressure on the issue of republican independence, inducing a shift to the right in presidential policy. Negotiations over a new Union Treaty had begun in June 1990 but the draft published in November 1990 failed to meet any of the republics' aspirations, asserting the primacy of federal over republican law, retaining much central control of economic and natural resources, keeping Russian as the state language and, perhaps most astonishingly, not granting the right to secession, a right which had been contained in every previous Soviet constitution (Walker, pp.183-4).

The end of 1990 was indeed perceived to be a dangerous period. In December 1990, Shevardnadze resigned as Foreign Minister, warning that 'a dictatorship is approaching' (Dunlop 1991, p.4). In January 1991, such a prospect seemed much closer as active military intervention into the Baltic States was instigated to prevent their outright secession. Gorbachev claimed to have no prior knowledge of the action, but such a denial was ridiculed both by supporters and opponents of the intervention. The events in Lithuania and Latvia also served to polarise political forces still further. In debates leading up to the military action, the leading bodies of the CPSU revealed a complete impotence to propose any alternative course (Buzgalin, pp.97-8). While the CPSU Politburo ultimately welcomed the crackdown, as did most of the higher bodies of the various republican communist parties, state bodies at all levels, including those controlled by communists, generally condemned the intervention (Wishnevsky, p.3). Figures usually associated with more conservative views, such as Russian deputy Aleksandr Rutskoi, also condemned the action, indicating a potential shift of sections of the security apparatus away from the Soviet centre towards strengthening the Russian state (ibid, pp.1-2).

## The Development of a Workers' Movement

The process of polarisation and fragmentation in the wider society and political system was reflected and influenced by the emergence of an organised workers' movement. I utilise this expression although it conveys the impression of a rather more comprehensive and all-embracing phenomenon than was actually the case in practice. This movement is usually associated with developments arising out of the July 1989 miners' strike although other organisations claiming to represent workers' interests had come into existence before then. Building on the emergence of a plethora of workers' clubs, *Sotsprof* (Socialist Association of Trade Unions) had been founded in April 1989 by figures associated with the nascent Socialist Party as an umbrella organisation for embryonic independent trade unions, and the Union of Workers of Lithuania was founded on 2 July 1989 (Shablinskii, p.72).

The miners' strike represented, however, a real turning point in the development of the workers' movement. Its mass character and organisational form provided an impetus to the formation of new trade unions and organisations which began to emerge separate from and often as the result of breakaways from the official unions belonging to AUCCTU. This 'bottom-up' process was a major element in the fragmentation of the official unions, but it was paralleled by a 'top-down' process of differentiation initiated by layers of the official trade union bureaucracy itself which sought to pre-empt the emergence of breakaway organisations through controlled splits and reconstruction which would keep their positions and privileges intact.

*The Kuzbass Workers' Union*

During the course of the July 1989 miners' strike, strike committees were established throughout the Kuzbass coalfield. Under the agreement with the government, these committees should have disbanded by 1 August. However, instead of disbanding they renamed themselves workers' committees and were soon brought together under an umbrella organisation: the Kuzbass Regional Council of Workers' and Strike Committees (Aves 1992, p.148). This organisation was formed ostensibly to monitor the implementation of Resolution 608 but it also underwent a rapid process of politicisation. A consequence of this process was the proposal at the third conference of Kuzbass workers' committees on 5-6 September 1989 to found the Kuzbass Workers' Union (STK) and adopt its statutes. The fourth conference of Kuzbass workers' and strike committees in November 1989 confirmed STK's establishment and accepted amendments to its statutes (Katsva, p.193).

The programme of tasks and goals contained in the statutes was thoroughly political, albeit contradictory in some of its positions, a fact which reflected the reality of the political environment at the time. The demands amounted to a thoroughgoing democratisation of the Soviet state: a reactivation of the soviets as the basic organs of government, self-management of the economy, and the realisation of social justice. It was in its economic demands, however, that the programme revealed its inconsistencies and the influence, in particular, of liberal currents. While calling for the creation of 'an economic system of socialism', the programme argued that such a system would be based 'on the interaction of various forms of property, including national, state, co-operative, individual and mixed ...' (Soyuz Trudyashchikhsya Kuzbassa, p.125). A potentially major step forward to an independent workers' movement was STK's decision to establish its own weekly newspaper titled *Nasha Gazeta* ('Our Newspaper'), which first appeared on 6 February 1990, merging a variety of sectoral papers which supported STK.

Despite the political character of its programme there was some debate as to whether STK was a political party or an independent trade union. This focused on whether STK should be designated a 'social' or 'socio-political' organisation. Some delegates argued that the latter formulation signified the formation of, in effect, a political party, which would be premature. In reality, STK was somewhere between a party and a trade union organisation and its statutes confirmed its ambivalent character as a 'socio-political organisation ... uniting all working people', although the latter phrase was more aspiration than reality (Tsentr po Izucheniya Obshchestvennykh Dvizhenii, p.280). Despite the majority's agreement with this formulation, the Kemerovo committee continued to oppose STK's formation (Clarke et al. 1995, p.92).

The intertwining of political and economic activity was an inevitable consequence, however, of the character of Soviet-type systems, as Solidarity had discovered in Poland. Addressing workers' basic demands for better wages and conditions soon became a directly political question, especially as the state's ability to satisfy those demands diminished. In practice the unitary nature of the Soviet system also blurred the division of labour between STK and the Regional Council of Workers' Committees; each adopted the same structure and even the same president: Teimuraz Avaliani (Clarke et al. 1995, p.92).

The ill-defined relations between STK and the Regional Council were apparent in the preparations for the 1990 local and regional elections. A statement published in the chemical workers' paper *Za Bol'shuyu Khimiyu* under the headline 'Candidates of the Kuzbass Workers' Union' noted that the Regional Council had nominated 63 candidates for the regional soviet, 55 percent of whom were members of the CPSU, while candidates for city soviets had been nominated by city workers' committees. In the same issue a draft 'STK Pre-election Platform' was published which had also, in fact, been adopted by the Regional Council. The Platform followed the statement that 'Soviet society has entered a phase of profound political and economic crisis' with a wide-ranging programme of political and economic reform (10 January 1990, p.3).

Notwithstanding the overlap between the two organisations, an evolution can be observed in STK's political and economic programme from the statutes adopted the previous November, which can only be attributed to the growing influence of the liberal opposition. In contrast to the original statutes which called for the 'establishment of an economic system of socialism', the Pre-Election Platform made no mention of socialism, and called for the 'liquidation of the command-bureaucratic system in the economy', adding private ownership to the property forms mentioned in the statutes. In addition, the Platform demanded 'the political sovereignty of the Russian Federation, the foundation within the republic of corresponding state institutions and structures, and the precise definition of the competences of the Union, republics and local organs of power' (ibid), although no such demand had been made in the statutes, which had called in general terms for the 'attainment of the power of the people through the broad representation of socially active workers in the soviets at all levels' (Soyuz Trudyashchikhsya Kuzbassa, p.124).

In January 1990, Avaliani resigned from his position as president of the Regional Council during the course of its negotiations with the government over the implementation of Resolution 608. Avaliani considered that the Regional Council's position had become one of complete support for the introduction of a market economy, whereas he opposed this, in effect supporting Ryzhkov's plan for some degree of reimposition of central controls to try and stabilise the economy. He was replaced as president by Vyacheslav Golikov (*Nasha gazeta* 8 February 1990). Clarke et al argue that it was the drawn-out character of the negotiations with government, and the latter's persistent obstruction, which finally drove the Regional Council into the arms of the democratic opposition, although the publication of the Pre-Election Platform so early in January would suggest that this evolution had already substantially taken place before negotiations became deadlocked.

The influence of the workers' committees can be gauged from the fact that candidates from the workers' committees were elected to local and regional soviets in March 1990, including eleven of the twenty deputies to the Russian Congress of People's Deputies, although they failed to break the grip of the local party apparatus (Clarke et al. 1995, p.95). This development was mirrored in Vorkuta where 10 members of the Democratic Workers' Movement (DRD), based on the Vorgashorskaya strike committee and established in autumn 1989, were elected to the city soviet in March 1990 (Aves 1990, p.22).

It seems scarcely surprising that the enthusiasm of supporters of the liberal opposition for STK and the workers' movement in general appeared unbounded. Vasilii Seliunin greeted STK as:

> an organisation which might become such an alternative force, an alternative structure, and if we have such a structure in place somewhere by next spring or summer, then it might perhaps be able to take the leadership of the country into its own hands. I do not imagine that the current party structure can keep control of the situation in the country for long. Then such a structure will be needed in which the people can believe (quoted in Redlikh, p.67).

Seliunin's overoptimistic prognosis was a thorough misinterpretation of STK's real character. By mid-1990, after almost a year of struggle, STK's membership was estimated at between 4000 and 8000 (Aves 1992, pp.148-9). Additionally, despite the inclusion in STK of workers' committees from outside the coal industry, the interests of mineworkers were paramount which meant that issues not always of direct relevance to other groups of workers, such as the implementation of Resolution 608, were usually prioritised.

*The Confederation of Labour*

Between 30 April and 2 May 1990, the foundation of the Confederation of Labour (KT) occurred at a conference in Novokuznetsk in the Kuzbass. The origins of the conference lay in a meeting of representatives of workers' clubs, workers' and strike committees, and independent union organisations held in Moscow in September 1989, which established an organising committee for a congress of independent workers' movements and organisations (Monusova 1992b, p.53). The conference brought together an impressive array of 334 delegates from independent workers' organisations and democratic political organisations, primarily from the various coalfields of the USSR, but also from other Union republics (Temkina 1990b).

The interweaving of the political and economic crisis produced varied responses to the perceived need for an organisation capable of defending the interests of working people. As in the discussion around the formation of STK some argued that such an organisation should be primarily a political party, whereas for others it meant the formation of independent trade unions (Speranskii, p.16). The Confederation of Labour, as its name implied, sought to provide an umbrella which could accomodate both orientations (Temkina 1990b). Leonid Gordon noted that the formation of the Confederation constituted 'the first attempt on the part of the workers' movement to create an organisation with a political colouration on a countrywide basis' (p.72). Gordon adds, however, that although the Confederation was not a 'pure' trade union organisation, because of the priority given to political tasks, neither was it 'a political party in the true sense because the defence of professional interests must play one of its principal roles' (ibid). The structure of KT was left deliberately loose, the conference establishing a Co-ordinating Council and electing a Representative Council, but with no clear idea of the relationship between them. It was also intended to establish co-ordinating centres in various parts of the USSR (Speranskii, p.19).

The foundation of KT was greeted both within the burgeoning Soviet workers' movement and abroad as 'an event of genuinely great significance in the political life of the country', and as the formation of a Soviet analogue to Polish 'Solidarity' (*Nasha gazeta* 8 May 1990, p.1). Such an affinity was explicitly stated in KT's Declaration of Basic Principles:

> The complexity and uniqueness of the situation, the combination of political, social and economic tasks requires a search for new forms of democratic workers' movement as did Polish workers in founding "Solidarity" (Konfederatsiya Truda, p.150).

The potential significance of the conference was also signalled by the presence of such diverse figures as Lev Ryabev, Deputy Chairman of the USSR Council of Ministers, and Lane Kirkland, head of the AFL-CIO.

The formation of KT was unquestionably important, bringing together for the first time representatives of workers' clubs and organisations on a countrywide scale, but such a diversity disguised the predominance of the miners, and specifically the Kuzbass miners, within the movement. In his report to the conference, Golikov correctly identified the beginnings of the workers' movement in the strikes of July 1989, but glossed over the fact that these were *miners*' strikes (*Nasha gazeta* 8 May 1990, p.2) and that, since then, the overwhelming number of days lost through strike action had been for nationalist goals (especially in Azerbaijan) rather than as a result of the miners' example spreading to other groups of workers (Teague & Hanson).

Clarke et al indicate that by the end of 1990 KT was virtually a shell. This resulted from a combination of two main factors: first, infighting between socialists and anarchists on the one hand, and pro-liberal forces on the other, over KT's political and economic orientation and, second, the concentration of groups of workers on building their own independent unions. The latter preoccupation particularly affected the core of KT, the miners. The most vociferous proponents of an independent union were the Kuzbass Regional Council and strike committees who subordinated the task of consolidating KT during 1990 to the struggle inside the official mineworkers' union. Attempts to rebuild KT after the 1991 strikes also came to nothing (Clarke et al. 1995, p.125). In practice, therefore, the differing strategies for the development of the workers' movement could not be accommodated within the framework of KT and the strongest groups of workers, especially the miners, pursued their own strategies for the strengthening of their own organisations.

*The Independent Miners' Union*

The requirement to hold a congress of miners of the USSR was contained in one of the points of Resolution 608 and the official Union of Coal Industry Workers organised such a congress (Extraordinary XV Congress) at the end of March 1990 in Moscow. It had been envisaged at the time of the agreement ending the July 1989 strike that such a congress would enable the new leadership which had emerged through the strike committees to undertake a thorough cleansing and reorganisation of the union. Such an outcome proved impossible, however, because the 123 rank-and-file worker delegates were outnumbered by representatives of other grades including management and especially union officials (*Ugol'* May 1990, p.2). On the first day of the congress, Bulat Mukazhanov, a delegate from the Karaganda coalfield, read out a declaration condemning the composition of the congress, demanding the establishment of an independent union of miners outside of AUCCTU, and proposing the organisation of another congress. Eleven delegates and 70 guests then walked out (*Nasha gazeta* 1 May 1990, p.1). The congress meanwhile continued, electing a new leadership comprising former party apparatchiks, changing the name of its leading organs and the name of the union itself to the Union of Coal Industry Employees, and agreeing to hold a new congress in August (Vasil'enko).

Given the politicisation of workers in the coal industry it was perhaps surprising that at the heart of the conflict within the official union was not so much major political differences as a feeling among many underground workers that their interests were being subordinated to those of all other employees in the industry, including ministry officials and mine directors, who all belonged to the same union. Reorganisation of the union therefore potentially entailed the establishment of an organisation capable of defending the interests of underground workers alone. Following the declaration and walk-out at the official miners' congress, an organising committee was established to prepare a more authoritative congress, representative of rank-and-file opinion, which it was decided to hold in Donets'k from 11-15 June. The appeal for delegates made it clear that the congress was to found a new miners' union, and that representation from underground workers was to comprise 80 percent of the delegates, with 20 percent allocated to workers from other sections of the industry (*Nasha gazeta* 1 May, p.1).

At the congress delegates voted to form a new independent miners' union but could not reach agreement as to whether this meant a thorough overhaul of the existing union, or the establishment of a completely new organisation. Nor was there any consensus as to who could join the new union: underground workers, all workers at a mine, or all workers in the industry. It was agreed that such questions would have to be discussed in the labour collectives (Temkina 1990a). The main programmatic resolution passed by the congress also revealed the continuing political evolution of the miners. The principal problem was that the government had promised to transform the economy and had failed. What was needed was a 'government with sufficient skill and decisiveness to end the monopoly of state ownership and the actual monopoly of the CPSU in politics, and to undertake a genuine transition to the market and to democracy'. As the existing government did not fit the bill the congress called for its resignation, the elimination of most ministries (including that of the coal industry) and other intermediate links, and for the formation of a new government enjoying the trust of the people (Materialy, p.51). The congress decided to treat the forthcoming miners' meeting in Moscow, arranged by the official miners' union, as a completely separate event, and therefore established their own organising committee to set a time and date for their own next congress (*Izvestiya* 16 June 1990).

In October the Second Congress of miners took place in Donets'k at which a new union, the Independent Miners' Union (NPG), was created. The congress was dogged, unsurprisingly, by organisational wrangles. When it was finally agreed to debate the question of establishing a new union, two distinct but irreconcilable positions were apparent: renovate the existing union, or form an entirely new one. Ultimately, a majority voted in support of the latter position (*Nasha gazeta* 30 October 1990, p.2), ignoring an appeal from Gorbachev for a 'common search for a real way out of the crisis' and for the creation of an 'atmosphere of civil peace and harmony' (*Rabochaya Tribuna* 23 October 1990, p.1). Despite the congress's decision, NPG's membership only ever consisted of a small minority of miners although larger numbers were prepared to follow their lead. The Congress also called for the liquidation of the 'pro-communist AUCCTU', a process which, ironically, was taking place at almost exactly the same time (Stolpovskii, p.137). Even amongst this layer of most politicised workers, the degree of disillusionment with the political scene was revealed by a survey of delegates: only 36 percent could see a political movement capable of improving the country's situation; 38 percent saw none; and 25 percent did not respond (Mandel 1991, p.161).

### *The 1990 strike and relations with Yeltsin*

The elevation of Yeltsin to the de facto presidency of the Russian republic in May 1990 was a turning-point for the future development of both the USSR and the workers' movement. Thereafter, the workers' movement was no longer confronted simply with a state to which it was increasingly hostile and against which it could undertake industrial action, but also an emergent Russian state headed by a figure in whom substantial numbers of workers, or at least their leadership, had a high degree of confidence.

The high priority accorded by Yeltsin to relations with the workers' movement was emphasised by his meeting with delegates to the June miners' conference in Donets'k. Yeltsin appealed to the miners for a period of grace in taking industrial action, in order for the new Russian government to enact necessary economic reforms. Yeltsin argued that any strikes would not only affect the Soviet economy but would also be detrimental to the nascent Russian economy. As a consequence, instead of its previously considered option of an indefinite national strike, the conference called a one-day warning strike directed specifically against Gorbachev and the Soviet centre for 11 July, the anniversary of the 1989 strike, and at the same time as the 28th Congress of the CPSU. An indefinite strike also entailed significant risk as many felt that the military, which had suffered hammer blows in Afghanistan and Eastern Europe, might be provoked into launching a coup if the country were paralysed.

On 23 June, Yeltsin met representatives of the Kuzbass Regional Council of Workers' Committees, which had issued an appeal to labour collectives to prepare for strike action. The meeting took place against the backdrop of the election of the conservative Polozkov as First Secretary of the newly-formed Russian Communist Party (RCP) and the Russian

Supreme Soviet's decision on state sovereignty. Having initially viewed the foundation of the RCP as a possible vehicle for opposing Gorbachev and the Soviet centre, Yeltsin told the miners that the defeat of his own candidate and Polozkov's election meant 'the collapse of the party, the end' (*Russkaya Mysl'* 29 June 1990, p.9). It had become clear that no section of the CPSU could be used as a means of promoting reform; it was now time to form a new party (ibid). The delegation was impressed with Yeltsin's assurances regarding the possibility of the Kuzbass becoming a free economic zone, and the removal of the Russian coal industry from the tutelage of the central ministry. Golikov promised that any action taken by workers would be in support of the Russian Supreme Soviet and that this was facilitated by a de facto situation in the Kuzbass where workers' committees acted as alternative power structures to the Soviet centre. For the Kuzbass delegates it really did seem that they and Yeltsin were of one mind and that, in such circumstances, the workers' movement could play a huge role in the realisation of Yeltsin's programme (ibid).

Faced with the patent failure of *perestroika*, the miners' leadership increasingly saw the only solution to their problems in a shift to republican control of the mines, self-financing, and the sale of coal on the world market for hard currency. Their demands therefore focused on the resignation of the Soviet government, new elections for the USSR and republican soviets, nationalisation of CPSU property and the depoliticisation of the army, KGB and police (Rutland 1990, p.372).

Declarations of sovereignty by other republics and the consequent struggle to enact a 'republicanisation' of economic structures and resources, also had an effect on the workers' movement. The Regional Union of Donbas Strike Committees (RSSKD) had only supported the call for the July strike 'after an apparently rancorous discussion', although it would appear that their political demands were identical to those of the Kuzbass (Marples 1990, p.16). The new government of Vitalii Masol also applied pressure on the miners not to strike, arguing that the main problem confronting them was Moscow's obstruction of plans to develop the Donbas. In addition, the production of coal in Ukraine for the first five months of 1990 was already 413,000 tons below the required level of delivery to the steel industry and further losses could not be tolerated (ibid, pp.16-17).

Clarke and Fairbrother contend that as a result of a growing rift within the miners' movement between its increasingly politicised leadership and a rank-and-file, whose main interests lay in the fulfilment of economic demands, the strike received poor support (1993c, p.155). This view should be qualified as, at this stage, the political authority of the miners' leadership was sufficiently great to be able to mobilise substantial numbers around limited action. The published figure suggest that the strike received good support in all mining regions although there was undoubtedly some exaggeration of the level of support: a majority of pits in each coalfield struck for the full 24 hours, and a number of pits struck for a token two hours. In Kuzbass, because of support from local and regional soviets, enterprises outside of the coal industry also took action, involving about 300,000 workers in that region alone (*Nasha gazeta* 17 July 1990, p.1; *Soviet Labour Review* 2(8), August 1990, p.6). The general argument around emerging differences is, however, a valid one which becomes particularly pertinent in relation to the proposed political strike in January 1991 and the strike in March-April 1991.

In August 1990, Yeltsin embarked on a marathon 22-day tour of the Russian Republic, during the course of which he fulfilled a promise made at his meeting with Kuzbass delegates that he would visit the Kuzbass in the near future. Addressing miners in various parts of the coalfield, Yeltsin denounced the Soviet centre and the conditions in which miners were forced to live, and assured his audience that the newly sovereign Russian state had thrown off the shackles of Soviet ministerial control. In Novokuznetsk, he was asked by the Regional Council to sign a document, which they had drawn up, which repeated the miners' main demands for enterprise independence, depoliticisation of the KGB and armed forces, and for the formation of a government of popular trust. Yeltsin signed without hesitation, dramatically reinforcing his reputation with the miners (*Nasha gazeta* 21 August 1990, p.1; Dunlop, 1993, pp.50-1).

`Yeltsin's cordial relations with the miners reinforced his own social base and helped gain acceptance among the miners' leadership of his liberal project to transform Soviet political and economic structures. In turn, the impact of the miners' movement was felt throughout the working class as it encouraged actions in other industries which achieved swift concessions from the centre. In conditions of declining ministerial control, the traditional Soviet collaboration between workers and managers manifested itself in the application of concerted pressure on the centre for more resources for their own particular industry. Clarke and Fairbrother conclude that 'the threat of workers' action was therefore a powerful force in the disintegration of the centralised administrative-command system and official trade union structures' (1993c, p.146).

## The Fragmentation of the Official Unions

At the same time as NPG was being formed AUCCTU was undertaking its very own belated process of *perestroika* at its 19th Congress in Moscow. As was noted in the last chapter, AUCCTU had begun to reorient itself at its September 1989 plenum in the aftermath of the 1989 miners' strike and, in a situation where sovereignty was constantly being asserted by the USSR's constituent republics, the maintenance of AUCCTU as a centralised all-Union organisation was thoroughly untenable. A cosmetic change took place in April 1990 when Shalaev was replaced as First Secretary by Gennadii Yanaev (*Izvestiya* 18 April 1990). Yanaev had not been in post very long before he was elevated to the CPSU Politburo and Secretariat at its 28th Congress. The post of AUCCTU first secretary then remained unfilled until the October Congress, during which time second secretary Vladimir Shcherbakov acted as leader, suggesting that plans were already in hand for the organisation's transformation.

AUCCTU had patently failed to defend workers in conditions of declining living standards. In a poll taken in June 1990, 22 percent of those questioned expressed 'total confidence' in the unions, 18 percent 'some confidence', and 31 percent a 'complete lack of confidence' (Stolpovskii, p.137). Signs of the changing attitude of AUCCTU to the Soviet government could already be seen in August 1990 at a conference in Moscow of leaders of its constituent unions. Measures for the transition to a market economy, outlined by Leonid Abalkin, were greeted with scepticism unless they were underpinned with substantial social protection. AUCCTU called for a package of measures to be taken to the USSR Supreme Soviet to protect workers and confirm that full employment continued to be state policy (*Soviet Labour Review* 4(8), December 1990, p.6). If AUCCTU were to be renovated it would have to develop a structure in keeping with the loosened republican ties and would also have to cease its traditional role of 'transmission belt' of the party's wishes and adopt a programme to defend workers' interests.

The fracturing of the structures of AUCCTU had already begun with the decision to establish a separate trade union federation for the Russian Republic. The new organisation, the Federation of Independent Trade Unions of Russia (FNPR), was founded in March 1990. From an initial membership of only four organisations FNPR had expanded by July 1990 to 66 and, by the time of its founding congress in October 1990, comprised 33 sectoral unions and 77 trade union councils (Klochkov, p.19). The number of sectoral committees was expanding because under AUCCTU few unions had structures at the level of the RSFSR. The adoption of the appelation 'independent' was an attempt to project a completely new image of an organisation which had broken with the past practices of Soviet trade unions. This image was rather dented by the FNPR's choice of Igor Klochkov, a former secretary of AUCCTU and chair of the organising committee for the founding congress, as its first president. His political opinions were of the Russian patriot variety: strengthening the Russian state and its independence within the Soviet Union, while also emphasising the rebirth of the Russian soul, language and literature (Barsenkov et al., p.306). What could be said about Klochkov was that he could see which way the wind was blowing. For him, the development of a market economy and the establishment of a Russian state were very much an inevitability with which the trade unions had to come to terms.

The renaming of AUCCTU as the General Confederation of Trades Unions (VKP) with Shcherbakov as its Chair did suggest, however, that a root and branch transformation had not in practice been implemented. Nevertheless, the key organising principle of the old organisation, democratic centralism, had been replaced by a much looser structure, and it was no longer beholden to the party through the *nomenklatura* mechanism. Shcherbakov emphasised VKP's new orientation by declaring that the unions must be the government's 'constructive opponents' (*Soviet Labour Review* 4(8), December 1990, p.7).

## The Miners and the Deepening Crisis

Despite its undoubted political impact, by the end of 1990, the workers' movement as a broad-based phenomenon was in decline. In reality the level of grass-roots activism had diminished considerably with few workers' and strike committees functioning effectively. In September, at the 5th Conference of the Kuzbass Workers' Movement, STK had been transformed into the 'political wing of the workers' movement', constituting, in the opinion of miners' leader, Aleksandr Aslanidi, an embryonic workers' party (*Nasha gazeta* 25 September 1990, p.3). Thereafter, however, it played no meaningful role in political events. The accent was on the creation of independent sectoral trade unions, but even that task was complicated by the increasing focus on republican institutions, which cut across workers' unity at a Union-wide level.

At the end of December 1990, a delegation of Kuzbass miners met with Yeltsin, expressing the opinion that 'a reactionary wave is growing in the country, and the centre is reinforcing all-Union structures, which are obstructing radical reform' (*Nasha gazeta* 1 January 1991, p.1). The workers' committees considered that the Russian government had done everything in its power to implement the demands of the miners but could progress no further in the current circumstances. They therefore presented a new package of political demands to Yeltsin, which included the dissolution of the USSR Congress of People's Deputies, the resignation of both Ryzhkov and Gorbachev, the formation of new state structures only after the conclusion of a new union treaty between sovereign states, the depoliticisation of the security forces, and the nationalisation of CPSU and AUCCTU property (ibid).

The military intervention in Lithuania in January 1991 provoked considerable differentiation within the ranks of the bureaucratic elite, for the use of force ultimately destroyed the only chance of keeping a voluntary, revamped Union together. The Kuzbass workers' committees also responded by attempting to organise a political strike, beginning on 18 January. Arguing that 'neither the President, the USSR Supreme Soviet, nor the USSR Congress of People's Deputies are capable of changing our lives for the better' the Appeal issued by the strike committees called for a general political strike with demands for the resignation of all institutions of the Soviet state, the abolition of the post of President, and the transference of all power to the republics; the withdrawal of all forces from the Baltic States; and the abolition of all party structures in the security apparatus, state institutions and enterprises (*Nasha gazeta* 18 January 1991, p.1).

The strike was, however, a failure. On 17 January Golikov called off the action in acknowledgement of the fact that, despite general agreement with the proposed slogans, there was little support for strike action in the labour collectives (*Nasha gazeta* 22 January 1991, p.1). The reportage in *Nasha Gazeta* suggests a leadership rather out of touch with reality. The strike was portrayed as the last, final throw, which would ignite a mass movement to prevent a military coup which had already begun in Lithuania (ibid). In the event it was shifts within the elite against the intervention, rather than workers' actions, that brought a swift end to the immediate crisis and something of a restabilisation.

## The Miners' Strike March-April 1991

It was not long, however, before the miners were able to exert some genuine influence over the course of political events in the USSR. In March 1991, the most important strike movement since July 1989 began. From the very outset it was a contradictory movement. Unlike the July strike, however, this was not a strike which snowballed from a spontaneous beginning, and whose demands struck an immediate chord with miners in all coalfields across the USSR. What was particularly noticeable was the different agendas pursued by different coalfields, and the initial lack of a response from a majority of miners. In the beginning, only Kuzbass pursued an overtly political strategy, whereas other coalfields raised primarily economic demands.

The strike movement was the product of the burgeoning economic crisis, manifested especially in rising prices and goods shortages, and conflict between Soviet and republican economic structures. In response to heightened inflation, the Second Miners' Congress had instructed the newly-created NPG to conclude a general collective agreement with the Soviet government establishing a framework for local contracts (Mandel 1991, p.163). No government response had been forthcoming.

In Ukraine, the pits had been transferred to republican jurisdiction in January 1991, but the maintenance of the price of coal at 1990 levels, while all other prices were rising, precipitated a crisis in the Ukrainian coal industry (Filtzer 1994, p.103). In January 1991, the directors of a number of mines attempted to provoke a strike in order to force the republican government to raise coal prices. While the miners were sympathetic to such a demand there was little support for a management-induced strike (ibid). The financial crisis in the coal industry did, however, mean that miners' demands for higher wages could not be met, precipitating a call from the Donbas regional strike committee for a strike on 1 March. The miners' demands remained economic, centring on raising wages by 200-250 percent, which was in line with the inflation-proofing of wages contained in Resolution 608. The main nationalist movement *Rukh* refused to support the strike fearing that it would damage the Ukrainian economy (Mandel 1991, p.164).

In the neighbouring Rostov coalfield the miners demands were also entirely economic: 100-150 percent pay rise, indexation of wages to rising prices, and improved pensions for underground workers. When these demands were rejected, a strike began in the coalfield, but initially only affected eight out of 49 pits (*Izvestiya* 12 March 1991). The overwhelmingly economic motivation for the strike from many ordinary miners is supported by Ladnyi's observation that in the Rostov coalfield and its 'Siamese coal twin', the Donbas, miners returned to work almost immediately after the announcement of the pay increase (p.243).

In Kuzbass, the workers' committees called a 24-hour strike for 4 March following the proposal issued by Kemerovo Regional Soviet that enterprises currently under all-Union control should be transferred to republican jurisdiction (*Izvestiya* 27 February 1991). This action, accompanied by the usual political demands, was taken on the understanding that parallel action was building in the other coalfields albeit around different demands. At the same time, NPG leaders called a nation-wide coal strike demanding the resignation of both Gorbachev and his government. Even before the strike, the miners' focus had shifted to addressing the Russian authorities to try and achieve a republic-level settlement (Cook 1993, p.195).

The strike was slow to get off the ground and 'lacked organisation, momentum or direction' (Clarke & Fairbrother 1993d, p.164). In Donbas, Mikhail Krylov, co-chair of Donets'k strike committee, argued that for Ukrainian miners any action was about fulfilling the demands made in 1989, whereas the Kuzbass miners were calling for the dissolution of the very government to which they were addressing their demands. Krylov added out of obligatory solidarity that, of course, they supported the Kuzbass political demands but the action was untimely and had to be co-ordinated (*Izvestiya* 12 March 1991). This was only achieved at the end of March with the formation of the Interregional Co-ordinating Committee of NPG and workers' committees which formulated a list of common economic and political demands (Clarke & Fairbrother 1993d, p.164).

Unlike in 1989 the Soviet government refused initially to negotiate with the strikers, claiming that the demands were political rather than economic. By the beginning of April, however, it had little choice as the strike wave rumbled on. The negotiations proved futile: representatives from the Kuzbass refused to participate on the grounds that their demands *were* political, and the concessions made by the government were inadequate. Almost simultaneously with the discussions, the decision of then prime minister, Valentin Pavlov, to raise retail prices by more than 50 percent and food prices by a devastating 240 percent, and to withdraw high-denomination banknotes came into force. This completely scuppered any chance of a settlement provoking not just miners to come out across the Soviet Union but also serving to ignite strike action across a number of industrial sectors. In Minsk, in the first two weeks of April, more than 60 enterprises went on strike advancing political as well as economic demands, included the holding of multiparty elections (Mihalisko).

The denouement of the strike began on 23 April with the signing of the

Novo-Ogareevo agreement between Gorbachev and the leaders of the remaining nine Soviet republics over the shape of a revamped Union. Shortly afterwards Yeltsin hurried to Kuzbass to persuade the strikers to return to work. Symbolically, on 1 May, Yeltsin signed an agreement in Novokuznetsk transferring jurisdiction of the coal industry to the Russian Federation. Miners were given a large degree of control over the disposal of their coal and over the form of industry privatisation. Kuzbass miners did not return to work, however, until 10 May so that they could have an opportunity to inspect the document (Aves 1992, p.151).

Irrespective of the motivation for the strike it undoubtedly had a profound political impact. First, the 1991 strike differed from its 1989 counterpart in the overt degree of both material and moral support received from other sections of workers, revealing the degree of estrangement from Gorbachev's regime (Moskoff, pp.216-7). Second, the 'official' trade union organisations were divided in their response. VKP, whose allegiance to the structures of the USSR was still apparent, nominally supported the miners' economic demands but condemned the strike as an extreme measure organised by 'political adventurers' (Cook 1993, p.196). FNPR, on the other hand, threatened a general strike if the government refused to meet miners' representatives, indicating that its leadership had recognised the real balance of forces and wished to consolidate its position within the Russian republic (Clarke & Fairbrother 1993d, p.165). Third, the continuing legacy of the social contract was apparent during April and May 1991, when more than 8,000 strikes are recorded, primarily against the price rises resulting directly from government policy, rather than the previously experienced gradual inflation (Cook 1993, p.186). Fourth, and most important, the strike 'forced the realignment within the ruling stratum in which the balance of power shifted decisively in favour of the reformist faction' (Clarke & Fairbrother 1993d, p.167). Yeltsin now had the whip hand: the coal industry in Russia came under republican jurisdiction, and the outlines of a new 'union' were established through the proposal for the '9 + 1' talks, popular support for a revised Union Treaty having been gained in a referendum held on 17 March (White 1993, pp.178-9). Jonathan Aves suggests that '[t]he miners' strike of March-April 1991 was arguably the most significant occasion on which mass popular action coordinated by independent political movements ... changed the political fate not only of the Russian Federation but of the Soviet Union as a whole' (Aves 1992, pp.151-2). Dunlop concurs with this view arguing that:

> the miners played a key role - indeed arguably the pivotal one - in inducing the

> RSFSR Congress to grant emergency powers to Yeltsin and to approve the holding of the June 1991 election of a Russian president. The vehement miners were also, clearly, a major factor inducing Gorbachev to terminate his politically dangerous "shift to the right" (1993, p.107).

The leaders of Democratic Russia were also in no doubt that the apparent political compromise between the centre and the republics 'was possible only thanks to the pressure of the strike movement and democratic forces' (*Russkaya Mysl'* 3 May 1991, p.2). Nevertheless, for the miners themselves, none of the 'political' demands were realised, and their only success was in economic terms: increased pay. Little else changed for the mining regions themselves.

## The August Coup and the Collapse of the USSR

In June 1991, Yeltsin was elected President of the Russian Republic, gaining 57.3 percent of the vote (White 1993, p.171). Unlike Gorbachev, Yeltsin had put his popularity to the test and won, even though that popularity was not as high as it had once been. The gaining of popular legitimacy was the culmination of a process through which increasing power had been transferred to the nascent Russian state and enabled Yeltsin to participate in the '9 + 1' talks from a position of strength.

The signing of the new Union Treaty, which had been agreed at those negotiations, was the trigger for the so-called August coup. The Treaty proposed that only the areas of defence, foreign policy, energy, communications, transport and budgetary questions would be dealt with 'jointly' by the centre and republics, all other affairs being devolved to republican control (ibid, p.179).

While the coup proved the last throw of the dice for those institutions, such as the KGB and MVD, whose power would be decisively weakened by such a treaty, for Yeltsin, it provided the opportunity to present himself to the world as the genuine leader of Russia's democratic forces. Before this event, the West had generally maintained their support for Gorbachev and had opposed the disintegration of the USSR, fearing the potential dangers of the fragmentation of the Soviet military and nuclear arsenal. The collapse of the coup revealed the extent to which even institutions which had previously derived their power from the Soviet centre had become fractured. Power fell into Yeltsin's hands and he was able to dictate terms to Gorbachev on his return to Moscow. The declaration of independence by Ukraine on 24 August set the seal on the future of the Soviet Union - it did not have one. All that remained was to negotiate the most amicable terms for the break-up.

While the situation was in the balance, Yeltsin appealed to workers to strike against the attempted coup but the response was poor. In Kuzbass, only 41 mines responded to the call, indicating general exhaustion among miners, and once again a reluctance to be involved in actions for directly political ends (Clarke & Fairbrother 1993e, p.173). Christensen's suggestion that one-third of Soviet mines were shut down after the first day of the coup seems rather wide of the mark (p.101). It has to be said that the coup was even welcomed by some groups of workers, tired of the chaos and constantly deteriorating living standards and hoping for some stabilisation.

## Conclusion

This was a period replete with ironies, but ironies explicable in the context of the development of the Soviet state and social structure. The first such irony was that the 'workers' state was undermined by the very social class it was supposed to defend, although it has to be said that the majority of workers remained quiescent, trying to survive the deteriorating conditions rather then reacting positively to overcome them. The second irony was that the burgeoning workers' movement provided the footsoldiers for the liberal opposition, who were committed to the USSR's transition to a capitalist system. The promotion of democratic demands by the liberal intelligentsia struck a chord with many workers, who proved incapable of formulating a programme which could have created a united front in pursuance of democratic aims while treating critically the liberals' economic programme, the implementation of which would have had dire consequences for workers' living standards and for the workers' movement itself. A third irony emerged as a consequence of the workers' and miners' movement becoming more and more synonymous during this period. The formation of NPG, divorced from the old trade union bureaucracy, political structures and ministerial and enterprise management, represented a major step forward in the creation of an independent workers' movement. But, despite the formation of more overtly political organisations and a confederation, which sought to pull together the disparate strands of independent working class politics, the miners insisted on their role as 'Leninist vanguard' and increasingly defended their own particularistic interests. The leadership of the new organisations, most of whose members were in the Kuzbass, became tied politically to Yeltsin and the liberal opposition and subordinated the general struggle for democratic rights and defence of workers' living standards to the promotion of the interests of one industrial sector through reliance on the actions taken by the new Russian government against the Soviet centre. This political relationship was to have serious practical consequences as many of the leaders of the miners' movement were co-opted into the newly-emerging state structures of the Russian Federation, creating a new form of corporatism, and denuding the movement of experienced grassroots activists.

# 5 Labour, State and Democracy in Russia

With the collapse of the USSR in December 1991, the new Russian government appeared to be confronted with the daunting task of achieving three interlinked transformations: the establishment of a capitalist system, a liberal democratic polity and the stabilisation of a new state. Patently, Russia's economic transformation was not to be a repetition of the genesis of capitalism in Britain, and to a lesser extent the other early capitalist states, where a capitalist class developed primarily through the internal erosion and transformation of feudal relations. Creating capitalism in Russia has instead entailed not just institutional changes and the development of market relations but the forging of a capitalist class itself. Moreover, this process has had to be accomplished in the environment of an already existing global capitalist economy and subject to its considerable pressures. In addition, the economy in 1991 was in a crisis excerbated by the disintegration of the Soviet Union and disruption of economic ties with other republics. Nor was the establishment of domestic political institutions a straightforward matter: first, a divide existed within the elite based on the different relations of production of the old Soviet system and of emergent capitalism; second, although a temporary consensus had been achieved within the elite in opposition to the Soviet state, the disintegration of the latter raised the question of how far agreement continued to exist over the 'rules of the game'; third, despite the emergence of a variety of informal organisations during the *perestroika* period, these had not crystallised into political parties and interest groups linking society and political institutions; fourth, although Yeltsin enjoyed a high degree of legitimacy, as a result of his recent popular election, and his role in the collapse of the Soviet system, this did not make him a democrat. It now seems clear that Yeltsin's priorities did not concern genuine democratisation but the consolidation of the Russian state and the position of the presidency within it. This represented not only a continuation of the Russian strong state tradition and a reinforcement of Yeltsin's own power and privileges, but also a response to Russia's subordinate position within the global economy. Russia's evolution in the 1990s can thus be seen as a variant of dependent democratisation, in which the appearance of liberal democracy is coupled with a more authoritarian reality.

The previous chapters have indicated how labour influenced the democratic trajectory of political change in the former Soviet Union. Significant sections of workers promoted demands and took actions which directly undermined the old authoritarian structures but, under the influence of the liberal opposition, support for democratisation became entwined with demands for the introduction of a capitalist economy. At the same time, a majority of workers organised in the former 'official' unions (FNPR) remained ambivalent about change and generally inactive. Russia's independence removed the structures of the Soviet state but created a new set of problems. For FNPR, which still organised by far the greatest proportion of workers albeit because of their control of social benefits, a major question was how to exert influence on a government set on implementing a radical economic transformation that would bring inflation and unemployment and consign what was left of the 'social contract' to oblivion. For the new independent unions, especially NPG, there was a different set of problems: their militancy had brought to power the forces they had supported against communism and, to a point, they had been rewarded for their loyalty with big pay rises in 1991. It would be very difficult, however, to oppose Yeltsin's government openly even if its policies were detrimental to workers' interests.

## The Political Economy of Russia's Transformation

### *The international context*

The orientation to integration into the global capitalist economy required Russia's membership of the big Western financial institutions: IMF, World Bank, European Bank for Reconstruction and Development (EBRD) and OECD. It also led Russia's new leadership to eschew the possibility of creating a smaller union of '2 + 5' (Russia and Belarus plus the five Central Asian republics) when the USSR collapsed because of the doubts which would have arisen about Russia's 'European' credentials. The establishment of the Commonwealth of Independent States (CIS) in December 1991 was designed to sound the death-knell of the USSR rather than replace it with anything substantial. Russia nevertheless claimed to be the continuation of the Soviet state, assuming the entire external debt of the former USSR as well as its nuclear arsenal. Integration has not, however, proved a panacea. Russia's debt burden has continued to grow rapidly, from about $40 billion at the end of 1991 to $87 billion by 1993, most of which was in convertible currency owed to official creditors and commercial banks in the West, Germany being owed a massive $50bn (Stent, p.128). By 1995, the servicing of this debt was estimated to be at a level twice that of the value of Russia's exports of goods and services (Pichugin, p.21). The IMF, which Russia joined on 1 June 1992, has sought, together with the other international institutions, to impose its own agenda on Russian politicians and interests in order to integrate Russia into the world economy as a subsidiary, semi-peripheral area primarily responsible for the production of raw materials, particularly gas and oil. This is perfectly in keeping with their policies towards other crisis-ridden economies. The Russian government accepted this agenda as its priority was to resolve Russia's massive economic problems and thereby establish its own legitimacy. The net result was that the 'government's agenda was worked out with, and reflected, the concerns and prejudices of Western agencies, governments and theories' (Robinson, p.595).

Both the IMF and World Bank have subsequently intervened heavily in Russian internal politics in the guise of advocating strictly economic terms and conditions. Moves have had to be made towards making the rouble convertible and Russia's external debt has had to be restructured under the IMF's close supervision (Evstigneev, p.7). In March 1995, the IMF insisted that the Russian government increase the volume of GDP, sharply reduce inflation, impose strict control over monetary emissions, dramatically decrease the budget deficit, remove most tax benefits and transfer the tax burden onto the fuel-energy sector, liberalise foreign trade, complete privatisation, rapidly introduce land reform, and create social security mechanisms insofar as they would not threaten financial stabilisation (ibid). The World Bank has also played an important role with proposals for the restructuring of sectors of the Russian economy, most notably the coal industry.

In return for increased integration, Western governments consistently supported Yeltsin as the only person capable of implementing the transformation, even when he appeared to act precipitately, for example in 1993 against parliament or in the conflict in Chechnya, or shifted away from an overtly pro-Western orientation in foreign policy. Yeltsin's personal habits and his less than robust health also caused great anguish in the West, but the alternative, either in the form of the nationalist Liberal Democratic Party of Russia (LDPR) or especially with the emergence of the reconstituted Communist Party of the Russian Federation (KPRF) always seemed much more of a danger to Western interests.

*Economic transformation*

Under the impact of the Gorbachev-era reforms the old *nomenklatura* had disintegrated as a mechanism for allocating people to positions within the party-state, destroying the power of those located in the central institutions. At the same time, Yeltsin utilised his control of the nascent Russian state to 'bribe' enterprises to transfer their jurisdiction from Union to Russian control, reinforcing the power of enterprise directors – the so-called industrial *nomenklatura*. In addition, Yeltsin had offered similar incentives to Russia's regions. Thus, in his struggle to destroy the Soviet state, Yeltsin had promoted social forces which ironically represented a major obstacle both to economic transformation and to the consolidation of the Russian state (Nagy, pp.65-6).

As well as controlling economic structures, the industrial *nomenklatura* enjoyed considerable influence in the Russian Congress of People's Deputies, the Supreme Soviet and especially its Presidium (Sakwa 1996, pp.119-120). As a counterweight Yeltsin assumed the position of acting prime minister as well as president and appointed a group of neo-liberal reformers who had fewer links to the old *nomenklatura* to positions in the government and the ever-expanding institutions of the presidency. From the viewpoint of the reformers, headed by Yegor Gaidar as deputy prime minister in charge of economic reform, the successful implementation of a transition to capitalism entailed the destruction of the *nomenklatura*'s political and economic power.

Yeltsin's neo-liberal team wished to implement a strategy of 'shock therapy' modelled on the Polish 'Balcerowicz Plan'. Shock therapy is both a political and an economic strategy designed to effect a transition from Soviet-style socialism to Western-style capitalism in the shortest possible time. By opening up the economy to the enervating forces of the global market and transferring state assets to private hands, the theory goes, old interests will be shattered and the basis created for the emergence of a nascent capitalist class. The 'over-riding strategic objective' is, according to Murrell, to 'take decisive steps to ensure that the existing structures and interests cannot derail reform' (p.113). The pursuit of so-called 'macroeconomic stabilisation' also entails a drastic deterioration in the living standards of the working population through enterprise bankruptcy, the collapse of production, mass unemployment, and high inflation alongside stagnating wage levels. Shock therapy therefore reinforces dependent democratisation for the following reasons: first, it is a technocratic recipe to transform the social and economic foundations of the state without the participation of the wider society; second, it claims that political democracy can only be created on the bedrock of market relations; third, 'democracy' is narrowly equated with the procedures of liberal democracy; fourth, as shock therapy advocates Lipton and Sachs make clear, forms of industrial democracy are also explicitly rejected as 'shifting to a Western European ownership structure will of course require that enterprise governance be removed from the workers councils and managers and placed squarely in a supervisory board (or board of directors) controlled by the owners of the enterprise (Lipton & Sachs, p.308).

Gaidar outlined the proposed economic policy in a speech to the Russian parliament on 28 October 1991, and the strategy was implemented in earnest on 1 January 1992 through the liberalisation of prices. It was not until 27 February 1992, however, that a more detailed 'Memorandum on the Economic Policy of the Russian Federation' was adopted by the Russian government (Smith 1993, p.177). Thus, it was not until almost two months into the implementation of shock therapy that a detailed programme was produced and this was specifically addressed to the IMF rather than to a domestic audience (Hedlund, pp.151-2).

In January 1992, prices on most goods were liberalised causing a dramatic increase in inflation which reached an astronomical 245 percent in that month alone but subsequently declined to a still comparatively high 38 percent and 30 percent in February and March respectively (Smith 1993, p.179). Gaidar's 'shock therapy' did not, however, address the problem of the monopolisation of the Russian economy and the freeing of prices allowed enterprises to utilise their monopoly positions to increase prices without increasing production. The 'monetary overhang', which had built up as a result of huge currency emissions in 1991, was eliminated almost at one fell swoop as 'the purchasing power of personal savings plus cash more than halved during the first quarter of 1992' (ibid). With it, however, went any domestic resources for future mass privatisation, a key element of the neo-liberals' programme. In addition, the reformers deliberately pursued a path designed to maximise Western rather than domestic support, dismissing the criticism of their policies levelled by the Supreme Soviet and pushing it into the arms of the directors' lobby (Hedlund, p.152).

The industrial *nomenklatura*, especially in those industries suffering considerably from the collapse of production and raging inflation and unable to survive without state subsidies, responded by creating Civic

Union, thus marking a return to the political arena (Shevtsova, p.14). Throughout the latter half of 1992 and through 1993, Civic Union sought to modify the course of economic reform by negotiating over its character and by influencing the composition of the government. Despite the support of international economic and political institutions, the fragility of Yeltsin's social base made the search for a compromise essential. According to Shumeiko 'Yel'tsin believed that he *needed* the support of directors and workers to maintain social harmony and political power' (McFaul, p.209). During 1992 a series of concessions was made: in June 1992, Yeltsin appointed three figures considered close to the directors' lobby, Vladimir Shumeiko, Georgii Khizha and Viktor Chernomyrdin, to the government, and Viktor Gerashchenko as head of the Russian Central Bank, an appoinment which 'in effect marked the end of "shock therapy"' (Shevtsova, p.13). During autumn 1992, Yeltsin met with Civic Union leaders on several occasions, finally instructing Gaidar to work out a compromise plan of economic reform which could be presented to the Seventh Congress of People's Deputies in December. Gaidar's position as prime minister was, however, the main problem for Civic Union and, in December 1992, Yeltsin finally succumbed to pressure from parliament to remove him. He was replaced by Chernomyrdin, formerly director of Gazprom, the gigantic gas industry complex.

By the end of 1992, therefore, the strategy of 'shock therapy' had been derailed and the directors' lobby appeared to be in the ascendancy. Cook argues that 'the Yeltsin government effectively left in place the fundamental problem of Soviet industry that reform is intended to resolve - the thousands of inefficient, overstaffed, obsolete production facilities that tied up labor, investment funds, energy, and materials' (1994, p.79). She does not indicate, however, why the government felt obliged to pursue this course. The fact was that the industrial *nomenklatura* were too entrenched for their interests to be attacked head-on. A compromise was required, of which the maintenance of subsidies was one element and the method of privatisation was the other.

### *Privatisation*

The industrial *nomenklatura* had already enhanced its position under *perestroika* through the 'spontaneous' privatisation of state assets, a process colloquially referred to as 'grabbing' (*prikhvatizatsiya*) to distinguish it from legal privatisation (*privatizatsiya*) (Clarke 1994, pp.166-7). From the *nomenklatura*'s point of view the legislative framework for privatisation proposed by the reformers, through which enterprise stock would be sold mainly to outsiders with only a small share going to the labour collective, was a non-starter as it would entail the removal of a significant number of existing directors (Cook & Gimpelson, p.468). The alternative proposed both by directors' organisations and trades unions was for a form of privatisation which would exclude outsiders and potential foreign investors by transferring ownership to the labour collectives. Faced with the comparative unity of the directors' lobby and a lack of unanimity among radical reformers over the form privatisation should take, the government was forced to negotiate (Kisovskaya, p.83). The outcome was a compromise which emerged from a government-Supreme Soviet conciliation commission in April 1992 (Cook & Gimpelson, p.469). As a consequence, the original form of privatisation was employed purely in respect of small businesses and retail outlets while the bulk of industry was to be privatised in a way much more favourable to existing management.

The form of privatisation envisaged the distribution of vouchers to the value of 10,000 roubles to all Russian citizens, and three alternative methods of privatisation were proposed which made significant concessions to the directors' and trade unions' desire for labour collective ownership. In particular, the second method of privatisation provided for a majority share-holding on the part of the labour collective. The prospects for privatised enterprises were subsequently enhanced by the presidential decree issued in December 1992, ensuring that both state and private enterprises had equal access to government subsidies.

Workers also gained some leverage over the privatisation process, which could be halted in the event of labour-management conflict, and through access to shares. Undoubtedly, notions of social justice and of the genuinely collective interest of the workforce (usually excluding management) have in many cases been retained. While the final version of the privatisation programme did not accord with the original intentions of the proponents of 'shock therapy', the benefit for the government was that 'a very rapid, state-controlled, mandatory programme of privatisation' would be implemented (Cook & Gimpelson, p.469). The political character of the privatisation programme was also made explicit by Anatolii Chubais, chair of the State Property Committee (GKI), who subsequently remarked that 'voucher privatisation ... was a large-scale programme to a great extent of a socio-political, rather than economic, character. It was the fundamental means of creating the socio-political preconditions for the resolution of economic problems' (quoted in Diligenskii, pp.68-9).

Despite the concessions on privatisation, subsidies, and government composition, Civic Union continued to oppose the government's overall economic programme, and while accepting the character of privatisation, objected to its pace, arguing that a strong state sector would be required for a long period (Kisovskaya, p.84). Nevertheless, the impact of privatisation on property rights affected the political behaviour of the industrial *nomenklatura*, which in turn influenced its relationship with the executive and legislature. As the privatisation programme unfolded from late 1992 onwards, the benefits to enterprise directors became increasingly tangible, the second option being the favoured method of privatisation in three-quarters of cases (Rutland 1997, p.162). In addition, a fresh impetus was given to 'spontaneous privatisation', 2590 cases of illegal privatisation being discovered by the Interior Ministry in the first five months of 1993 alone (Kholodkovskii, p.73).

Throughout 1993 the Supreme Soviet debated the course of the economic transformation and privatisation in particular. Those critical of the speed and character of voucher privatisation proposed a 'fourth variant' of privatisation which would have transferred ownership to the labour collective over a period of three to five years (Kisovskaya, pp.90-1). The popularity of the existing privatisation programme, however, rendered such an additional variant redundant.

As directors began to turn their control of enterprises into *de facto* ownership, their interests became increasingly fragmented. For the managers of enterprises, whose position was sufficiently secure not to require government intervention, collective lobbying was not a priority, whereas for those in a parlous state, regardless of whether they had been privatised or remained under state control, the capacity to extract vital funds frequently required collaboration rather than opposition. Enterprise directors became more inclined to passive support of the regime and less concerned with the developing conflict between the presidency and the Supreme Soviet, which became increasingly divorced from major social forces. The parliamentary leadership, centred around its speaker Ruslan Khasbulatov, became more and more focused on establishing the ascendancy of parliament in relation to the presidency, and Yeltsin, sensing the growing isolation of parliament, began to seize the opportunity to assert the predominance of the executive. The institutions of the executive were built up over a period of time by taking advantage of the hazy relationship between legislature, executive and judiciary expressed in the oft-amended 1977 Soviet Constitution. A highly centralised institutional matrix was established, 'reminiscent of the CPSU Central Committee apparatus in its size, complexity, and policy-making powers', which comprised the presidential administration created in August 1991, the Security Council formed in spring 1992, and the Presidential Council created in 1993 (Willerton Jr, p.47).

By September 1993, the balance of forces had changed to such a degree that Yeltsin was able to move decisively, issuing decree No.1400 which dissolved parliament. In October, the Constitutional Court, the supposedly supreme judicial body which had declared Yeltsin's action unconstitutional, was itself dissolved. The impact on domestic political forces was profound. By unilaterally clearing the way for the adoption of a new constitution and elections to a new parliament, Yeltsin drove a wedge into the liberal camp from which they have never completely recovered. More dramatically, a confrontation ensued between the armed forces, which remained loyal to the president, and supporters of the old Supreme Soviet, which culminated in the shelling of the parliament building and the eventual surrender of pro-parliamentary forces. Buketov suggests that international factors played a major role in determining the decision to carry out the assault on parliament, which followed on the heels of the IMF's refusal to allot its previously promised $3 billion because of the slowness with which economic reform was being implemented. Only a strengthening of the executive and a decisive weakening of the political opposition could ensure that such reform was carried out successfully (Buketov 1995a, p.15).

The December referendum to approve the new constitution and parliamentary elections provided further confirmation of the weakness of Russia's democratic institutions: the turnout in the referendum officially declared at 54.8 percent was subsequently revealed to have been below the required 50 percent (Steele, p.391); and the election result produced a dramatic result, the largest single party being the nationalist Liberal Democratic Party of Russia (LDPR). Under the new constitution, however, the powers of the new bicameral parliament, the Federal Assembly, which comprises a lower house, the State Duma, elected on a nationwide basis, and an upper house, the Federation Council, consisting of two representatives from each of Russia's 89 regions, are considerably inferior to those of the president. The cohesion of parliament is also undermined by the feebleness of the political party system. With the exception of the liberal Yabloko and the reemergent KPRF no political parties have been able to develop any stability or coherence, suggesting profound problems in their linkages with civil society and especially interest groups.

Yeltsin's attempt to create a strong state was not, however, entirely successful. The desire to maintain the unity of the Russian Federation led at the end of 1994 to war with the breakaway republic of Chechnya. The outcome was a disaster, with considerable loss of life among both the civilian population and Russian forces. The pursuance of the conflict also further undermined support for Yeltsin among reformers and bolstered opposition especially in the form of the KPRF. The Kremlin was also perceived to be increasingly beholden to a comparatively small group of wealthy financiers, commonly referred to as the 'oligarchs'. Their wealth and influence was boosted after the completion of the voucher privatisation process in 1995 through the notorious 'loans for shares' deal. Through this mechanism the aim was to provide companies with shares in key industries, especially in the energy and communications sectors, in return for loans to the government. In practice, the government provided the money subsequently loaned back to them, and the auctions were rigged to allow purchases at knock-down prices and to keep out foreign interests and other competitors (Hedlund, pp.256-60). The oligarchs' gratitude to Yeltsin was subsequently expressed in their bankrolling of his 1996 presidential campaign and the orchestration of media support.

The general contours of Russia's economic and political system can be summarised as follows:

- First, the voucher privatisation of state assets resulted in the transfer of *de jure* ownership to enterprise workforces, but allowed *de facto* control to be retained by the old *nomenklatura*; at the same time, foreign investment in Russian industry has been kept to a minimum (the Russian economy accounts for less than one percent of global foreign direct investment). Privatisation, therefore, entailed neither substantial new investment in industry nor its restructuring to make it more efficient and competitive on the world market. Far from unleashing unbridled competition, privatisation reinforced monopoly and enterprises' dependence on the state. Profits are being made but essentially through the medium of trade and the manipulation of rates of exchange, rather than through the generation of surplus value in production.
- Second, as in the Soviet economy, money plays a secondary role to non-monetary transactions and barter arrangements. A vicious circle of credit and debt has built up between enterprises, between enterprises and their workforces, between enterprises and the state, and between the state and society (see Commander and Mummsen 1998). Despite

the inviability of most of Russia's enterprises, few have been forced into bankruptcy and closure because of the impact this would have on the elite, and in terms of social unrest.

- Third, because money is scarce but nevertheless essential, banks have become powerful institutions and, under their aegis, new conglomerates (so-called Financial-Industrial Groups or FIGs), have begun to form, seeking to vertically integrate all stages of the production process (Johnson). In addition, criminal groups (*mafiya*) also exercise a growing influence, creaming off substantial resources which are not productively invested or channelled to the state in the form of tax revenue.
- Fourth, integration into the global economy is primarily through the following processes: as a provider of raw materials, especially oil, natural gas, and precious metals; as a debtor state; and as an exporter, usually illegally, of capital. In these respects, Russia bears all the hallmarks of a Third World state. As with other Third World states, the international financial institutions have only been prepared to provide assistance in return for economic liberalisation, while political support was maintained for Yeltsin as the guarantor of economic transformation.
- Fifth, Russian 'democratisation' has entailed the construction of a centralised but paradoxically weak state where power resides in a presidential apparatus riddled by corrupt practices and linkages to dominant economic interests. The ability of civil society to exert influence has been severely constrained by the calamitous economic situation and the general weakness of interest groups and political parties.

## Trades Unions and Transformation

The response of workers and trades unions to the reform process has been generally muted and reveals the complex relationships which exist between workers and managers at an enterprise level and between enterprises and the state. The following factors have had a constraining and at times, debilitating effect on the capacity of trades unions to influence the direction of events after 1991. First, an overarching framework, frequently referred to as 'social partnership', was established to regulate state-union relations even before the collapse of the USSR. Second, the essentially collaborative relationship between unions and enterprise management, which pertained in the old Soviet system, has continued into the post-Soviet era. This has not only manifested itself at an enterprise level but also in forms of political organisation. Third, as we have discussed in previous chapters trades union organisations have fragmented along sectoral and ideological lines, generating different strategies as well as animosities. Fourth, even union members have had little confidence in their own organisations as means of defending their interests, making it difficult at a national level to instigate coordinated and effective action. Finally, the headlong collapse of the Russian economy with its attendant inflation and threats to job security has had a detrimental effect on union membership and levels of activism.

*'Social Partnership'*

As the collapse of the Soviet Union became an inevitability, the Russian government's priority was to ensure minimal disruption to the transformation process. This particularly applied to the trades unions which emerged comparatively intact from the upheavals of 1991. The chosen path was partially a continuation of the Soviet practice of integration of the trades unions into the state but with a veneer of West European social democratic neo-corporatism. In January 1992, a quasi-corporatist body, the so-called Tripartite Commission on the Regulation of Social and Labour Relations was established by presidential edict. The Commission, which involved trade unions, government and 'employers' (realistically enterprise management), was designed to negotiate a comprehensive annual agreement (Kirichenko & Kudyukin, p.131). In addition, the Commission would be able to review and set wage levels, monitor working conditions, and mediate in industrial disputes. In return for this direct input into policy-making unions were to take a no-strike pledge (Cook 1994, p.70). Sensing an opportunity to exercise some influence, FNPR agreed to be involved in the tripartite arrangements despite being subjected to criticism from its largest regional organisation, the Moscow Federation of Trade Unions (MFP), which urged the FNPR leadership not to enter into any kind of social partnership as it would mean losing the right to strike and the unions becoming party to anti-worker decisions (*Solidarnost'* 16, 1991, p.6).

The Commission, co-ordinated by State Secretary Gennadii Burbulis, comprised 14 representatives from each of the three sides. Of the seats allocated to the trade unions, nine were from FNPR, one each from NPG and the Independent Union of Civil Aviation Pilots, and three from *Sotsprof*, the leadership of which was politically close to Aleksandr Shokhin, the then labour minister and architect of the Commission. The latter allocation, in particular, was bitterly opposed by FNPR who argued that such an insignificant organisation should not have such potential influence. The composition of the trade union section meant, of course, that potential opposition from FNPR to the government's course would be undermined by those sitting on the same side, who were generally supportive of government policy. Managers were also represented by several organisations including the Russian Union of Industrialists and Entrepreneurs (RSPP) and Congress of Russian Business Circles representing managers of banks, insurance and stock companies.

The purpose of such arrangements can be viewed from two angles. On the one hand, there was a genuine desire on the part of their social-democratic framers to establish a system of 'civilised' industrial relations derived from the experience of Germany, Sweden and Austria. On the other, was a rather more practical concern about the potential response of workers to the impact of shock therapy. Broad sectors of workers had taken action against government instigated price rises in spring 1991, and workers' reactions to the threat of mass unemployment were as yet untested. Having FNPR involved in the Commission was a means of buying off its leadership, which, in any event, was not directly hostile to economic reform, by creating a veneer of participation in decision-making and, secondly, by constraining it through having a substantial element of the trade union side composed of organisations openly supportive of the government. The involvement of organisations representing the industrial *nomenklatura* and the newly-emerging class of entrepreneurs was also a way of trying to neutralise opposition from enterprise management.

The initial experience of the Commission was one of comparative success. In March 1992, a General Agreement was negotiated, which provided for state regulation of a limited number of consumer and energy prices and a quarterly review of minimum wages and pensions. FNPR promised to refrain from strikes on matters regulated by the Agreement and management agreed not to close factories or lay off workers (Cook 1994, p.72). In addition, more than 40 tripartite industrial sector agreements had been signed by September 1992 (Kirichenko & Kudyukin, p.131). It has also been argued that the Commission, in bringing unions and government together, helped to negotiate settlements to industrial disputes and defuse a potentially difficult situation. Towards the end of 1992, however, FNPR assumed a more oppositional stance to government policy and the

Commission became caught up in the accelerating conflict between executive and legislature. Burbulis refused to appear on the same TV programme as FNPR leader, Igor Klochkov, and the Commission 'became mired in acrimony' (Teague 1993, p.38). In December 1992, at a meeting of the FNPR Council, Klochkov indicated his disquiet, claiming that the Commission had become simply a talking-shop (*Trud* 19 January 1993). Nevertheless, despite threats to withdraw, FNPR continued to participate in the Commission, the alternatives being severely limited.

Cook concludes that '[t]his corporatist approach to state-labor relations seems ill-advised for a government which wants to implement radical economic reform' (Cook 1993, p.211). This would seem to be true but assumes an homogeneous approach on the part of the government. In reality, different visions of the future of Russian capitalism can be detected, which did not all accord with neo-liberal 'shock therapy'. She might also have added that none of the prerequisites for successful corporatist arrangements were in place: single peak organisations representing distinct economic interests in an expanding economy. Kudyukin notes that the activities of tripartite bodies at various levels:

> were linked not so much to the real relationships of social forces and to the demands which these social forces were putting forward, as to the desire to "be like civilized countries". For the present, social partnership in Russia remains a superficial political game which has no effect on the real relationships in the sphere of labor (p.2).

Nevertheless, the Commission continued to play a role despite these pessimistic assessments because it provided a forum for direct negotiation with the government at a time when the unions had few means of influence.

### *Reactions to shock therapy*

The first major threat to workers' living standards was a rapid 40 percent fall in real wages as prices were liberalised (*Izvestiya* 21 February 1992), but FNPR's verbal support for the reform programme left it in a weak position to defend its membership, forcing it to advance primarily economic demands, such as the indexation of incomes (*Izvestiya* 11 January 1992, p.2). Workers in more militant and economically important sectors, such as the miners, responded to price liberalisation with massive pay demands and strike threats. Wishing to avoid any confrontation at this stage, the government responded by buying the miners off with big concessions, tripling their wages in the process. A strike by miners in the Kuzbass in March was mediated by the Tripartite Commission and wages were increased (Cook 1994, p.73).

The worst hit workers were those in the so-called 'budget sector', dependent on allocations from the Treasury. Early strike threats in the budget sector were preempted by a 45 percent pay increase (*Pravda*, 25 January 1992, p.2) but the squeeze on the budget sector was such that teachers and health workers continued to be badly affected and, backed by the FNPR, undertook nationwide strikes in March and April 1992, demanding that their monthly pay be increased to the average industrial wage (*Nezavisimaya gazeta* 6 May 1992, p.2).

What is perhaps surprising, however, is that, in the face of this onslaught on their living standards, an overwhelming majority of workers did not resort to strike action. In an analysis of strike data for the first quarter of 1992, the newspaper *Trud* concluded that, compared to the previous year, there had been a significant shift away from strikes in productive sectors of the economy to strikes in non-productive sectors. In the first quarter of 1991, 120 enterprises had suffered strike action and lost production amounted to 107 million roubles, whereas in the first quarter of 1992, only 35 enterprises were affected and losses amounted to a mere 35 million roubles. The main reason for this is that industrial workers had already gained large pay increases and were more likely to be cushioned from the effects of rampant inflation through the facilities provided by their enterprise. As a consequence, more than 90 percent of strikes had occurred in the unprotected and under-funded budget sector: of the 49,000 who had been on strike, 22,000 had been teachers and 14,000 health service workers (*Trud*, 25 April 1992, p.2).

Teachers and health service workers in the Russian republic continued with industrial action in April and May. The main demands of health workers in Moscow were for total state funding of medical institutions, in a situation where the majority of the city's inhabitants were unable to pay for medical services, and a 500 percent increase in wages (although a 180 percent rise had already been agreed in a Presidential decree but not implemented). The dispute was temporarily resolved through the use of the Tripartite Commission, which helped negotiate a settlement giving an 80 percent increase to all budget-sector workers and 160 percent to teachers (*Izvestiya* 16 May 1992, p.2).

The potential divisions between groups of workers in different economic sectors, particularly those linked to the world economy could be seen in May 1992, when oil and gas workers struck demanding higher pay and the freeing of oil and gas prices. In response, wages were tripled and prices increased but the government was not prepared to instigate complete deregulation. Oil and gas production during 1992 declined sharply (Cook 1994, pp.73-4; *Rossiiskaya gazeta* 3 June 1992, p.1).

As a consequence of concessions, parliamentary legislation and enterprise management, wages increased rapidly during 1992. Between January and September 1992 average industrial wages quadrupled from 1801 to 8140 roubles per month but real wages fell as prices increased by twice as much over the same period. The government rejected FNPR's demand of full indexation but conceded partial indexation in the General Agreement of March 1992 and subsequent measures (Cook 1994, pp.75-7).

In the spring and summer 1992, a new phenomenon afflicting the Russian economy, inter-enterprise debt and the non-payment of wages, provoked a new wave of strikes affecting Kuzbass, Krasnoyarsk, Novosibirsk, Kamchatka and the Russian Far East. Apart from the payment of wages, demands were also raised in respect of the cancellation of enterprise debts, extension of credits, indexing of wages and working capital, all of which completely undermined government efforts to liberalise the economy (Cook 1994, p.75).

A further impact of shock therapy was a fall of employment in the state sector by six million in 1992. Much of this decline can be attributed to workers shifting to generally better-paid employment in the burgeoning private sector. Official unemployment during the same period grew much more slowly than had been anticipated, rising to 518,000 by December 1992. Seventy percent of the registered unemployed were women who had been employed primarily in white-collar occupations, but many employees were retained by enterprises on a part-time basis, sent on extended holidays or with 'administrative leave', that is unpaid but still on the enterprise's books (*Komsomolskaya Pravda* 9 June 1992, p.2). The surprisingly low level of unemployment indicated the degree to which shock therapy had not brought about a fundamental change in the relations of production. Subsidies continued, little was done about enterprise debt, the State Bank under Gerashchenko softened its monetary policy, and there was a failure to implement bankruptcy legislation, as a result of resistance from the Supreme Soviet.

The unions sought to present themselves as 'responsible' elements in a chaotic situation. FNPR leaders insisted that their disagreements were not with the strategic thrust of Yeltsin's programme, only with specific details. In response to a projected fall in production by the end of 1992 of 25-30 percent and potential mass unemployment, FNPR proposed an investment programme to maintain production, with priority being given to the energy sector, agriculture, food, medical and consumer goods. Value-added tax would be staggered depending on social need and prices on oil, gas and coal would be controlled by the state (*Trud* 4 April 1992). Shortly afterwards, FNPR President Klochkov asserted, in a speech to the Sixth Congress of People's Deputies, that the main problem of reform was the continued existence of monopolies, and that privatisation should be accelerated while 'taking into account the interests of the labour collectives' (*Trud* 10 April 1992). He further argued that, in the main, Yeltsin's programme coincided with that of the trade unions, who were 'opposed to exacerbating the political and class struggle' and could become a 'powerful force for consolidation' (ibid).

Nevertheless, during 1992, FNPR's stance to the government became increasingly oppositional but it also came under increasing internal pressure over its strategy of support for budget sector workers to the perceived neglect of other groups of workers. In October 1992, FNPR's call for a 24-hour strike against government policy led to the withdrawal from FNPR of the mining and metallurgical union, led by Boris Misnik, which comprised two million members. In an interview shortly afterwards, Misnik argued that 'the actions of the FNPR's leaders do not leave any opportunity for the independence and self-activity of member organisations. All of our efforts to change the position of the FNPR leadership were unsuccessful' (*Nezavisimaya gazeta* 12 November 1992, p.2). Although both mining and metalworking sectors were heavily dependent on government support, it is also clear that the split was provoked by an element of personal ambition which generated opposition to the split within the union (Clarke 1993, p.157; see also *Trud* 12 January 1993).

A balance sheet of FNPR's activity during 1992 in the newspaper *Trud* was decidedly negative, suggesting that delay in reforming the unions' structures and developing a policy appropriate to the conditions of economic transition had pushed different sectors into dependent action (*Trud* 5 January 1993, p.1). *Trud* also suggested that this was not a problem of FNPR alone but also of new unions indicating a profound disorientation among all organisations claiming to represent workers' interests. While a degree of success had been achieved in terms of wage agreements, no mechanism existed to ensure that they were implemented (ibid). The same could be said about the General Agreement, obtained through the Trilateral Commission, only 15 of its 50 points having been implemented (*Trud* 19 January 1993).

One 'success' for FNPR during 1992 had been the institutionalisation of its relationship with enterprise directors through the establishment in July of the Russian Assembly of Social Partnership (RASP), which according to Connor was 'more event than organization' (1996, p.48). The following autumn, FNPR entered into a more serious arrangement by joining Civic Union. On the face of it this identification of workers' and managers' interests seems a rather paradoxical development, but, in the context of the breakup of the Soviet Union, it was extremely logical. As we have discussed before trade unions at all levels of the Soviet system played the role of an adjunct to management in fulfilling the plan. In addition, enterprises played the crucial intermediary role in the social contract by disbursing social benefits to the workforce. The collapse of the planning mechanism enhanced the role of the enterprise within the economic system while leaving production relations relatively intact. In this context, unions continued to be responsible for the management of the enterprise's social security fund and collaborated with directors to obtain essential subsidies from the state. It made sense, therefore, to extend this relationship to the overall struggle for resources at a governmental and parliamentary level.

Partly because of this developing political relationship the increasing conflict between executive and legislature had a major impact on the trade unions. Just prior to the April 1993 referendum, which was in effect a vote of confidence in the president, Yeltsin met with leaders of about 30 independent trade unions, including miners, metallurgists, and aviation, who expressed their support for him, for the privatisation programme, and for early parliamentary elections (Connor 1994, pp.335-6). FNPR, on the other hand, in the increasingly difficult economic and political conditions, had tried to remain neutral in the dispute between Yeltsin and parliament, trying to manoeuvre between the two structures (Shubin 1995b, p.7). This conflict coupled with growing popular discontent created some space for opposition but FNPR continued with a cautious policy. The leadership eventually formulated a 'Plan of Collective Action' to build its political base and which was to have been backed by a wave of political strikes in autumn 1993. In practice, however, nothing was done to further its implementation (Clarke 1993, p.157).

When it came to the showdown FNPR was the only trade union federation to oppose the decree dissolving parliament, declaring the closure of the 'legally elected Supreme Soviet and Congress of People's Deputies' a 'coup d'etat' (Buketov 1995a, p.19). Soon afterwards communications between FNPR headquarters and the outside world were disconnected (*Segodnya* 28 September 1993, p.2). The assault on the official unions between FNPR headquarters and the outside world were disconnected (*Segodnya* 28 September 1993, p.2). The assault on the official unions continued when, on 24 September 1993, first deputy prime minister, Vladimir Shumeiko, signed a directive prohibiting financial organs from collecting union dues, thus undercutting FNPR's financial base (Cook 1994, p.84). On 28 September 1993, Yeltsin signed a decree transferring management of the social security fund from the unions to the government who would manage social insurance 'with the participation of ... trade unions' (*ITAR-TASS* 28 September 1993). While such a move could have virtually removed FNPR's *raison d'etre*, in practice, the unions continued as the agents responsible for the management of the funds, thus maintaining their key function and preventing disintegration.

The unity of FNPR was undermined from within by MFP, indicating a major divide in the FNPR bureaucracy, which argued that Yeltsin had acted 'unconstitutionally' rather than 'anti-constitutionally' and warned trade-unionists 'not to be drawn into bloodshed while all means of defending the constitutional order have not been employed' (Buketov 1995a, p.20). While Klochkov argued that the executive had rejected dialogue and the search for agreement, his call for resolute action to defend the Supreme Soviet was opposed by MFP which argued that a peaceful outcome through compromise was essential. This compromise could take the form of the voluntary dissolution of the Supreme Soviet and the preparation of simultaneous parliamentary and presidential elections, while retaining the existing government in post until the outcome of the two elections was known. Provisions were made to defend FNPR property, to work illegally in the event of a crackdown, to have an alternative leadership in reserve should the existing leaders be 'neutralised', and even to transfer FNPR headquarters to another city (*Segodnya* 28 September 1993, p.2). Preparations were also made for an all-Russian strike and to call an extraordinary FNPR congress for 28 October (*Segodnya* 28 September 1993, p.2; 14 October 1993, p.2).

Following the decisive resolution of the conflict in Yeltsin's favour and allegations by a number of union organisations that he had been complicit in the armed conflict, Klochkov agreed to resign on 11 October. He was replaced by MFP leader Mikhail Shmakov who was immediately faced with a political crisis within FNPR in respect of its strategy and the government's threat to suspend its financial operations. In addition, FNPR's opposition to Yeltsin's actions against parliament had led to demands from unions unaffiliated to FNPR, primarily the newer independent unions such as NPG and *Sotsprof*, for the redistribution of

FNPR property and resources and for the removal of the right of FNPR-affiliated unions to disburse social welfare benefits in the enterprises. In the event, FNPR's financial operations were not suspended, its property was not affected, and its control of social security funds was limited rather than removed. This suggests that Klochkov's replacement by Shmakov, who projected an image of willingness to collaborate with government and to keep the unions out of 'politics' was enough to earn FNPR a reprieve (see the interview with Shmakov in *Segodnya* 28 October 1993).

The impression of moderation was continued at FNPR's extraordinary II Congress in late October, when the formation of a new association was discussed which could bring both 'old' and 'new' unions together under one umbrella. This was a position pushed by tripartite commission chair, Vladimir Shumeiko, who would have preferred that the government negotiate with a unified trade union side. Ultimately, the congress rejected this possibility, the new unions also being unwilling to be absorbed (*Segodnya* 30 October 1993). The position of Shmakov and his co-thinkers in the leadership was also reinforced at the congress through the decision to discuss a draft document titled 'Freedom, Justice, Solidarity' which was based on MFP's platform. It was finally adopted with few amendments in April 1994 (Shubin 1995b, p.8).

## Trade Union Strategy 1994-96

After the 1993 elections trade unions, regardless of their political orientation, were confronted with two major problems. First, how to bolster their influence on decision-making in the new configuration of political forces represented within the Duma and within the institutional matrix which issued from the new Constitution adopted in December 1993. Second, how to gain influence among their own memberships, which for the FNPR in particular was staggeringly low.

In respect of the first problem, FNPR immediately began to reassess its strategy towards elections both at a national and local level. A problem existed for FNPR and a number of sectoral unions in that their constitutions did not envisage participation in the electoral arena, but this was not an insurmountable problem. The next national elections were scheduled for December 1995, which gave the unions a reasonable period to assess the suitability of different political currents for any potential electoral bloc. The question of forming a political party which could defend trade union interests was also a topic of ongoing discussion

(*Rabochaya tribuna* 21 January 1994, pp.1-2). Since August 1991 a group around then MFP chair, Mikhail Shmakov, had had an orientation to the formation of a political party linked to the unions (Shubin 1995b, p.7). In pursuit of this goal Shmakov had aligned himself with the emerging Party of Labour (PT), headed by Aleksandr Buzgalin, a former leader of the CPSU's Marxist Platform, long-standing socialist dissident, Boris Kagarlitsky, and Andrei Isaev, leader of the anarcho-syndicalist KAS-KOR. The aim was to establish a socialist party based on the trade unions, modelled loosely on the British Labour Party. At the time, Shmakov's desire to back PT seemed to create the real possibility of such a party coming into existence. Now that Shmakov was leader of FNPR, however, the project of building a Party of Labour, which had been useful in the conflict with Klochkov, was abandoned, condemning it, in the absence of alternative sources of institutional support, to a lingering death. Electoral strategy for the foreseeable future would be based on the formation of a bloc with suitable partners.

Prior to the elections FNPR strove to increase its influence through face-to-face discussions with leading figures in the new Duma and with Yeltsin himself. This stance was assisted by the continuing existence of the tripartite commission in which FNPR still participated, despite criticism of the degree to which the provisions of general agreements were being implemented (*Rabochaya tribuna* 21 January 1994, p.2). FNPR's position in the eyes of the government was also enhanced by Shumeiko's argument that the trade unions should be unified under one organisation, thus undermining the influence which the new trade unions had previously enjoyed with the government.

The stance of the new government, and of Yeltsin himself, had also moved, as a consequence of the December 1993 elections, to one which unambiguously placed more emphasis on the role of the Russian state than on radical economic reform (Tolz, p.1). Indeed, the 'neo-liberal' element of the government had been substantially removed, creating a government, in FNPR's view, more sympathetic to the trade unions, and more capable of halting the economic crisis. FNPR was, therefore, afraid of taking any actions which might bring down the government and hasten the return of the neo-liberals (Shubin 1995b, pp.8-9).

The new approach of the government was illustrated by the discussions around the so-called Civic Accord. Within Russia, tensions between different elements of the federation, rising crime, and potential social unrest prompted the drawing up of the Civic Accord and a number of conciliatory gestures, such as an amnesty for the organisers of the 1991 coup and of the 1993 parliamentary opposition, in an effort to stabilise society. The main purpose of the Accord, signed on 28 April 1994, to create some sort of unity between Russia's constituent elements, was only partially achieved. The Accord was not signed by a number of major political parties including the KPRF, the Agrarian Party and Yabloko (Tolz, p.3). Within FNPR also, there was discord, only 31 of its 42 member unions agreeing to sign. FNPR saw the Accord as an additional means of exerting pressure on the government, but the apparent failure of this strategy, led to some other unions withdrawing support for the Accord, although a majority of FNPR remained signatories. A Conciliation Commission was formed out of the Accord, chaired by Sergei Filatov, head of the presidential administration, which gave FNPR yet another means of direct access to the government, but it was difficult to see what role such a commission could play that the tripartite commission did not already fulfil (Buketov 1995b, p.31).

Deteriorating economic circumstances and the FNPR's seeming lack of activity prompted a change of tactics in the direction of mass action. On 7 September 1994, at a conference of regional and sectoral trade unions in St. Petersburg, Shmakov argued that the government's anti-inflation policy had led to the following problems: a fall in production, because of less demand and purchasing power, which had created unemployment, and a crisis of non-payment resulting in wage debts of more than three trillion roubles. Officially, 4.5 million were unemployed, representing five percent of the working population, with a further five million working part-time. In Shmakov's opinion, unemployment could rise to 11 million. The trade unions had to work out a plan of action, the main element of which would be a nationwide day of protest on 27 October (*ITAR-TASS*, 7 September 1994). The two main demands of the protest, which would consist of meetings, marches, rallies and strike action where appropriate, would be the preservation of jobs, and payment of unpaid wages (*ITAR-TASS* 13 September 1994). An appeal was sent by FNPR to Yeltsin, Chernomyrdin, Shumeiko and the chair of the State Duma, Ivan Rybkin, warning them that the action would be taken unless the government responded to the unions' demands (*Rabochaya tribuna* 1 October 1994, p.1). After warnings first to call off the protest as it contravened the Civic Accord, and then not to make it too 'political', Shmakov reassured potential supporters that the protest action would pursue purely economic goals and that FNPR had dissociated itself from attempts to give a political complexion to the events, which had been called 'only to correct the government's course' (*ITAR-TASS* 26 October 1994).

Increasingly, FNPR's search for a strategy revolved around the forthcoming parliamentary elections, and this prompted a call for a fresh day of action on 12 April 1995. This attracted support on a larger scale than 27 October and, despite FNPR's efforts to limit the demands to purely economic questions, political demands including for the resignation of the government and president were raised in a number of regions (*Rabochaya Politika* 1995, No.2, p.25). The 1 May demonstrations were also significantly bigger and more widespread than in the previous two years, partly as a result of mobilisations by the KPRF (ibid, p.32).

*Strikes*

While trade union activity had remained fairly quiet during 1994, the continuing deterioration in living standards made a new rise in strike activity almost inevitable. It was the coalfields that were most affected by strikes along with teachers and healthworkers in the cash-strapped budget sector. The coal industry represents the most interesting example of changing attitudes to reform as, of course, miners were in the vanguard of democratisation and had been most influential within the workers' movement in support of radical economic transformation. Early manifestations of discontent over the inflation generated by shock therapy had been countered by rapid concessions on wages. By February 1995, however, a new wave of strikes began to hit the coalfields in response to the general decline in living standards, and more specifically chronic non-payment of wages, and the prospect of mass pit closures and redundancies. In contrast to previous stoppages, these actions were led primarily by the former official union *Rosugleprof*. Even NPG, whose leadership had been reluctant to lead any action which could undermine the reform programme because of its support for Yeltsin, had since late 1993 been involved in sporadic actions to redress declining conditions.

In the early years of economic transformation, the strategic location of the coal industry in terms of the reliance of other industries on its output, the large number of people employed, and the miners' political support for Yeltsin meant that it had escaped major restructuring. Nevertheless, output had fallen catastrophically between 1988 and 1994 from 416.5 million to 261 million tons (Morvant, p.57). The target for 1995 was 264 million tons but actual output was only 250.1 million tons. Eventually, capitalist transformation demanded that the Russian Coal Company, *Rosugol'*, be reorganised to make it 'leaner and fitter'. *Rosugol'* boss, Yuri Malyshev, warned that reorganisation would take six years and involve the closure of

100 uneconomical pits, 70 of them by 1998 (*Interfax* 30 June 1995). The World Bank also drew up a programme for restructuring the industry, recommending the closure of 80 pits by the year 2000, and the diversion of current subsidies to fund a social safety net. It was willing to lend the Russian government $500 million for relocation and retraining. Morvant suggests that a 'consensus on the need to restructure the industry' existed between unions, management and government, but that differences existed over the pace of change (Morvant, p.58). Nevertheless, pits were being closed and workers made redundant. In 1995, 57,000 mining jobs were lost and the level of government expenditure on pit closures rose from 1.5 percent of its total subsidy in 1994 to 8.5 percent in 1995 and was expected to rise to 15 percent in 1996 (*Finansovye Izvestiya* 26 January 1996, p.2).

Non-payment of wages had become an endemic feature of the economy and the source of most resentment among workers (see Table 5.1). In the coal industry 2,200 billion roubles were owed at the beginning of 1995 by enterprises to which coal had been delivered, and 1,300 billion roubles were owed from the federal budget (*Segodnya* 3 February 1995, p.2). The level of wage arrears was coupled in the coal industry with concern over the degree of state subsidy. Many pits are unprofitable: at the beginning of 1995, approximately two-thirds of Kuzbass pits were making a loss (*Izvestiya* 20 January 1995, p.5). As a consequence of these factors strikes in the coal industry became almost a daily occurrence, particularly at those pits with the lowest productivity and fewest prospects for survival without state support (*Finansovye Izvestiya* 26 January 1996, p.2). Formerly loyal followers of Yeltsin were turning into his bitter opponents.

On 1 February 1995 work ceased at the 26 pits in the Rostov-on-Don region governed by the *Rostovugol'* coal association as 75,000 miners went on strike. They were owed 230 billion roubles in arrears (*Izvestiya* 4 February 1995, p.2). A further 50,000 miners struck in neighbouring Krasnodar krai (ibid, p.1). Here workers had not been paid since November 1994. On 2 February 1995, following strikes against wage arrears in Rostov and Krasnodar regions, *Rosugleprof* called a 24-hour all-Russia warning strike for 8 February, demanding that the government immediately pay what it owed in subsidies for 1994 and January 1995 and accelerate efforts to solve the non-payment problem. More than half a million miners took strike action - the largest stoppage since the 1989 strike and, for the first time since the split in the miners' union in 1990, a degree of co-ordination was achieved between the two unions. The strikes resulted in government concessions to demands for increased subsidisation of the coal industry and for the rejection of the World Bank plan for rationalisation, averting a threatened indefinite all-Russia strike for 1 March, which would have demanded the resignation of the government and early elections for the president (*Segodnya* 3 February 1995, p.2).

**Table 5.1 Total wage debt, billion roubles at December 1995 prices, end period**

| | *1992* | *1993* | *1994* | *1995* | *1996* |
|---|---|---|---|---|---|
| Industry | 1034 | 2653 | 5019 | 7734 | 18185 |
| Agriculture | 397 | 2092 | 3009 | 2571 | 4855 |
| Construction | 541 | 840 | 1686 | 1941 | 5310 |
| Transport | | | | 1134 | 3305 |
| Health | | | | | 2108 |
| Education | | | | | 3667 |
| Culture | | | | | 396 |
| Science | | | | | 888 |

*Source*: Clarke 1997, p.2

Strikes continued to occur on a local basis throughout 1995 until, on 25 January 1996, the executive of *Rosugleprof* voted for a nationwide strike to begin on 1 February. Union leader, Vitalii Bud'ko, claimed that 4,500 billion roubles continued to be owed to the coal industry, of which 1,000 billion were wage arrears. On 26 January, against a background of the strike threat and persistent picketing of the government building by angry miners, prime minister Chernomyrdin agreed to allocate immediately 600 billion roubles to pay off wage arrears up to the end of 1995. This was not sufficient to mollify the unions, however, who also demanded that the government draw up a schedule for funding the industry and for mines to be allowed to retain a greater amount of funds to pay wages. The unions also demanded that government funding of the industry for 1996 be increased to 10,400 billion roubles. On 31 January, the newly-elected State Duma, in which the KPRF was the largest single party, passed a resolution in support of the miners' legitimate demands and sent a delegation to meet with Yeltsin.

It was not, however, possible to avert the strike which began on 1 February with widespread support. *Rosugleprof* subsequently claimed that 80 percent of coal enterprises had been involved although some mines rejected strike action altogether as inappropriate in the current climate.

Nevertheless, the government response was to make immediate concessions: 10,400 billion roubles would be allocated to the coal industry during 1996, of which 5,100 billion would be paid in the first six months; Chernomyrdin indicated that a new wage agreement would shortly be signed between the government and unions; the promised 600 billion roubles was also received on 1 February. In response to these developments the *Rosugleprof* executive voted on 2 February by six to five to suspend the strike immediately from 3 February, although warning that, if the government did not deliver on its promises, the strike would be resumed on 1 March.

### *Electoral strategy*

The absence of an independent political profile on the part of the trade unions is exemplified by the variety of orientations they adopted in relation to other political forces in the run-up to the December 1995 parliamentary elections: FNPR finally ended up in an alliance with its traditional allies, enterprise management; NPG became part of the bloc organised by Speaker of the State Duma, Ivan Rybkin; and the mining and metallurgical union ended up supporting the social-liberal Yabloko.

FNPR had begun to co-operate with other political forces in late 1994, forming a very loose alliance with the Socialist Party of Working People (SPT), the most moderate offshoot of the CPSU, and Yuri Skokov's Commodity Producers' Federation of Russia (*ITAR-TASS* 29 October 1994), but the persistent refusal of the government to make concessions to the unions' demands pushed it towards adopting a more 'political' strategy.

The decision to create the pre-election association Trade Unions of Russia (PR) was taken by FNPR on 17 February 1995. The FNPR's decision to participate in the December elections represented a shift away from mass mobilisation as a means of influencing political decision-making towards involvement in the legislative process itself. This is an unusual step for an interest group to take even in Russia's comparatively corporatist system. As Shubin notes, turning the entire trade union federation in a political direction initially avoided the problem of alignment with one particular political party, which had been posed during previous discussions around creating a 'labour' party and risked the possibility of a split (1995a, pp.32-3). Despite claims that FNPR's massive paper membership could deliver a sizeable vote, the reality was that lack of confidence in the unions ensured that collaboration with other parties, and the negotiation of electoral blocs, was only temporarily postponed if PR was to have any chance of overcoming the five percent hurdle to representation in the Duma.

On 31 March 1995, at a conference of chairs of the sectoral trade unions belonging to FNPR, Mikhail Shmakov argued that the trade unions were faced with an alternative: either to engage in mass protests or to prepare to participate in the forthcoming December elections. In his opinion, participation in the latter would be a more efficient usage of the FNPR's resources, enabling the unions directly to influence legislation in respect of economic policy, working conditions, and the rights of unions themselves, thus raising the profile and authority of FNPR (Buketov & Nikul'nikov, p.5). It would be irresponsible, Shmakov argued, to exacerbate the current social crisis (*RIA Novosti* 31 March 1995). Rather than ends in themselves, the mass protest actions planned for 12 April and 1 May could be seen as stages in the electoral campaign. Such a counterposition of electoral campaigning and mass actions clearly revealed where the FNPR leadership felt happiest: small-scale negotiations with anybody prepared to listen.

The next step was the formation of an organisation separate from but intimately connected to the FNPR. This was done through 'Russian trade unions - to the elections!' (RPNV), established on 1 June (*ITAR-TASS* 2 June 1995) and subsequently registered at the Ministry of Justice on 24 June (*Radio Russia* 24 June 1995). RPNV's sole function was to plan for the elections and negotiate with potential bloc partners. FNPR's strategy was to create a centre-left bloc drawing in as many forces as possible but, as the notion of left and right has always been problematic in the Russian context, quite who would be included in or excluded from the centre-left was never clearly defined. In addition, no political party, apart from the KPRF, had a mass base, while others expressed the interests of a particular economic sector (for example, the Agrarian Party of Russia) or bureaucratic elements in various parts of the state. Pro-Yeltsin forces established 'Our Home is Russia' (NDR), headed by prime minister Chernomyrdin, to try and organise the disparate elites into a so-called 'party of power', and also created an ever so slightly left-of-centre analogue of NDR around Duma Speaker, Ivan Rybkin (Rybkin bloc) to try and attract wider forces.

The political orientation of RPNV was centre-left and, thus, any choice of partners had to be from those with the same broad ideological standpoint (*Solidarnost'* No.13, 1995, pp.8-9). According to Andrei Isaev, editor of *Solidarnost'* and adviser to FNPR leader Mikhail Shmakov, collaboration with big fish such as the KPRF was dependent on the latter becoming a centre-left party (*Solidarnost'* No.8 1995, p.4). In the event, the KPRF felt, not surprisingly, that it had sufficient strength on its own and decided to run as an independent party.

FNPR soon discovered that a left-centrist bloc was not going to coalesce around RPNV, and oriented instead to the already established Rybkin bloc, of which Shmakov had previously been critical because of its fundamentally pro-governmental character. As a condition for joining the bloc, RPNV insisted on the prioritisation of the unions' social demands and a fair representation of union candidates on the bloc's list. As neither of these conditions were fulfilled, RPNV began to seek other partners (Buketov & Nikul'nikov, p.12).

Unfortunately, there was only one other likely organisation: the Russian United Industrial Party (ROPP). On 5 September, the conference of RPNV voted for a bloc with ROPP to create 'Trade Unions and Industrialists of Russia - the Union of Labour' (*Soyuz Truda* - ST). The emblem of ST was reminiscent of a sawn-off hammer and sickle and its programme was essentially corporatist: its main slogan being 'Wages, Jobs, Law and Order!' (*Zarplata, Zanyatost', Zakonnost'*) (*Solidarnost'* No.18, 1995, p.4). Isaev explained that such an alliance was possible only in the current conditions where the fundamental social cleavage ran between the government and industry (representing the rest of the country) rather than between workers and management.

The newer independent unions also participated in the elections, but their small size placed even more of a premium on finding significant partners. In July 1995, the Confederation of Labour of Russia (KTR), which united the new unions, had declared that it was impossible to ally with any of the electoral blocs. Soon afterwards, KTR joined the liberal Democratic Russia (DR) to form the 'Democratic Russia and Free Trade Unions' bloc. The bloc was never registered, however, because it failed to gain the requisite number of signatures (Buketov & Nikul'nikov, p.7). Meanwhile, NPG found its way into the Ivan Rybkin bloc. NPG leader Aleksandr Sergeev argued that their own 'centre-left' position accorded with that of Rybkin, so an alliance was a natural continuation of their policies in pursuit of a 'socially directed' course of reform (*Delo* 37, September 1995, p.1). *Sotsprof* activists, on the other hand, found themselves travelling in different directions, some entering the 'For the Motherland' (ZR) bloc and others going with NDR (Buketov & Nikul'nikov, p.8). Altogether, the trade unions were represented by a total of 236 candidates on the lists of various parties and blocs. Unsurprisingly, the largest number of candidates, 101, was on the list of the ST, while both

APR with 34, and Yuri Skokov's Congress of Russian Communities (KRO) with 15 had significant numbers (ibid, p.7).

The result of the election was one of resounding failure on the part of virtually all the blocs supported by unions irrespective of their orientation. Overall, ST gained 1.59 percent of the vote, although in some particularly badly hit regions it did rather better. Nevertheless, it failed to overcome the 5 percent hurdle. The one union which did manage to get a candidate elected through its own efforts was 'Miners of Russia' based on *Rosugleprof*, who were reluctant to participate in ST. The programme of 'Miners of Russia' extended beyond defence of the coal industry to that of all workers, and initially there was a desire to affiliate to a larger bloc. Opinion poll evidence, however, suggested that there was a reservoir of support for the miners, even in non-mining districts (Borisov 1995), and as a consequence 'Miners of Russia' decided to stand alone, winning one seat through Vladimir Katal'nikov in Rostov region. Amongst other parties, KPRF received more than 50 percent of the vote in the Kuzbass, a reflection of the degree of disenchantment with Yeltsin and the impact of the reforms.

## Conclusion

Russia's experience during the 1990s and into the twenty-first century throws into relief much of the literature on democratic transitions, in which there is a tendency to view the development of democracy as an inexorable process once the previous authoritarian regime is overturned. This is reiterated every time Russia survives another election without bloodshed or widespread electoral fraud. By some commentators' criteria Russia is now the proud possessor of a 'consolidated' democracy. By any objective criteria Russia has made steps forward in permitting competition between political organisations and the expression of dissenting opinion, but the political system is severely flawed by the domination of the presidency and its associated apparatus, and by the weakness of civil society, which was energised under perestroika, but has subsequently become stunted and politically inactive. In such circumstances, the reemergence of the trade unions as an influential force throughout society, rather than in one or two specific sectors, appears to be a prospect for the medium, rather than the short, term.

The difficult conditions which applied in post-Soviet Russia did not make for the development of a dynamic trade union movement, which could advance the cause of democracy. Trade unions are at their most effective when the economy is expanding and concessions can be more readily obtained. Russia's economy in 1992 was in crisis, a situation excerbated by the implementation of price liberalisation. For the former official unions in FNPR, the low level of support from rank-and-file members, who mainly retained their membership for the social benefits unions continued to disburse, made it difficult for the leadership to mobilise around demands and campaigns and pushed them to seek compromise. For the new independent unions', on the other hand, support for Yeltsin's government and the programme of radical economic reform compromised their capacity to defend their members interests and in most cases has reduced their membership and influence.

At the heart of the unions' problems has been the lack of consciousness of ordinary workers of their real interests, which are instead identified with 'their' enterprise and its management. As a consequence, workers have been unable to establish viable and genuinely independent organisations which could constitute a labour *movement* encompassing both unions and political parties capable of articulating workers' interests at a national level. Success in winning concessions has usually been dependent on the strategic importance of the industrial sector rather than on the inherent strength of the unions. Thus workers in energy, particularly oil and gas, with its high levels of hard currency earnings, were swiftly bought off, while workers in the 'budget sector', with no economic leverage, recorded the highest levels of strike action but saw their earnings fall constantly in comparison with the highest earning sectors.

Efforts to create a 'civilised' industrial relations climate through the tripartite commission must also be considered a failure. The objective conditions for the establishment of corporatist structures simply were not present in Russia in 1992. First, the government could make no meaningful concessions to labour because of the economic crisis; second, the interests of the three sides, and especially employers and labour, were indistinct and difficult to distinguish from each other; third, both 'employers' and trade union sides were fragmented between different organisations and not all-embracing 'peak' organisations, as a consequence of which there was no guarantee that any agreement reached within the commission could be implemented.

The fortunes of FNPR throughout this period have been inextricably linked to those of enterprise management. This continuation of Soviet practice is a consequence of the economic crisis, especially in those sectors (the overwhelming majority) which still depend on government subsidy to survive, and of the form of privatisation, which brought only a juridical change in the ownership of much of industry rather than an actual shift in the relations of production. In the cases where unions have taken action, for example around such issues as wage arrears, demands have been directed at the government rather than enterprise management. At a political level, independence was also severely compromised through alliances between unions and a plethora of different parties which did little to advance workers' interests and generally resulted in abject failure in the 1995 elections.

# 6 Labour, State and Democracy in Ukraine

Ukraine's evolution as an independent state has been heavily influenced by its geopolitical situation. On the one hand, Ukraine has the problem of how to deal with its gigantic neighbour to the east, on whom it is dependent for energy and a sizeable proportion of its trade, and, on the other, the sheer size and location of Ukraine makes it attractive economically and in security terms for Western states. The gravitational pull exerted from these two different directions has created considerable tensions, which have threatened to tear the fledgling Ukrainian state asunder. In such circumstances, it has been possible for different interest groups to exercise some influence over political decision-making.

## The Legacy of the USSR

Ukraine had only briefly tasted independence between 1917 and 1921 and, even then, its existence was constantly threatened by the Civil War between Reds and Whites resulting from the Bolshevik Revolution. Before that, as Solchanyk observes, 'Historically, mainstream Russian political thought never considered Ukraine to he anything other than 'Little Russia' (Malorossiya) and Ukrainians as an offshoot of a larger all-Russian (*obshcherusskii*) nation' (Solchanyk, p.49). While most of the historical territory of Ukraine was incorporated into the Soviet Union in the early 1920s, the ethnically Ukrainian region of Galicia, which had formerly been part of the Austro-Hungarian empire, ended up as part of the newly-reconstituted Poland. It was only with the Hitler-Stalin Pact of 1939, which carved up the Polish state, and then in the aftermath of the defeat of Nazism that all Ukrainian regions were absorbed and consolidated into the Ukrainian Soviet Socialist Republic. The Nazi invasion had, however, given an impetus to nationalist currents in Ukraine which saw an opportunity to be rid of the primary obstacle to Ukrainian independence - the Stalinist bureaucracies in Moscow and Kyiv. After the war, guerilla warfare continued in parts of western Ukraine until the late 1940s against what was considered to be illegitimate reoccupation by Soviet forces.

The pressure to resist Russification led Ukrainian leaderships, particularly after destalinisation, to make some concessions to nationalist sentiments. This was especially the case with Petro Shelest, who despite neglecting western Ukraine, spoke and promoted Ukrainian as a matter of course, demanded more investment for Ukraine and 'took seriously the promise of Ukrainian autonomy enshrined in the Soviet Constitution' (Subtelny, p.511). Shelest's 'Ukrainianisation' of the Communist Party of Ukraine (CPU) during the 1960s undoubtedly generated disquiet in Moscow and he was replaced in May 1972 by Volodymyr Shcherbytsky, a member of Brezhnev's 'Dnipropetrovs'k Mafia'. Shcherbytsky subsequently followed a more pro-Moscow line, but the ease with which the CPU had been previously 'Ukrainianised' suggests that its takeover of the nationalist movement when it emerged under *perestroika* was not altogether unexpected.

Ukraine was an important component of the USSR in a variety of ways: it was the second largest republic with a population of around 52 million at the time of independence; the CPU was an important source of cadres to the CPSU and all-Union apparatuses; economically, Ukraine's central and western regions were the Soviet Union's 'breadbasket'; the Donbas was a major industrial region although, during the Soviet period, its development was kept deliberately behind that of Russia and was characterised by poor productivity and low incomes resulting from inadequate central investment. Two-thirds of Ukraine's exports comprised heavy industrial goods or energy in the form of coal or petrochemicals (Lukinov, pp.35-6). In addition, Ukrainian industry was primarily run by Moscow-based ministries: in 1987, only 6-7 percent of its industrial potential was controlled from Kyiv. As Gorbachev's economic reforms took effect this increased to 45 percent but all basic industries remained under the control of Moscow (ibid, p.31). Keeping Ukraine in a subordinate position to Moscow was thus crucial to the maintenance of the Soviet Union itself.

Industrialisation helped create the ethnic profile which has been so important in post-Soviet Ukraine. The workforce of the coalmining and steel industries of the Donbas was provided predominantly by an influx of ethnic Russians. By 1989, 22 percent of Ukraine's population were ethnically Russian, primarily in the East and Crimea, but an even higher proportion spoke Russian on a day-to-day basis. During the 1960s, the working class became the dominant social force and increasingly assertive. Workers were even more highly concentrated than in other parts of the USSR with two-thirds working in factories of more than 1000 employees and was becoming increasingly ethnically homogeneous: in 1970, 74 percent of workers were Ukrainian as a result both of Russians taking better jobs and being replaced by Ukrainians and of the industrial development of central and western Ukraine. The ranks of the working class were also swollen by an influx of youth, frequently well-educated and looking for the better pay associated with manual jobs, whose expectations were also considerable. Those expectations were, however, dashed by the 'stability of cadres' of the Brezhnev era which produced a lack of social mobility (Krawchenko, p.212). The conditions were, therefore, already developing both socially and economically for the emergence of a nationalist current when *perestroika* created the conditions for its maturation.

In Ukraine, the movement for greater autonomy from Moscow was initiated by *Rukh* (Popular Movement for Perestroika) founded in September 1989, but the fragmentation of the Soviet state and communist party led to the emergence of a faction within the Ukrainian CP which also saw its interests in autonomy from Moscow. This faction, backed by large sections of the apparatus and *nomenklatura*, successfully usurped the struggle for independence from *Rukh* and declared Ukraine independent on 24 August 1991, following the collapse of the attempted coup. Independence was subsequently confirmed in a referendum on 1 December 1991. At the same time, the *nomenklatura*'s success was confirmed in elections for Ukraine's first president by the victory of erstwhile party ideologist Leonid Kravchuk who soundly defeated former dissident, Vyacheslav Chornovil, while extolling the 'thousand-year-old tradition of Ukrainian statehood' begun by Kievan Rus' (Dawisha & Parrott, p.39).

The results of both election and referendum revealed that support for an independent state overwhelmingly permeated all sections of the Ukrainian population and all regions of Ukraine. Ethnic differences within Ukraine were buried before the prospect of a territorial Ukrainian state, in which things could only get better if the nettle of independence were grasped and the economic and political transformation of the vestigial structures of the Soviet state completed. The ship of Kravchuk's state soon began to founder, however, partially as a result of the very event which had precipitated the birth of independent Ukraine - the collapse of the USSR and specifically its economic links - and partially as a consequence of concentrating on establishing Ukraine's statehood to the detriment of political and economic transformation.

## Ukraine under Kravchuk

### *Economic transformation*

The elation with which independence was greeted masked the shock which the disintegration of the USSR administered to the Ukrainian economy. In 1990, Ukraine's national income per capita was ten percent higher than Russia's and in 1991 the cost of Soviet oil, on which Ukraine was heavily dependent, was less than one percent of the world market price (Aslund 1995, pp.125-6). These favourable conditions rapidly changed. Demand from the former Soviet Union for Ukrainian heavy industrial, and particularly military, goods dropped by 30 percent between 1991 and 1992. In addition, the prices of oil and gas imports from Russia began to rise towards world market prices. Oil imports declined between 1991 and 1992 from 51.1 million tons to 34.1 million tons and high levels of subsidy were maintained in order to keep domestic prices low. Independence for the former republics of the USSR led to the introduction of customs tariffs, restrictions on cross-border transport and the disruption of trade and production links between enterprises previously under the jurisdiction of a single ministry in Moscow (Dabrowski, pp.123-4). In this context, unrest in the Donbas generated understandable demands for links with Russia to be restored and for participation in the CIS economic zone as 70 percent of supplies to eastern Ukraine came from Russia and 85 percent from the former Soviet Union (Jung, p.52).

In January 1992, Ukraine followed Russia's lead in price liberalisation provoking an immediate 250 percent rise in prices. The government of Vitold Fokin, dominated by elements of the old *nomenklatura*, did little to respond to changing circumstances, maintaining Soviet-style controls over foreign trade, undertaking little reform of industry and continuing to subsidise its most uncompetitive elements. At the same time, independence brought with it costs previously borne by the USSR budget, particularly in respect of the maintenance of a defence force. The result was a budget deficit equivalent to 27.8 percent of GDP in 1992 and 10 percent in 1993, massive capital flight, a collapse of production and a hyperinflationary spiral fed by the gradually increasing costs of vital resources imported from Russia (Dabrowski, pp.126-7). The scale of the devastation was such that officially GDP fell by 52 percent between 1990 and 1994 (Aslund 1995, p.127).

Ukraine endeavoured to establish its credentials in international financial circles by joining the IMF in March 1992 and by creating its own, albeit transitional, currency, the kupon (karbovanets). The intention was to introduce a genuinely convertible currency, the hryvna, when economic circumstances had stabilised. The kupon, initially introduced into circulation at parity and in parallel with the ruble, soon developed an inflationary spiral of its own, with goods being sold at distinct ruble and kupon prices. The growing economic problems were 'solved' by the emission of more and more currency, fuelling a situation of hyperinflation which reached a staggering 10,200 percent in 1993, and furthering demands for higher wages. Such were the monetary emissions of the National Bank of Ukraine that Russia expelled Ukraine from the ruble zone (Aslund 1995, p.127).

This headlong decline of the economy even took place when Ukraine was still cushioned to a certain degree from the ravages of the global economy. In 1992, Ukraine received 22 percent of its GDP in subsidised Russian credits (Aslund 1995, p.127). By September 1993, Ukraine's trade deficit with Russia had risen to six trillion karbovantsi (1,594 billion roubles) but even this was not the real figure as Russia's continued sales of key commodities at below world market prices implied a capital transfer to Ukraine of 1.2 trillion roubles, equivalent to 30 percent of Ukraine's GDP (Dabrowski, p.125).

The approach of the new Ukrainian regime to economic transformation clearly distinguishes it from its Russian counterpart. The Fokin government had no intention of implementing a 'shock therapy' programme and price liberalisation was more an unavoidable consequence of events in Russia. A privatisation programme was drawn up in July 1992, which bore a marked similarity to the Russian version. It envisaged privatisation through the issuing of vouchers to the population, with labour collectives having priority in the purchase of their own enterprise. As in Russia, this method was the one generally favoured by enterprise directors as it kept control in their hands. The difference was that the Ukrainian programme was not so much the result of compromise between a radical liberal government meeting stiff resistance from entrenched interests, as a consequence of a *commonality* of interests between the regime and the industrial *nomenklatura*.

## *The character of the state*

After the August coup the Communist Party of Ukraine (CPU) had been declared illegal and, in the absence of its framework, representatives of the old *nomenklatura* who dominated the Ukrainian parliament, the *Verkhovna*

*Rada*, cohered through their desire to hold onto political power, creating a shadowy 'party of power' (*partiya vladi*). The existence of the 'party of power' within both executive and legislature made a viable separation of powers very difficult to achieve, especially as Ukraine remained without a proper constitution until June 1996. Kravchuk was also determined that Ukraine should be a strongly-centralised unitary state, establishing a system of regional presidential representatives in March 1992, who exercised control over local government (Birch & Zinko, p.23).

Ukraine's constitutional problems were exacerbated by the situation in Crimea, whose predominantly ethnic Russian population, strongly supported some degree of autonomy within Ukraine, if not outright independence. Crimea's status was also bound up with the question of the old Soviet Black Sea Fleet, which was based at the Crimean port of Sevastopol, and therefore concerned Ukrainian-Russian relations both in terms of ethnicity and security. To make matters even more complicated, the Crimean Tatars, expelled from their homeland to Siberia by Stalin for alleged collaboration with the Nazis, were permitted to return.

Kravchuk's concentration on the stabilisation of the Ukrainian state to the detriment of a viable economic programme alienated large sections of his former base in eastern Ukraine, but increased his support in nationalist western Ukraine. As a consequence, the 'party of power' became increasingly riven between its industrially-based, Russia-oriented eastern section and its more agriculturally-based, Europe-oriented western component. The growing rift was demonstrated by the degeneration of the working relationship between Kravchuk as head of state and Leonid Kuchma, former director of the gigantic Yuzhmash missile plant in Dnipropetrovs'k, who was appointed prime minister in September 1992. Kuchma, aware of the dire state of Ukrainian industry, particularly in the East, wished to accelerate the pace of economic reform but could not gain Kravchuk's agreement to proceed.

## Trade Unions under Kravchuk

Even before independence, and under the influence of the emergence of a liberal opposition to the Soviet regime, increased labour militancy and the development of a nationalist movement, trade unions in Ukraine had begun to fragment. Donets'k had been the site of the split in the miners' union in 1990 and in June 1991 the All-Ukrainian Association of Workers' Solidarity (VOST) was established in counterposition to the former official union federation the Federation of Trade Unions of Ukraine (FPU). VOST immediately identified itself with Ukrainian nationalist organisations *Rukh* and the Ukrainian Republican Party (Milovidov, p.12), electing URP activist Stepan Khmara onto its executive (Crowley, p.52). As Crowley notes, the nationalist orientation of VOST effectively excluded large sections of the labour movement in the Russified east (ibid). Even NPG, who were the main representatives of independent unions in the Donbas, were castigated at VOST's founding conference for their membership of an all-Union organisation (Milovidov, p.12). By June 1992 VOST claimed a membership of four million in eight regions of Ukraine but proved ineffective in mobilising workers for a number of all-Ukrainian strikes (Crowley, p.52).

A consequence of the problems of VOST's nationalist orientation was the establishment in May 1992 of an alternative association of independent unions, the Consultative Council of Free Trade Unions of Ukraine, which comprised the NPG, independent pilots, air-traffic controllers and train drivers unions. The Council was immediately drawn into round-table discussions with Kravchuk alongside FPU. When the government was slow in implementing an agreement regarding collective contracts, the independent unions called a strike which began on 2 September 1992, affecting the industries in which they had influence. Political demands, calling for the resignation of Fokin's government and parliamentary elections also emerged. Because of the impact of the strike on such services as public transport it was not well supported by ordinary people and enabled the government to act against the strikers via the media and through the use of the 1989 Soviet law on labour disputes. In addition, the strike was supported neither by FPU, which had reached a separate agreement with the government, nor by nationalist organisations which accused the independent unions of potentially undermining Ukrainian sovereignty. Nevertheless, the strike was solved by the government agreeing to drop prosecutions of strike leaders, sign the tariff agreements and give the strikers air time on state television to present their case (Crowley, pp.53-55).

## The June 1993 Strikes

The strikes which affected Ukraine during 1992 and early 1993 were soon to be eclipsed by a strike wave in eastern Ukraine, which produced a genuine political crisis and hastened the democratic evolution of the

Ukrainian state by provoking the holding of early elections both for the *Verkhovna Rada* and the presidency. The strike centred almost inevitably on the coal industry in the Donbas but, because the economic crisis affected the entire region, there was also a reaction from other generally more quiescent workforces, such as steelworkers, who had been cushioned from the extremes of economic collapse. The demands raised by the strikers and their supporters were primarily political from the outset: autonomy for the Donbas, and referendums of (no) confidence in the president and *Rada* as a prelude to early elections. Traditional economic demands remained in the background.

### *The Ukrainian coal industry*

At the time of the June strike the Ukrainian coal industry comprised 277 underground mines run by 23 mine associations, of which 20 associations and 254 pits were in the Donbas, employing 1.2 million workers, five percent of the Ukrainian labour force (Sagers, p.399, *Financial Times* 18 March 1994). Coal output, 189 million tons in 1985, had decreased markedly to a mere 115.7 million tons in 1993. This was due to diminishing coal reserves together with desperately low productivity, resulting from the use of obsolete equipment and continuing high levels of manual labour, exacerbated since the end of 1991 by the decreasing availability of mining machinery from Russia (Jung, p.52). The industry could thus only survive through heavy subsidisation. The Ukrainian coal industry is also the most deadly in the world, four or five miners dying for every million tons of coal brought to the surface, and pays the lowest mining wages in Europe. In addition, the coal industry contributes three percent of global emissions of methane, resulting in very high levels of pollution in Donets'k and other cities of the Donbas (*Financial Times* 18 March 1994).

### *Causes, demands and organisation*

While the immediate backdrop to June 1993 is one of increasing economic and political crisis, the strikes were not an isolated incident but the culmination of a series of threats and stoppages going back to the previous autu million. In April 1993, a three-day strike organised by all unions in the coal industry, but not supported by miners in western Ukraine, led to increased subsidies for the coal industry.

The raising of Russian energy prices was the official reason for the massive increase in the cost of basic goods in Ukraine by between 200 and 500 percent announced on 5 June 1993. This followed a government announcement that the minimum wage would be 6,900 karbovantsi with effect from 1 June (*Pravda Ukrainy* 3 June 1993). The FPU had criticised this amount for being way below even the government's own estimate of the minimum income required (22,100 karbovantsi).

The strike began spontaneously at the Zasyad'ko pit in Donets'k on the afternoon shift of 7 June as a result of workers' indignation at the price rises and failure on the part of management to provide clarification when requested (*Gorod* No.25, 24 June 1993). Why it began at this particular pit is a slight oddity as it was renowned as a 'scab' pit which had not been involved in either of the two major strikes after 1989 (July 1990 and March-April 1991). Zasyad'ko had been rapidly turned round from being a poor producer to a highly profitable enterprise with well-paid workers after the appointment of Efim Zvyagil'skii as mine director in 1979. Zvyagil'skii left that particular position to become mayor of Donets'k in November 1992, became a Vice-Premier during the course of the strike and was to play a major role in its ultimate resolution (*Alternativa* 21-27 June 1993). It seems significant, however, that the Independent Miners' Union (NPG) was very weak at the pit with only about a dozen members. Donbas NPG had been planning a strike for 21 June but the Zasyad'ko strike threw all of NPG's calculations out of the window and resulted in a more haphazard organisation of the strike than had been envisaged (*Novosti i Sobytiya* No.21, July 1993). Nevertheless, other pits soon took Zasyad'ko's lead - Krylov's own pit and NPG stronghold, Oktyabr'skaya, quickly followed suit when the workers learned of the actions (for details of the sequence of events at Zasyad'ko see Borisov & Clarke).

Both the local NPG and the local mine directors moved quickly to control the strike movement. For the NPG it was an opportunity to enhance their influence and strike a blow against the central government whose policies had seemed detrimental to the livelihoods of miners in the Donbas. For directors the strike was a convenient pretext for action aginst central government in pursuit of greater autonomy for the Donbas and reestablishment of the traditional economic links which had previously existed with Russia. A package of documents regarding the implementation of regional autonomy had apparently been lodged with the Ukrainian government some two months previously but no reply had been received (*Trud* 10 June 1993). Zvyagil'skii and the local directors were so supportive of the desire to spread the strike that they laid on transport for workers wishing to attend the continuous rallies in Oktyabr'skaya Square in Donets'k, and encouraged enterprises outside of the coal industry to take action also. Within a matter of days most pits in Donbas were idle.

A government commission headed by Viktor Pynzenyk, vice-premier for economic reform, met with strike leaders and directors of the Donbas coal concerns within a couple of days of the strike beginning, but the strikers rapidly withdrew from negotiations believing them to be a waste of time as the commission offered no solutions to their demands and was without any real power to negotiate. Within four days, in an effort to break the deadlock, Zvyagil'skii was whisked to Kyiv in the guise of a new vice-premier with responsibility for ending the dispute, although Krylov has suggested that he had already been lined up for the vacant position before the strike began (*Novosti i Sobytiya* No.21, July 1993).

The initial demands, which emerged spontaneously, centred on economic questions: a revision of prices; removal of high income tax rates; raising the minimum wage; indexation of incomes. However, after the intervention of NPG, the main demands became essentially political with economic demands playing a secondary role. In an echo of the demands of the 1991 strike, the major demands became the holding of referendums of (no) confidence in Kravchuk and the *Verkhovna Rada*. The other main demand was for regional economic autonomy for Donbas, later extended to cover the four eastern provinces of Donets'k, Luhans'k, Kharkiv and Dnipropetrovsk (Borisov 1993a; Borisov & Clarke). This latter demand was linked to the restitution of relations with Russia through the medium of the CIS and the removal of tariff barriers affecting trade. The demand for Russian to be recognised as a second state language in eastern Ukraine was also raised. It was emphasised, however, that these were not demands for the creation of a federal Ukrainian state. The nature of the demands reflected a growing dissatisfaction with Ukraine's predicament. Workers in eastern Ukraine had supported independence because of the potential material benefits rather than through the identification with Ukraine's linguistic and cultural heritage characteristic of western Ukraine. Initially, Kravchuk stressed the territorial character of independent Ukraine, which encompassed a variety of ethnic groups, but subsequently shifted, as his political base moved westwards, to a Ukrainianisation of public life. In addition, the hyperinflation accompanying Ukraine's minimal economic reform had been associated with Viktor Pynzenyk and former first vice-premier, Igor Yukhnovskii, both from western Ukraine. In contrast with 1989, the miners did not claim to represent, and were not seen to represent, the interests of society against the state; indeed, members of the same organisations involved in the strikes were often overtly hostile to the actions because of the potential damage to Ukraine as a nation-state.

The June strikes also differed from 1989 in that the existence of three miners' organisations meant that mass meetings, attendance at which was more orchestrated than in 1989, played a less important role in the exercise of rank-and-file control over the strike leadership. The initial strike committee was elected from representatives of the pits present in Oktyabr'skaya Square, but operated more as a mechanism for legitimising the actions of an already existing leadership drawn from the NPG and the Donets'k City Strike Committee (which had its origins in the 1989 strike). The affiliation of workers to different mining unions also resulted in some mutual hostility. In some pit towns where strike committees were slow to get off the ground they had to be 'jumpstarted' mainly by NPG (Borisov 1993a). Vladimir Limarenko, chair of the trade union committee at the Lidievka pit, complained that, as a result of this type of intervention, the Lidievka strike committee was completely inexperienced. He accused the City Strike Committee of failing to organise the strike properly and Mikhail Krylov in particular of betraying the interests of miners, rather paradoxically by pursuing demands narrowly associated with the miners, rather than those which would raise the living standards of all Ukrainians (*Golos lidievki* 26 June 1993). Another worker at Lidievka expressed the view that the strike was organised from above and ended in victory for Zvyagil'skii, the regional authorities and Kravchuk himself (ibid). Krylov himself was not afraid to respond, accusing Lidievka of 'gaining a taste' for the strike only towards its end (*Novosti i Sobytiya* No.21, July 1993).

## The Impact of the Strike

The impact of the strike was considerable both economically and politically. At its peak 238 Donbas mines, 44 mine construction offices, 16 ore dressing works and 400 other enterprises in various branches of the economy were reportedly affected and losses amounted to 6 billion karbovantsi and 3.414 million tonnes of coal (*BBC Summary of World Broadcasts* 19 & 26 June 1993). The strike also exacerbated tensions between the various branches of power whose actions had provoked the strike in the first place. In a television broadcast on 10 June, Kravchuk offered no real concessions and appealed to strikers to return to work for the sake of the economy. His only positive move was to appoint Zvyagil'skii to the post of first deputy premier with responsibility for ending the dispute in which capacity he replaced Pynzenyk as head of the government negotiating team.

As the strike widened, the prospect of a resolution seemed no nearer and economic losses mounted, Kravchuk realised that the demand for referendums of (no) confidence had to be accepted. After suggesting a compromise, involving simultaneous new elections to the *Verkhovna Rada* and a referendum of confidence in himself, which was rejected by parliament, he set about convincing the *Rada* that calling the two referendums was essential to end the strike. In any event, the result of the referendums would not be constitutionally binding. Faced with an ultimatum from Donets'k that a campaign of civil disobedience would commence on 17 June if the political demands were not satisfied, the *Verkhovna Rada* finally bowed to the pressure on 16 June and agreed to the two referendums being held on 26 September.

The resolution of that particular issue led to a major rift between Kravchuk and Prime Minister Kuchma. Kravchuk attempted to create a special economic committee to be headed by Kuchma but effectively stripping him of many of his prime ministerial powers. Kuchma, not for the first time, threatened to resign. Kravchuk responded by withdrawing the decree establishing the committee when he realised that he was, in effect, assuming full responsibility for Ukraine's dire economic plight (*Nezavisimaya gazeta* 23 June 1993). It was clear, however, that Kravchuk and Kuchma depended for their support on different constituencies and had different strategies for overcoming the crisis.

Following the government's important concessions, the government commission and the council coordinating the strike signed a protocol on 18 June calling for a return to work on 19 June. Some workers condemned the co-ordinating council, however, for putting their names to an agreement and calling for a return to work before all its provisions had been ratified by the *Verkhovna Rada*. The co-ordinating council did however maintain a pre-strike stance pending the adoption of the documents (*Pravda Ukrainy* 22 June 1993).

At a conference of mine representatives held in Donets'k on 23 June on the initiative of both NPG and the Union of Coal Industry Workers (PRUP), criticism of the co-ordinating council continued and it was condemned for 'betray[ing] the interests of the miners' movement'. It was proposed that the strike continue (*BBC Summary of World Broadcasts* 26 June 1993). According to *Interfax*, 80 mines were still on strike in Donbas on 24 June.

The strike seems to have petered out, however, once it became clear that the main economic demands around regional autonomy had been granted. Apart from agreeing to the referendums, the other major concessions involved the government promising a package of measures worth 13 trillion karbovantsi - roughly half of Ukraine's expected tax revenue for 1993 (*Financial Times* 23 June 1993). The minimum wage was raised to 20,900 karbovantsi and miners received the biggest wage rise to a guaranteed salary of between 290,000 and 350,000 karbovantsi with underground workers receiving an additional 40,000 karbovantsi. Ivan Illin, deputy minister of finance, said that 'agreeing with the miners' demands [would] lead to a 15-fold increase in consumer prices. This is hyperinflation' (*Financial Times* 23 June 1993). The big gainers were, however, enterprise directors whose debts were eliminated and fines imposed for overspending on wages wiped out.

The question of workers' independence was again raised in August 1993 with the conclusion of a 'programmatic agreement' between the Donets'k Workers (Strike) Committee and Igor Markulov's Liberal Party of Ukraine (LPU), whose main cadres were once leading members of Donets'k Komsomol. The essence of the agreement was that LPU guaranteed to attract western investment to Donbas coalmines and to ensure that resources were made available for workers made redundant from the closure of unviable pits to be retrained without any loss of wages or benefits. The centrepieces of the new Donbas economy would be a car industry centred on Donets'k and Kharkiv and financed by $200m and a revamped agricultural sector. How LPU was to achieve these goals was left unanswered. The agreement, which appeared to place no obligations on the Strike Committee, was subsequently strongly defended in the pages of its newspaper (see *Novosti i Sobytiya* nos. 28 and 29) as purely an economic and not a political arrangement. Markulov, equally explicitly, said that it was a political alliance (*Novosti i Sobytiya* No.29, September 1993, p.3). The Strike Committee's stance seems extraordinarily naive in a system in which politics and economics continue to be so intimately linked and reveals the desperation of certain sections of the trade unions to associate themselves with anyone, other than communists or nationalists, who offers a way out of the crisis even if the evidence of their capacity to do anything to remedy the situation is flimsy to say the least. For their part, LPU gained considerable publicity and assistance in the development of their base in the run-up to the forthcoming elections.

### *Impact on the trade unions*

FPU had been led since November 1992 by Oleksandr Stoyan, previously a 'senior consultant in the president's political service', and while Kravchuk was president the FPU was much more accomodating to the president's line (Crowley, p.56). On the other hand, the *Rada* was seen as hostile to the demands of the trade unions. Stoyan pointed out that only two deputies in the old *Rada* came from the unions whereas half the deputies represented directors' interests and, as a consequence, 'have not investigated the changes happening in the trade union movement and do not comprehend their consolidating role in the construction of a law-based, democratic Ukrainian state' (Stoyan, p.16). Stoyan bemoaned the fact that the parliament 'had not adopted a single law needed by the trade unions and had even deprived them of rights they had enjoyed before', in particular, the right of trade unions to initiate legislation. On this basis the failure of trade unions to engage in politics and parliamentary elections had been a big mistake (ibid, pp.16-17).

It was within this framework that FPU offered its support to the strikers. The FPU leadership had met on 8 June, declared a state of 'pre-strike readiness' from 10-15 June, and called a day of action on 16 June, which involved a lobby of the *Verkhovna Rada*. FPU were initially more supportive of the economic demands, concentrating on the fall in living standards as a result of rising prices and on the consequent need to raise the minimum wage (*Profspilkova Hazeta* 19 June 1993, p.1). In an interview in *Trud*, Stoyan argued that the responsibility for the crisis lay firmly at the door of the *Verkhovna Rada*, which had 'become a brake on the road to the stabilisation of society', thus distancing FPU from criticisms of Kravchuk, and that 'the basic demands from the localities are economic and concern primarily the resignation of Parliament in its present form' (*Trud* 17 June 1993). In a speech to the *Verkhovna Rada* on 14 June, Stoyan emphasised the need for a collective effort, naturally involving the trade unions, to find a way out of the economic crisis; the demand for a referendum of confidence in the *Rada* and president would only be supported if the workers' demands were ignored (*Profspilkova Hazeta* 19 June 1993, p.2). By 16 June, Stoyan indicated that FPU supported Kravchuk's proposal for simultaneous elections to the *Rada* and a referendum of confidence in the president and that he also supported Kuchma's request for extraordinary powers to deal with the economic situation (*Trud* 17 June 1993). Stoyan's leadership during this period suggests a strategy of low-level 'responsible' activity to try and pressure the *Rada* and government into talks with FPU, which was ultimately outflanked by Kravchuk's capitulation to the demands for referendums.

The strike's concentration in the Russified east was responsible for the reverberations felt even in the newer unions. NPG was affected by a *de facto* split. While the Donbas miners emphasised the political character of their demands, NPG leader in Kyiv, Aleksandr Mril', pursued a similar line to that of FPU, issuing an ultimatum which argued that 'in order to stabilise the situation in the Donbas' it was necessary 'to resolve the economic demands of the striking miners immediately'. It would only be in the event of the government's continued failure to grant these demands that political demands would be advanced and an all-Ukrainian political strike called (*Pravda* 11 June 1993). NPG leaders in Donets'k were furious at this misinterpretation of their key demands and also at Mril's failure to acquaint himself with the real situation by visiting Donbas (see *Novosti i Sobytiya* No.24, July 1993, p.2).

Unions associated with the nationalist movement, *Rukh*, were even less supportive. VOST, in a rather tendentious interpretation of the word 'solidarity', argued that the strikes could not be supported as they were the work of pro-Russian remnants of the old communist regime and were thus subversive of Ukraine's independence.

The political and economic crisis in Ukraine continued to rumble on unabated. In September, Kuchma finally and definitively resigned as prime minister to be replaced temporarily by Zvyagil'skii. The referendums agreed for 26 September also disappeared after the *Verkhovna Rada* agreed to hold elections both to the *Rada* itself in March 1994 and for the presidency in June 1994. Despite much union sabre-rattling and threatened national strikes, no action was taken over this abrogation of what had been the strikers' main demand in June.

In November, a number of small 'independent' trade unions under the leadership of NPGU formed a new confederation Free Trade Unions of Ukraine (VPU) (*UNIAR* 10 November 1993). Both VPU and FPU argued the need for setting a realistic minimum wage and social security level and for indexation of wages which had been removed earlier in the year. In the absence of a decision by the government to introduce such measures VPU demanded the government's resignation and called an all-Ukrainian strike for 18 January 1994. Faced with the threat of a renewal of the June strikes, and with elections looming, the government capitulated, reducing a number of food prices from 1 January 1994, allowing banks to extend credit to enterprises to pay wages and promising to index pay.

VPU, however, pressed ahead with its strike call, demanding the government's resignation and the appointment of a prime minister with power to implement all necessary market reforms. The call was not, however, supported in western Ukraine by VPU or by VOST, which along with *Rukh* increasingly saw Kravchuk as the protector of the Ukrainian state, whose position had to be safeguarded at all costs. In the event, the strike was poorly supported and swiftly ended.

## Ukraine under Kuchma

### *The 1994 parliamentary and presidential elections*

The aftermath of the parliamentary and presidential elections seemed to leave Ukraine split down the middle. In both cases, forces advocating closer ties with Russia, the adoption of Russian as an official language and dependent for the overwhelming bulk of their support on the predominantly Russophone eastern regions of the country and the Crimea were narrowly victorious. Taken together with the demands that had arisen since the strikes in 1993 for greater regional autonomy, the results of the elections were not encouraging for the maintenance of the Ukrainian state in its original form. Kuchma has, however, shown himself to be quite adept at manoeuvring between the geopolitical forces which exercise the greatest influence on Ukraine: Russia and the West, and he has done this by compromising (if not reneging on) some of the policies he advocated at the time of his election, thus appeasing nationalist forces in western Ukraine.

Following the passage of a new electoral law in November 1993, a French-style electoral system with two rounds of voting was introduced for the March 1994 parliamentary elections. The new law, which has no party list element, limits the possibility of election for all but the most organised of parties. It favours those candidates with the highest local profile and influence, particularly those from the old *nomenklatura*. Parties on the centre-right condemned the new electoral law as undemocratic and designed to retain the old political system (*Nezavisimaya gazeta* 4 December 1993); *Rukh* in particular, suffered from the strict rules which stipulate a 50 percent minimum turnout for a result to be valid. Kravchuk's hope with the parliamentary elections was that turnout would be below the validating 50 percent, leaving Ukraine without an elected parliament but with an elected president, who could then assume total control. In the event, turnout on the first round was a very healthy 74.8 percent and 66.9 percent on the second round (Birch, pp.95-6). Many candidates lacked any party affiliation and, on average there were 13 candidates per constituency. consequently, only 49 deputies were elected on the first round and a further 287 in the more straightforward runoffs on the second. Failure to reach 50 percent turnout meant that only 336 out of 450 seats were filled after the second round of voting (ibid). The new electoral system has, therefore, done little to break the hold of the 'party of power' and those who enjoy privileged access to the decision-making process.

The main winners were undoubtedly the Communist Party (CPU), Socialist Party (SPU) and their rural counterpart the Agrarian Party, all of which retained strong ties with the old *nomenklatura* and constituted the largest bloc in the new *Verkhovna Rada*, albeit without an overall majority. The predominance achieved in March 1994 was gradually whittled away, however, as by-elections returned a variety of non-communist deputies, and the Agrarian Party in particular split along pro- and anti-reform lines.

Like KPRF, its sister party in Russia, the CPU's resurrection as the major electoral force seems truly remarkable given that its refoundation congress only took place in Donets'k in June 1993 (*Pravda*, 15 June 1993; 25 June 1993). It is perhaps less remarkable if the following factors are taken into account: first, the absence of radical economic reform left the old Soviet economic system almost unaltered but in a greatly deteriorated condition, providing workers and enterprise directors with a common interest in wresting resources from the centre; second, the crisis also generated a pressing need for a restoration of economic links with Russia which, coupled with the predominance of ethnic Russians in eastern Ukraine, produced a strong movement of support for parties advocating a return to some form of USSR and the creation of a federal Ukrainian state; third, in the CPU's case the first two factors were also linked to a high degree of support from the local *nomenklatura* (Arel & Wilson 1994a, p.14). The CPU seems to have taken a great deal of support away from SPU, which won only three seats in Donbas, but the latter was able to exert some influence through the election of its leader, Oleksandr Moroz, as speaker of the *Verkhovna Rada*.

The presidential election resulted in the narrowest of victories for Leonid Kuchma with 52 percent of the vote over Kravchuk. Kuzio has portrayed this as a 'contest between two branches of the Party of Power divided along language and foreign cleavages' and as such it was less a case of support for one candidate as greater antipathy toward the other (p.117). Kuchma presented a platform which tried to balance the notion of a sovereign and democratic Ukraine, albeit with a strong executive power, against the pragmatic need to strengthen economic ties with Russia. This latter position, together with his support for the recognition of Russian as an official language, inevitably raised the ire of the more nationalist west and earned the support of the Russophone industrialised east. Kuchma was also committed, however, to more rapid economic transformation, including privatisation and the liberalisation of foreign trade, which cut across the demands of the Donbas for greater state support, particularly for the coal industry (Kuzio, pp.128-9). The election results indicated that the country was split down the middle along the historic faultline of the Dniepr river - the left bank (east), under Russian control since 1654, showing heavy support for Kuchma, and the right bank including western Ukraine showing equally heavy support for Kravchuk (see Arel & Wilson 1994a).

Kuchma's election took place against a backdrop of rumbling unrest in the coalfields in both Eastern and Western Ukraine. In Western Ukraine demands were confined to the strictly economic question of the payment of wage arrears (*UNIAN* 17 March 1994), but in the Donbas such demands were once again mixed with calls for Kravchuk's resignation (*UNIAN* 31 March 1994). It was suggested that strikes in eastern Ukraine in late June were motivated by a desire to compromise Kravchuk before the second round of voting, some of the strike leaders belonging to Kuchma's campaign organisation (*UNIAN* 29 June 1994).

### *Economic transformation*

Kuchma has had two fundamental priorities: first the commencement of a radical economic transformation and, second, the securing of a constitution for Ukraine in which the president is the lynchpin of the system. These two elements are intimately related as Kuchma believes that a strong executive is essential for the enactment of economic reform, particularly given the weight of socialist and communist deputies in the *Rada*. In addition, successful economic reform is seen as essential for the continued existence of the Ukrainian state itself. First, such a reform would attract Western support, credits and expertise to restructure the economy, and would thus make participation in wider economic and political forums much easier; secondly, it is only through creating a sound economy that Ukraine can overcome its dependence on Russia, maintain a good relationship with its giant neighbour and at the same time defuse those currents, in Crimea and the east, which might seek a rapprochment with Russia.

Ukraine was characterised by hyperinflation and a collapse of industrial production in 1992-94. Under Zvyagil'skii, 'the Ukrainian economy became utterly stifled by regulations and confiscatory taxation ... [t]he obvious aim of [which] was to maximize the revenues of the old elite from corruption and fraud'. Zvyagil'skii himself fled to Israel in order to avoid charges of defrauding the state of $25 million (Aslund 1995, pp.128-

9). Foreign debt also rose considerably between 1991 and 1994 to about $7 billion, $5 billion of which was owed to Russia for oil imports and $1 billion to Turkmenistan for gas imports. As a result of this debt Ukraine was forced to cut its energy imports sharply, reducing the balance-of-payments deficit to $1.5 billion in 1994 (ibid, p.129).

Kuchma's objectives were, therefore, to bring inflation down to manageable levels, to halt the output decline and pay off much of the debt, especially to Russia. On coming to power, Kuchma indicated that he would not blindly follow the precepts of international institutions, attacking the IMF's 'model of forced liberalisation' (*Holos Ukrainy* 17 June 1994), and subsequently arguing that IMF monetary reforms were inappropriate to Ukraine's situation. Kuchma further declared that he intended to eradicate the 'shameful phenomenon' of unemployment, which for the IMF was a necessary concomitant of market reform (*Holos Ukrainy* 6 July 1994). This populist rhetoric helped to consolidate Kuchma's position in the aftermath of his election but the pressure from international institutions, if a structural transformation of the Ukrainian economy was to take place, was to become increasingly apparent.

Given his early declarations it was not surprising that Kuchma's first programmatic speech to the Ukrainian parliament on 11 October 1994 came as something of a bombshell. Borrowing from the experience of the Polish Balcerowicz Plan, Kuchma announced a programme of rapid economic transformation comprising price and trade liberalisation, a strict monetary policy leading to macroeconomic stabilisation, mass privatisation and land reform (Aslund 1995, p.134). Aslund argues that Kuchma had learnt a valuable lesson from the Russian experience in that, despite the perceived weight of anti-reform elements in the *Rada*, he was determined to obtain parliamentary backing for his proposals. He thus put his speech to the vote and gained overwhelming support (Aslund 1995, p.135).

Kuchma's reputation as a reformer quickly attracted substantial amounts of finance (around $5 billion by August 1995) but the conditions were stringent. Control of inflation was the main target of the IMF and became a condition of a standby loan negotiated in April 1995, which demanded a reduction of the monthly rate to between one and two percent. Kuchma argued that this was unrealistic although the aid helped to stabilise the karbovanets and reduce inflation in the first half of 1995.

### *Privatisation*

The pace of privatisation quickened under Kuchma, who reappointed

Pynzenyk as minister responsible for economic reform. Between 1992 and September 1995, 4,571 large enterprises and 15,270 small and medium-sized enterprises were privatised and, by mid-1995, 40.5 percent of total industrial output was being produced by privately-owned companies (Filatotchev et al., p.187). Filatotchev et al have noted that privatisation in Ukraine was characterised by the fact that '[t]here is very little shareholding by parties external to the enterprise, with foreign investors, investment funds, the state and industrial partners owning an average of 2-3% each' (ibid, p.197). As in Russia, privatisation has thus been primarily a mode of transference of state assets into the hands of labour collectives. This method has been criticised by Ribun who argues that rapid and effective reorganisation cannot be carried out without the involvement of Western firms, nor without the network of independent organisations and financial control bodies characteristic of Western capitalist economies (p.120).

Filatotchev et al suggest that *de jure* enterprise ownership by the labour collective has been translated into a high level of involvement in management and assemblies by workers themselves, but that the objectives of workers and management for the future of the enterprise are somewhat different and ultimately conflictual: workers wish to maintain job security and improve living standards; management are concerned with raising profitability. While even privatised enterprises continue to enjoy state subsidies, however, such different orientations can be reconciled (pp.197-200).

At the beginning of 1995, the government declared that 8,000 large enterprises and all small concerns must be sold off during the course of the year. The privatisation programme was reassessed in July, however, after the sale of only 95 firms in the first three months, and a simplified voucher scheme was introduced to encourage people to participate in the privatisation process, and control of privatisation was handed to one body - the State Property Fund (Filatotchev et al., p.187). Privatisation plans were also subsequently halved by the parliament which declared that 6,100 'strategic' enterprises should remain in state hands.

*Industrial restructuring*

The creation of a capitalist economy cannot be undertaken without a radical restructuring of industry. In Ukraine, there are a number of sectors which need to be addressed: defence, and various branches of heavy industry in particular. The problem with defence is that it was well integrated into the overall Soviet military sector, making it reliant particularly on Russia for components. Addressing this problem involves either the conversion of defence industries to civilian production or the replication of components production on home soil for those weapons for which there is a substantial market. Either way considerable investment is required in a sensitive sector. Other sectors such as coal and steel also need reorganisation. In the coal industry, output in 1994 was 94.4 million tons and this declined to around 80 million tons in 1995. The industry has avoided restructuring for rather different reasons than its Russian equivalent - the reluctance of the government to undertake any radical economic reform. Since Kuchma's election, however, coal industry restructuring has been placed on the agenda. As in Russia, international institutions, the World Bank and the IMF, have been actively promoting pit closures, reduced subsidies and the exposure of the industry to the full rigour of the world market, in return for which they have proposed loans to assist with softening the impact of redundancy.

On 18 November 1995, World Bank president, James Wolfensohn, expressed the World Bank's readiness to finance restructuring of the Ukrainian coal industry. He said that, although the Ukrainian coal industry was 'not uncompetitive', all uneconomic mines which could not be upgraded would have to be closed. In addition, the World Bank intended to finance welfare measures for miners at three pits which were scheduled for closure. Talks were also being undertaken to make $3 billion available as foreign investment guarantees in priority sectors. The same month First Deputy Prime Minister, Pavlo Lazarenko, suggested that only one third of Ukrainian mines were self-sufficient and that 64 would have to close, although he did not indicate any timescale.

## The Character of the State

Frequent conflict has emerged between president and parliament, particularly over such questions as who has the right to appoint the prime minister and other members of the government, and enact legislation, especially concerning economic reform. As a parting shot and in an effort to attract last-minute communist support, Kravchuk installed Vitalii Masol as prime minister. Masol was the last prime minister before independence and, as a representative of the old *nomenklatura*, was not inclined towards a radical reform programme. Despite his nominal power to appoint the prime minister, Kuchma had considerable difficulty removing Masol from his post, the latter finally resigned only in March 1995.

On 18 May 1995, the *Rada* approved a political reform law which expanded the president's powers to pursue economic and political reform and, at the same time, diluted the *Rada*'s powers. The law did, however, contravene 68 articles of the existing constitution and thus required a constitutional amendment to be enacted, which would have required a two-thirds majority of the *Rada* (301 of the 450 deputies). Such an amendment was opposed by the communist and socialist factions in the *Rada*, which comprised more than a third of deputies thus blocking any such move. In a situation of deadlock, Kuchma threatened to call a referendum of confidence in himself and the *Rada* unless a compromise was agreed. Given the *Rada*'s much lower popularity rating in opinion polls, the deputies backed down and a so-called 'constitutional accord', which required only a simple majority, was passed. The accord strengthened Kuchma's hand in a number of areas: first, the president alone was now responsible for appointing the government; second, the president's powers to pass decrees on economic reform were enhanced; third, the president gained control of local executive committees, while parliament lost control over regional and local councils, which became notionally independent (Lapychak, p.7).

In June 1996, a constitution was finally ratified by the *Rada*. Ukraine was declared a unitary state with Ukrainian as the only state language. Despite its unitary character, however, Crimea was granted special status as an autonomous republic albeit without a president of its own and with a representative of the Ukrainian president present on Crimean soil.

### *International orientation*

The reality of Russia's importance to Ukraine both in economic and security terms was demonstrated by the level of trade between the two states in 1994: Russia accounted for 39 percent of Ukraine's exports and 30 percent of its imports, while Ukraine accounted for 13 percent of Russia's trade (Rutland 1995, p.23). The importance of Ukraine to the West was also demonstrated by the visit of US vice-president Al Gore to Kuchma soon after his election victory and this was followed up by President Clinton's visit in May 1995. As well as the prestige of such high-level visits, material aid was also forthcoming - $700 million in 1994 in technical assistance and $1 billion in balance-of-payments support making Ukraine the fourth highest recipient of such support in the world (Aslund 1995, p.139; Rutland 1995, p.23). The motives for US aid are fairly transparent. On the one hand, the US wants to maintain an influence in Europe which extends to the borders of Russia, thus heavily constraining the latter's room for manoeuvre; at the same time, the US also wants to prevent Germany from developing into an hegemonic power on the European mainland, which could be achieved through a strategic alliance with Russia. Ukraine is the biggest state, both in terms of population and geographic area, between these two major players and thus potentially plays a key role in keeping the two states apart.

## The Response of the Labour Movement

With Kuchma's election the relationship of the trade unions to the president and parliament underwent a fundamental reorientation. Kuchma's desire to implement a rapid transition to the market and industrial restructuring, coupled with the crisis of non-payment of wages, produced a much more confrontational relationship between trade unions and president. The newly-elected *Rada*, on the other hand, was much more accomodating to trade union demands because of the large presence of socialist and communist deputies, not to mention Stoyan himself. As early as January 1995 the *Rada* approved the FPU's version of a law on wages as against that of the Cabinet of Ministers. The union version proposed that a guaranteed minimum wage should not fall below an agreed low-income threshold, a suggestion dismissed as too costly by the government (*UNIAN* 26 January 1995).

After Kuchma's election, the trade union movement continued to feel the effects of the cleavage between eastern and western Ukraine. At the Third Congress of FPU, held at the end of June 1994, delegates from the western oblasts of Lviv and Ivano-Frankivsk walked out in protest at a decision to join the Moscow-based General Confederation of Trades Unions (VKP). West Ukrainian delegates held out the possibility of secession from FPU but did not ultimately implement the threat.

### *Strikes*

As in Russia, the main issues animating Ukrainian workers have been wage arrears, social provision and industrial restructuring. In the coal industry, subsidies were severely cut in 1994 but still constituted $50 million per month, while 95 percent of production was accounted for by state orders, leaving only five percent to be disposed of by enterprises on the free market (*Financial Times* 18 March 1994).

Throughout 1995, 'guerrilla warfare' took place with strikes affecting individual pits but, after government failure to deliver on a promise to repay delayed wages, a nationwide strike took place on 2 October organised by the 'official' miners' union. About two-thirds of the country's 254 pits took part and only one-third of the daily quota of coal was extracted (*UNIAN* 4 October 1995). The strikers advanced demands for prompt payment of wages, an increase in wage rates, for a national wage agreement to be signed by 20 October, and for state policy toward the coal industry to be enshrined in legislation. While leaders of the former 'official' coal union intimated that the miners' demands would become more political if the government did not respond favourably, the Independent Miners' Union (NPGU) accused the official union of being 'provocative' in calling the strike.

Towards the end of October the first congress of Ukrainian miners took place in Kyiv. The congress reinforced the demands for the prompt payment of wages and the immediate payment of arrears and for a whole series of credits for the industry's restructuring. In addition, the miners demanded that government and parliament adopt a programme of market reform for the industry by the end of 1995 which would take into account union proposals. The first hint of a political demand also emerged with the suggestion of a signature-raising campaign in favour of Kuchma's resignation.

The problem for the government was how to solve the arrears crisis without additional monetary emissions, which would fuel the already severe inflationary situation. It was acknowledged that 29,500 billion karbovantsi were needed to pay wage arrears (*UNIAN* 11 November 1995). Despite meetings between ministries and unions, no agreement was reached and on 14 November 16 mines began indefinite strike action initiated by NPGU. This figure increased to 22 pits the following day. Losses were estimated at between 20,000 and 30,000 tons of coal.

In response to the miners' growing militancy and to undermine their strategic position the Ukrainian government increased coal imports from Poland, modernising the Lviv railway to cope with the increased traffic: whereas 2 million tons had been handled in 1994, this had risen to 5.3 million tons in the first six months of 1995 (*ITAR-TASS* 6 December 1995).

### *The February 1996 strikes*

1996 began where 1995 left off with a number of mines on strike in eastern

Ukraine. As well as wage arrears miners were demanding greater autonomy for the mines and more attention to social problems. By 30 January, the mineworkers' union decided that the situation was so bad that an indefinite nationwide strike beginning on 1 February was the only way of bringing the government to the negotiating table with serious proposals to end the crisis in the coal industry. Announcing the action, coal union leader, Viktor Derzhak, said that the strike was because of wage arrears and delays in paying for coal already delivered. He argued that decreased government subsidies had caused price rises and a fall in production. The government had responded by importing 20 million tons of oil at a cost of $520 million. Derzhak further argued that the IMF's desire to reduce the number of loss-making pits had resulted in the diversion of funds allocated to support those mines. An end to the action was dependent on the government meeting the union's demands (*ITAR-TASS* 30 January 1996). Other industries badly hit by debt and arrears, such as engineering and defence were supportive of the miners' action.

In response to the beginning of the strike Prime Minister, Yevhen Marchuk, suggested that the problems in the coal industry were inherited from the Soviet past and that reform had not been fast enough, a prime reason for the sacking of the previous coal industry minister. Structural reorganisation was, therefore, essential. He acknowledged that miners' wage arrears were growing but stated that, of the estimated debt of 30,000 billion karbovantsi, the government owed only 1,000 billion from the state budget. It could not therefore fund the arrears from the budget without creating rampant inflation. In addition, the government had already rendered assistance to the tune of 100,000 billion karbovantsi during 1995. In response, the unions accused the government of spending more money on importing coal from Russia and Poland than was the entire total of miners' wage arrears. According to Viktor Derzhak 11.5 million tons of coal had been imported in the first 8 months of 1995 at a cost of $525 million when the debt to miners was 73,000 billion karbovantsi ($390 million).

Accurate figures as to the number of mines responding to the strike call are virtually impossible to find: the coal industry unions and the government producing distinctly difference estimates. Because the strike focussed on economic issues rather than the character of the Ukrainian state as the June 1993 strikes had done, the miners of Western Ukraine, traditionally more supportive of the government, were also prepared to take action. According to union sources, 142 mines ceased extraction and a further 115 suspended deliveries; the number of employees involved in the action was around 700,000. The coal industry ministry reported, however, that only 30 mines with a workforce of 3000 were affected and that daily coal production had scarcely fallen. While it is true that a number of pits continued to mine coal, a majority withheld shipments to consumers, creating a crisis situation in electricity-generating and other coal-dependent industries. On 5 February, a conference of trade union activists in Donets'k decided to continue the strike, which was spreading out from its base in the Donbas to the Luhans'k and Cherkasy regions.

The Ukrainian government proved itself to be much more stubborn than its Russian counterpart in its dealings with the miners, a reflection of its comparative security. Marchuk persistently claimed that the government owed the miners nothing and that coal industry managers had been partly responsible for the strike by not allocating government funds correctly. Nevertheless, Marchuk said that 6,000 billion karbovantsi had been found by the government towards solving the wages problem and that a further 15,000 billion karbovantsi could be allocated. Overall, however, the government refused to negotiate with the unions until industrial action was called off.

While a substantial number of pits were either on strike or refusing to dispatch coal to consumers, pressure was growing on the unions to suspend their action. On 12 February, miners in Western Ukraine returned to work after a ballot and two days later the power workers' union appealed to the miners to end the strike because of the dire situation in electricity generating: fuel shortages, causing power stations to operate at 30 percent capacity, coupled with the exceptionally cold winter resulted in the Russian and Ukrainian power grids being disconnected threatening power cuts (*Interfax* 13 February 1996). On 15 February, the miners' unions voted to suspend the strike from the following day pending the promised negotiations with government. In a justification for the strike, union leaders claimed that the action had thrust the plight of the coal industry to the centre of the government's attention. In material terms, however, only 13,500 billion karbovantsi out of total wage arrears of 84,300 billion had been received by 14 February.

This experience shows a marked change from June 1993 when the wave of strikes in Donbas brought a rapid response from the government. It is true that the 1996 strike was less overtly political but, nevertheless, the fact is that Kuchma despite his origins in the Russian-speaking population had developed an alternative source of power, bolstered by improved relations with the West. The east of Ukraine is now in a much weaker position to threaten destabilisation, a fact illustrated by the maintenance of

Ukrainian as the sole state language despite Kuchma's election promise that Russian would be given the status of an official language.

## Conclusion

The apparent success of the workers' movement in forcing the Ukrainian president and parliament to accept political demands is deceptive. Almost immediately after the strike had begun, enterprise directors began playing a major role in manipulating its direction and its demands. This is particularly apparent with the case of Zvyagil'skii, who seems to have provided strike leaders with a list of demands around questions of regional autonomy which had been discussed some time before; the strike merely presented an opportunity for these demands to be presented to Kyiv with some industrial muscle to back them up.

The demands of strikers and directors in this instance seem to have coincided, highlighting a real problem in the development of an independent workers' movement in the former USSR - precisely that of independence. The trade unions which emerged in the aftermath of the 1989 strike called themselves 'independent' in order to emphasise that they were not an arm of the state and to distinguish themselves from the 'official' unions. However, while organisationally independent, the new unions have in the main been unable to devise any strategy independent of other social forces in society. Unlike in Russia, where the NPG was Yeltsin's main industrial prop, NPG in Ukraine was not beholden to the Kravchuk regime and played more of a role of defender of the Donbas coal industry. As in Russia, however, the continuing existence of the old relations of production in enterprises, providing a whole range of social benefits, and to a large extent reinforced by the weakness of the centre, made it difficult for unions to break away from their old role and strengthened the hand of many enterprise directors. In addition, the collapse of any form of socialist ideology created a vacuum into which a variety of political currents flowed, vying for workers' support. This has been exemplified in the Ukrainian case both by the agreement between LPU and Donets'k Strike Committee and the relationship between VOST and nationalist parties in Western Ukraine.

Ukraine shows clearly a number of features about the character of post-Soviet states. First, the fact that directors have promoted and used strikes as a means of achieving their own ends demonstrates that, at present, directors have little *collective* social weight although they may wield considerable influence within their own enterprise. Conversely, workers can display great social cohesion and power when mobilised but lack independent leadership and are frequently vulnerable within the enterprise. Second, the power of domestic social forces to influence the direction of state policy is intimately linked to the influence of external forces. The success of the June 1993 strikes resulted from Ukraine's dependence on Russia, the dire state of its economy and the fact that little Western support had been gained at that time; Kravchuk's support in western Ukraine was an inadequate counterweight to the industrial east. Kuchma's success has lain in his ability to attract the support of Western institutions on the promise of a rapid transformation of the Ukrainian economy, a rapprochement with Russia, whose leverage is now counterbalanced by Western credits, and the institutionalisation of presidential preeminence through the new constitution. Kuchma's power-base has also shifted westwards but opposition from the east has been mollified by easing economic relations with Russia. Kuchma was, therefore, able to create an equilibrium in Ukraine on which the miners' strike of February 1996 had comparatively little impact.

# 7 Theorising Transition and the Role of Labour

The fundamental arguments of this book have been as follows:

- the origins and progress of transitions to democracy lie in the interrelationship between the domestic and global political economy and, contrary to most of the literature on democratisation, cannot be reduced to the impact of domestic factors;
- the breakdown of authoritarian regimes and transitions to democracy cannot necessarily be reduced to elite activity;
- if democratisation is the consequence of pact-making among elites in states occupying a subordinate position in the global political economy the outcome will tend towards a form of *dependent democratisation*;
- the role of civil society and especially labour is vital to the establishment of political systems that transcend the *dependent democratisation* syndrome.

If the above points are taken into consideration when developing a comparative analysis of democratisation processes then it is possible to produce a different focus from that prevalent in the transitions literature. The starting point of any such analysis must be the shifts wrought in the global capitalist system as a consequence of the crisis of the mid-1970s. The end of the postwar boom threw into crisis all models of capitalist development, from the Keynesianism of the advanced capitalist states through to the industrialisation strategies of Third World states. It also badly affected Soviet-style industrialisation which, for rather different reasons, was also encountering problems. Under the influence of the dominant capitalist power, the United States, the outcome was the emergence of a new global orthodoxy: neo-liberalism, which provided the ideological framework for a new strategy of capital accumulation requiring a transformation of the production process and the relations between states and the global economy. This strategy has entailed comparatively high levels of unemployment and the globalisation of the 'reserve army of labour', a switch to 'flexible production', and the greater integration of peripheral regions into the global economy. It has also involved the very intelligent employment of the rhetoric of democratisation which was necessitated by first, the failure of the United States' intervention in Vietnam which had made support for authoritarian regimes politically difficult (although not impossible as the cases of Indonesia and Pinochet's Chile demonstrate) because of the high level of domestic resistance to such a policy; second, the need for a new regime type capable of successfully implementing economic liberalisation. The new formula promotes democratisation, especially of a procedural kind, and is thus more politically acceptable, but establishes regimes which are structurally dependent on the advanced capitalist world through the explicit linkage of economic assistance to neo-liberal economic reforms which facilitate integration into the global political economy ('structural adjustment'). This is a process I have termed *dependent democratisation*. In this sense recent transitions to democracy have usually involved both political and economic change and cannot be reduced simply to the replacement of the political regime. This does not mean, however, that such changes can or should be directly compared to the profound transformation taking place in the former Soviet bloc.

Nevertheless, in an effort to extend the analytical framework of the transitions literature, the changes in the former Soviet Union and Eastern Europe have increasingly been viewed as fundamentally similar to those taking place in other regions of the world. Schmitter and Karl considered that events in Eastern Europe and the former Soviet Union 'should be treated as part of the same "wave of democratization" that began in 1974 in Portugal ... [and] should (at least hypothetically) be regarded as parts of a common process of diffusion and causal interaction' (p.178). Moreover, whereas they had previously explicitly acknowledged the revolutionary character of the collapse of communism, they took issue with Michael McFaul for his characterisation of the Russian case as a revolution:

> I [Schmitter] disagree with his basic premise in categorizing the former USSR as uniquely revolutionary and, hence, am unwilling to rule out *ex hypothesi* that its logic of transformation, its constellation of political and social forces and even its eventual outcome will not differ fundamentally from what has happened in other regime transitions (p.181 fn).

Clearly, Schmitter and Karl were arguing that fundamental similarities existed between all cases of democratisation, irrespective of the region in which they occurred, and that so-called 'area specialists' (like McFaul) were incorrect in their insistence on the specificities of the former Soviet bloc. Valerie Bunce correctly criticises Schmitter and Karl, however, claiming that their overarching methodology emphasises the primacy of domestic over global factors, and the activity of elites over popular classes and strata thus ignoring 'the very explanatory variables that would seem to follow logically from these assumptions', especially the transformation of the global political economy (1995, pp.117-8). In addition, in a comparison of Eastern Europe with Latin America and Southern Europe, 'state socialism was different along vitually every dimension that economists, sociologists and political scientists recognize as important' (ibid, p.119). My fundamental argument has been that the changes in the Soviet Union and Eastern Europe have not been 'typical' of a democratic transition: their fundamental characteristic has been that of *systemic transformation* or *revolution*, through which the system's economic foundations as well as its regime have been radically transformed. To pursue an examination of this transition from the perspective of the literature on democratisation creates the danger of concentrating on 'purely' political questions - the provisions of the constitution, the relationship between institutions, electoral law, etc. - to the detriment of the socioeconomic issues: the transformation of property relations and the formation of new social classes.

## The Collapse of Communism

If the analysis presented in the previous chapters is extended to an examination of the factors and forces behind the collapse of communism in Eastern Europe, a totally different picture is revealed to that claimed by democratisation theorists for transitions in other regions of the world. First, the question of international influences is striking; second, the role of civil society in promoting regime collapse is much more apparent; and, third, pact-making between elements of the elite is very limited.

Let us look first at the international dimension. First, the relationship to the USSR is crucial: Gorbachev's reversal of the 'Brezhnev Doctrine', which had previously dominated Soviet-East European relations, was dominant factor affecting the timing of the downfall of Eastern Europe's 'communist' regimes. To attribute the upheavals in Eastern Europe solely to the changes wrought by Mikhail Gorbachev in the Soviet Union would, however, be a serious misreading of the dynamics of Eastern Europe's political and economic systems. As Walton and Seddon suggest, the crisis in the Soviet bloc had been 'accompanied since the early 1980s ... by increasing intervention on the part of the international financial institutions ... and the major capitalist states ... explicitly directed towards the capitalist development of Central and Eastern Europe' (p.289). During the 1960s and 1970s the process of détente enabled trade between the Soviet bloc and capitalist economies to increase from an average annual growth rate of about 11 percent in the period 1965-70 to an average of roughly 23 percent between 1970 and 1975. Over the same period imports increased from an annual average of 12.2 percent to 31.2 percent. This trade was accompanied by increasing balance-of-trade and balance-of-payments deficits which in turn fuelled foreign borrowing and indebtedness (ibid, p.8). Expansion of contacts with the West derived from the absence in Soviet-type systems of an economic mechanism for the extraction of the social surplus product. In order to avoid a threat to their political power and to bolster the 'social contract', ruling elites sought to obtain a 'surrogate' surplus.

In Poland, following violent workers' opposition to price rises in 1970, which brought about the withdrawal of the rises and the removal of communist party leader Gomulka, the Gierek regime sought to avoid reform and avert any future discontent through substantial borrowing from Western institutions. Foreign loans, it was hoped, could, quite literally, buy off industrial workers through higher wages and increased access to consumer goods. Gierek wished, in addition, to invest Western credits in the modernisation of Polish industry, which would then be equipped to make goods of sufficient quality to sell to the West in return for hard currency with which to pay off the debts. Unfortunately for Gierek, the economic crisis of the mid-1970s scuppered this strategy, decisively weakened the Polish economy and destroyed any semblance of legitimacy the regime enjoyed. The economic crisis of the late 1970s, debt at a level of $25 billion, and the attempts of the regime to impose a fresh round of price increases resulted in the formation of the mass workers' movement, Solidarity. After the imposition of martial law designed to crush Solidarity in December 1981, the new militantly anti-communist Reagan and Thatcher administrations invoked very damaging trade sanctions against Poland, exacerbating the economic crisis (Potts 1993, p.154). The 1980s in Poland were dominated by the regime's search for a solution to that crisis and a viable basis for its rule.

In Hungary, the accumulation of foreign credits was for a quite different purpose: the enactment of the most radical economic reform in the Soviet bloc. The reform, the New Economic Mechanism (NEM), was initiated in 1968 as part of the Kádár leadership's continued pursuit of legitimacy for the regime in the aftermath of the Hungarian Revolution of 1956. By the late 1970s, however, the NEM was running out of steam. Western credits helped to launch NEM Mark 2, which further loosened central control over the economy and encouraged petty entrepreneurship but with little success for improved economic performance. Indeed the economy experienced a decline in the first years of the 1980s.

Partly as a function of her small size and lack of natural resources, and partly as a result of the leadership's desire to make her less dependent on the USSR, Hungary became the most integrated of all East European states into the world economy. In 1982, Hungary became the first East European state to join those bastions of post-war capitalism, the IMF and the World Bank and, throughout the 1980s, struggled to implement a series of IMF-instigated austerity programmes designed to decrease the largest per-capita debt in the region.

The relationship to the international capitalist economy also had an impact on other East European states. The GDR gained almost the status of a member of the European Community as a result of its relationship to West Germany, whose constitution regarded the two Germanies for the purposes of internal trade as a single economic space. At the same time, however, the GDR accrued a large external debt which contributed to a decline in the conditions of the social contract and undermined the Honecker regime's room for manoeuvre. In Romania, the bloody uprising of December 1989 derived in part from the Ceausescu regime's pauperisation of large sections of the population in its efforts to pay off the external debt accumulated primarily in the 1970s when Ceausescu's estangement from the USSR attracted the support of Western governments.

The other side of the coin of international constraints on Eastern Europe was, of course, the USSR. The Soviet Union's links were not solely political and military, important as these elements were. The USSR also exercised considerable economic leverage primarily through the provision of raw materials, especially oil, gas and electricity, at below world market prices. This was done in order to secure the Soviet Union's political domination and worked well to alleviate the worst of the energy crisis of the mid-1970s and prevent the kind of social and political unrest experienced in other parts of the world. As the economic crisis worsened for the East European states the more this pattern of trade rebounded on the Soviet economy. The East European priority became one of paying off external debt, which meant earning more hard currency through sales of best quality goods, while offloading large quantities of poor quality produce through barter exchange as a means of paying for Soviet energy supplies. In addition, the gap between world prices for energy and those the Soviet Union charged its East European allies was ever widening. Implicitly, therefore, the Soviet Union subsidised Eastern Europe's ailing economies, contributing in no small measure to its own economic difficulties. The context of regime change in Eastern Europe is thus one of considerable international influence over deteriorating economic performance.

If we turn our attention to the actual collapse of the regimes, the role of civil society, with the partial exception of Hungary becomes apparent. In Poland, Solidarity continued to provide the opposition, both symbolic and actual, to the regime throughout the 1980s despite suffering considerable repression after 1981. Two waves of strikes in 1988 in response to the regime's imposition of austerity measures were crucial in bringing about a realignment of forces between the regime's liberal wing (itself the consequence of greater economic liberalisation) and Solidarity's moderate leadership. These strikes were not controlled by the traditional leadership of Solidarity, which had been fragmented as an underground movement, but were in the hands of a younger generation of militants. This fact was worrying not just to the regime but to the Solidarity leaders themselves and prompted a search for compromise on the part of moderate elements in both camps. This process was assisted by the intervention of Gorbachev who visited Poland in Summer 1988 in between the two strike waves and put pressure on the regime to negotiate with Solidarity. The result was the process of liberalisation associated with the recognition of Solidarity, the round-table negotiations and the restricted competition permitted for the elections to the Sejm and newly-established Senate in May 1989. Solidarity's resounding victory in those elections then prompted the previously loyal satellite parties in the government to desert the Communist Party and form a coalition allowing Solidarity to form the first non-communist government in August 1989.

In Hungary, the transition to democracy most conforms to the model established in the democratisation literature. The outcome of the long process of reform was to create a technocratic stratum which benefitted from increased autonomy and was a major force behind the transformation of the regime by promoting rifts in the elite. Such divisions paved the way for the development of an informal alliance between reformers and opposition which effectively neutralised the party apparatus (Bruszt). Technocratic elements achieved the party's separation from the state, the ending of the *nomenklatura* system and gained a vote of no confidence in the government in parliament even before negotiations began (ibid). As Bruszt observes, however, the downfall of the regime was not so much a function of mass mobilisation, of which there was comparatively little, as of elite compromise and the withdrawal of popular support for the regime (ibid).

It is no coincidence that Poland and Hungary, Eastern Europe's biggest debtor nations and whose economies were most inserted into the global political economy, were the two states which trailblazed the path away from Soviet control in 1989. Economic reform had undermined the stability of the *nomenklatura* by creating incentives for entrepreneurial activity and the shift to new property relations. The absence of economic reform in other East European states made for a rather more explosive mix: the sudden appearance of popular movements, buoyed by the changes taking place in Poland and Hungary, played an important role in undermining the regimes in the GDR, Czechoslovakia and Romania, whose regimes lacked a significant reformist wing.

The influence of workers in an organised manner on the demise of the regimes was, however, limited. Only in Poland and the Soviet Union did workers develop their own autonomous organisations to press political demands. In Czechoslovakia, a two-hour general strike symbolically demonstrated the workers' alienation from the regime, graphically revealing the latter's isolation, but scarcely represented organised labour's seizure of the struggle's leadership. In Poland, however, a unique set of circumstances, which included the regime's insistence on making workers pay for the crisis and the existence of a comparatively autonomous institution in the shape of the Roman Catholic church, paved the way for the emergence of an autonomous labour movement which unified opposition to the regime. In the USSR, as this book has hopefully shown, sections of workers proved able to take action and create their own organisations, advancing demands which served to radically undermine the regime. In both the Polish and Soviet cases, however, the workers' cause was itself damaged by their incapacity to develop ideological independence from the liberal intelligentsia.

**Labour and Democratic Consolidation**

Liberal democracy has been consolidated, historically, both in its first and second waves in conditions of economic expansion, industrialisation and the growth of the working class and its organisations. This is quite understandable if the development of liberal democracy is seen as a major component of a compromise between the bourgeoisie and organised labour. In the first wave, the strength of the burgeoning proletariat, whose demands included the expansion of democratic institutions as well as greater social justice, were accomodated by the development of parliamentary democracy, which enfranchised broad masses of the working population while simultaneously excluding them from access to the machinery of the state, and by the benefits which derived from colonial possessions and a growing economy. Realistic prospects of winning access to parliament, and even potentially of forming the government, promoted the growth of working class parties committed to changing the nature of the system, albeit gradually. By the end of World War II, social-democratic governments, committed to the expansion of the welfare state, nationalisation and limited planning, were actually in power. Even in conditions of comparative economic difficulty, following years of war-induced privation and destruction, these governments were able to deliver benefits to the working class which were subsequently reinforced through the expansion of the global capitalist economy and through the medium in many European states of corporatist structures which involved trade unions directly in policy-making.

The remarkable feature of the latest wave of democratisation is the *absence* of precisely the conditions which enabled such advances in the past: the 'third wave' was precipitated not by expansion of the global economy but by its profound crisis, and has involved a neo-liberal rejection of state-centred reform in favour of economic liberalisation. Despite marked dissimilarities in social structure and historical development, this is the main feature, along with profound social inequality, which the newly-democratising regimes in Latin America and the former Soviet Union share. As O'Donnell has noted, however, these conditions make it difficult to envisage a successful democratic consolidation (1986, p.11). For those echoing Barrington Moore's famous phrase, 'no bourgeois, no democracy', who consider the emergence of a capitalist class essential to democratic consolidation then the outlook is also pessimistic. When looking at the potential for different social forces to promote or retard democratisation, however, it is crucial to locate these forces historically. The bourgeoisie could act to promote democracy in the eighteenth and nineteenth centuries because it was a means of securing their own political power against entrenched feudal interests. Under what conditions is a bourgeoisie emerging in the postcommunist states? On the one hand, it could be argued that there are indeed strong parallels as the nascent capitalist class has to combat the entrenched interests of the old *nomenklatura* and, therefore, has a powerful impetus to promote democratic institutions. This is tempered somewhat by the fact that a substantial element of the new bourgeoisie comes from the old *nomenklatura* and retains much of the latter's disdain for democratic procedures and institutions. In addition, the international environment is totally different: the competitive pressures being exerted by the advanced capitalist states is enormous. These conditions force the capitalists in the post-communist countries, if they are to be able to compete, to drive down living standards and restrict workers' rights.

There are a number of additional features which apply more or less to all cases of post-communist development:

- the influence of opposition movements in the collapse of communism evinced more the weakness of the regimes than of the strength of civil society;
- the strength of popular feeling has not been translated into the formation in a post-communist context of strong political parties and interest groups;
- there has been a significant fall in production and a drastic decline in the standard of living;
- in the political system, executives have dominated over legislatures.

These factors have tended to be mutually reinforcing but at the heart of the problem, given that state control over interest group activity has substantially decreased if not completely disappeared, is the shape of the economy. The long-term picture, I believe, is that Russia and Ukraine will not undergo the 'economic miracle' which transformed a number of states in the aftermath of World War II, but will remain fundamentally semi-peripheral in the global political economy. This means that some sectors will continue to play an important and expanding role, for example, oil and gas in Russia and possibly some high technology industries in both Russia and Ukraine, but that much of industry will continue to produce poor-quality output because of lack of investment. Nevertheless, if there is a steady improvement in the economy, albeit punctuated by periods of stagnation and downturn, then interest group activity in general and trade union activity in particular could be encouraged. This has been the experience of the advanced capitalist countries where economic expansion has provided the resources to meet both workers' demands for higher wages and also to fulfill elements of a wider pro-labour agenda, such as improved health care, pension entitlement, and educational opportunities, generally achieved under the aegis of social democratic governments. One should be wary, however, of assuming a simple replication of the postwar experience in Russia and Ukraine. The differences between the two situations are very marked. In the first place, the trades unions have been unable to operate effectively as trades unions or to develop an independent political organisation. While the offshoots of the CPSU have proved to be the most well organised and viable political parties in both Russia and Ukraine, the fact that they encompass elements of the old *nomenklatura* has meant that they have promoted demands for industrial regeneration which accord with the interests of enterprise managers rather than organised labour. They have also pursued a nationalist agenda which envisages the creation of a revamped USSR based on the Slavic states of Russia, Ukraine and Belarus. Outside of the coal industry, health service and education, workers have been reluctant to take action because some provision of scarce goods and services continues to be made through the medium of the enterprise. While this remains the case, and in the absence of a clear transformation of production relations along capitalist / proletarian lines, workers will tend to see a common interest with enterprise directors in gaining resources from the centre, rather than a 'class' interest with other workers. The problem of breaking the link between workers and directors is illustrated by the June 1993 strikes in Ukraine, which began as a spontaneous movement against steep price rises but which were rapidly utilised by mine and enterprise management to push demands which would enhance their own position through greater regional autonomy and the renewal of economic ties with Russia.

Apart from this one significant period of action, Ukraine's workers have been reduced to comparative impotence. The 1996 miners' strikes in Russia and Ukraine provide an interesting parallel. In Russia, the looming presidential elections and Yeltsin's dire opinion poll ratings provided the context in which the miners could win swift concessions. In Ukraine, however, such conditions did not prevail and, in a dire economic situation, industrial muscle alone proved inadequate.

In such an unfavourable environment, and with little confidence in their own organisations, workers have been forced to adopt individualistic solutions: growing their own food, heavy reliance on other family members, sometimes criminal activity. At a national level, the trade unions have responded to their lack of influence by seeking alliances with directors' organisations. In 1992, FNPR joined Civic Union, an organisation initiated by elements of the directors' lobby, and was fully in agreement with the directors over the form of privatisation, which prioritised labour collectives. After the destruction of parliament and the 1993 elections, many directors withdrew from direct involvement in politics at a national level, having gained considerably from the privatisation programme, and concentrated instead on obtaining concessions for their own enterprise or economic sector. The unions' relationship to the directors changed accordingly during this period to a more sectoral approach, although the FNPR leadership attempted to highlight specific national problems, such as wage arrears, through days of action. The national alliance with the directors reemerged in 1995 with the formation of the Union of Labour electoral pact but failed dismally in terms of winning votes. The national campaign contrasted with the lower key but more effectively targetted campaign run by the miners' union, which saw one of its key activists elected to the Duma. Union of Labour's poor showing did at least place on the agenda the utility of the unions' continued collaboration with directors' organisations. Nevertheless, in the campaign for the 1999 parliamentary elections, the Union of Labour once again eschewed the creation of a party solely representing the interests of labour in favour of joining the Fatherland-All Russia (OVR) bloc associated with Moscow Mayor Yuri Luzhkov and former prime minister, Evgenii Primakov. The union-management link evident at enterprise level thus continues to be replicated at a political level.

Another major difference with the postwar situation is that the economic recovery of neither Russia nor Ukraine will be based on the regeneration of manufacturing and core industries, which in the West were heavily unionised. With the possible exceptions of oil and gas in Russia, it is difficult to envisage the recovery of such sectors. While it is conceivable that worker militancy will increase in these industries, their comparatively narrow base and geographical isolation make it unlikely that they will represent the vanguard of a wider labour movement. Indeed, such militancy might be harnessed to promote the interests of a particular industry.

Which sectors are affected by improving performance is therefore crucial to the emergence of labour as an effective force. If growth occurs in new, small business sectors, employing predominantly non-union labour, while traditional heavy industrial sectors stagnate, then labour's influence will remain marginal. The degree to which economic improvement has a national rather than a regional impact is also important for two states whose stability has been threatened by regionally-based interests. Russia has adopted a form of asymmetrical federalism, which has basically meant making different concessions to different regions and republics to keep them within the federation. In Chechnya, where no agreement was possible, military force has been exercised. This initially resulted in the regime's humiliation, but subsequent success has underpinned the Yeltsin succession. In Ukraine, the unitary character of the state has been threatened by various attempts to enhance Crimea's autonomy if not outright independence, and by the demands for increased autonomy for the Donbas. The results of Ukraine's 1999 presidential elections would suggest that regional differences continue to exist but that Kuchma has been successful in limiting their impact. Nevertheless, strong growth in specific regions, especially where this is combined with an ethnic component, could reignite separatist or at least autonomist currents. This would be unlikely in those regions most strongly committed to the existence of the nation state: western Ukraine and the regions of western and central Russia, but could be important for Crimea and eastern Ukraine and also for the eastern and southern regions of Russia.

If democracy is to be consolidated, therefore, a generalised economic upturn is essential. Disillusionment with the failure of economic reforms to improve the lot of the vast majority of Russian and Ukrainian people has reinforced a lack of participation within political parties and other organisations since independence. The most positive sign of attachment to the new political system has been the turnout for elections, which has generally been good, suggesting that this mechanism is considered a viable means of political change in both states. In itself, however, it is an inadequate indicator of democracy.

In the main, Russian politics has assumed a highly polarised form, rather than one based on agreement and consensus. This is illustrated by the control exercised by the state or 'oligarchs' over television and other forms of media, especially newspapers. During the 1996 presidential elections, the almost total support of the media for Yeltsin raised serious questions about the fairness of the campaign and result. This experience was repeated in Russia's 1999 parliamentary elections and 2000 presidential elections. Moreover, the result of the latter opens up the opportunity for a move in an authoritarian direction in order to implement marketisation (what might be termed the 'Pinochet variant'). Should this happen then labour's room for manoeuvre would be even more severely restricted. This is certainly a more likely prospect in Russia with the election of Vladimir Putin as president than in Ukraine where Kuchma, reelected president in 1999, has maintained a greater respect for democratic norms and civil rights.

The final dimension of democratic consolidation that needs to be addressed is that of international relationships. As a counterweight to Russia's influence, Ukraine has sought close ties with the European Union, NATO and other international institutions. If membership particularly of the EU is to be a realistic prospect then it entails meeting certain norms concerning human and civil rights, and the functioning of democratic institutions. For Russia, on the other hand, with its pretensions to great power status and as its intervention in Chechnya has demonstrated, such norms need not have such an influence. Such links have, however, created opportunities for both Russia's and Ukraine's trades unions to build links with those in the west and to affiliate to international trades union organisations. There is a stark contrast, however, between the pace of globalisation, which increasingly undermines the capacity of the nation state to influence economic activity within its own geographical boundaries, and the degree to which relations between labour movements have become internationalised in practice. Trades union demands, in a majority of cases, are still ineffectively confined to a national framework.

The overall picture painted in this book of labour's influence on the political transformation of Russia and Ukraine is unfortunately a gloomy one. Whereas workers' action played a significant role in the downfall of the USSR, a combination of circumstances has ensured that labour has not enjoyed similar influence in the postcommunist period. The biggest single problem has been its incapacity to create its own independent union organisations and a political party capable of representing its interests and projecting a coherent programme of change. In the absence of such a labour *movement* and in conditions of economic collapse the danger emerges of support for populist figures, a return to a form of authoritarianism and the failure of democratisation itself.

# Bibliography


Abugattas, L.A. (1987), 'Populism and After: The Peruvian Experience', in Malloy, J.M., et al. (eds), *Authoritarians and Democrats: Regime Transition in Latin America*, Pittsburgh, University of Pittsburgh Press, pp. 121-143.

Adamson, W.L. (1980), *Hegemony and Revolution: A Study of Antonio Gramsci's Political and Cultural Theory*, Berkeley, University of California Press.

Adler, G. and E. Webster (1995), 'Challenging Transition Theory: The Labor Movement, Radical Reform, and Transition to Democracy in South Africa', *Politics and Society*, 23(1), pp. 75-106.

Alekseeva, L. (1986), 'Zabastovki v SSSR (poslestalinskii period)', *SSSR: Vnutrennye protivorechiya*, 15, pp. 80-145.

Arel, D. and A. Wilson (1994a), 'Ukraine under Kuchma: Back to 'Eurasia'?', *RFE/RL Research Report*, 3(32), pp. 1-12.

Arel, D. and A. Wilson (1994b), 'The Ukrainian Parliamentary Elections', *RFE/RL Research Report*, 3(26), pp. 6-17.

Armstrong, P., A. Glyn and J. Harrison (1984), *Capitalism Since World War II: The Making and Breakup of the Great Boom*, London, Fontana.

Arnot, B. (1988), *Controlling Soviet labour: experimental change from Brezhnev to Gorbachev*, Basingstoke, Macmillan.

Ashwin, S. (1999), *Russian Workers: The anatomy of patience*, Manchester, Manchester University Press.

Aslund, A. (1989), *Gorbachev's Struggle for Economic Reform*, London, Pinter.

Aslund, A. (1995), 'Eurasia Letter: Ukraine's Turnaround', *Foreign Policy*(100), pp. 125-143.

Aves, J. (1990), 'The New Russian Labour Movement', *Slovo*, 3(2), pp. 16-27.

Aves, J. (1992), 'The Russian labour movement 1989-91: the mirage of a Russian Solidarnosc', in Hosking, G.A., et al. (eds), *The Road to Post-Communism: Independent Political Movements in the Soviet Union 1985-1991*, London, Pinter, pp. 138-156.

Baretta, S.R.D. and J. Markoff (1987), 'Brazil's Abertura: A Transition from What to What?', in Malloy, J.M., et al. (eds), *Authoritarians and Democrats: Regime Transition in Latin America*, Pittsburgh, University of Pittsburgh Press, pp. 43-65.

Barsenkov, A.S., V.A. Koretskii and A.I. Ostapenko (1993), *Politicheskaya Rossiya Segodnya. (Ispolnitel'naya Vlast', Konstitutsionnyi Sud, Lidery Partii i Dvizhenii). Spravochnik*, Moscow, Moskovskii Rabochii.

Bellin, E. (2000), 'Contingent Democrats: Industrialists, Labor, and

Democratization in Late-Developing Countries', *World Politics*, 52(January), pp. 175-205.

Berezovskii, V., N. Krotov and V. Chervyakov (1990), 'Ot dvizheniya rabochikh k rabochemy dvizheniyu', *Dialog* 14, pp. 53-58.

Bernhard, M. (1994), 'Riding the Next Wave: Recent Books on Democratization', *Studies in Comparative International Development*, pp. 50-73.

Birch, S. (1995), 'The Ukrainian Parliamentary and Presidential Elections of 1994', *Electoral Studies*, 15(1), pp. 93-99.

Birch, S. and I. Zinko (1996), 'The Dilemma of Regionalism', *Transition* 1 November, pp. 22-25, 64.

Borisov, V. (1993a), 'Zabastovka kak forma aktivnosti trudyashchikhsya v period provedeniya ekonomicheskikh reform (na primere zabastovki v Donbase, 7-20 iyunya 1993g.)', mimeo.

Borisov, V. (1993b), 'Samoorganizatsiya rabochego dvizheniya', *Sotsiologicheskie Issledovaniya* 2, pp. 42-44.

Borisov, V. (1995), 'Politicheskie perspektivy glazami izbiratelei', *Na Gora!*, Moscow, p. 2.

Borisov, V. and S. Clarke (1994), 'Reform and Revolution in the Communist National Park', *Capital & Class* 53, pp. 9-13.

Bova, R. (1991a), 'Political Dynamics of the Post-Communist Transition: A Comparative Perspective', *World Politics*, 44(October), pp. 113-138.

Bova, R. (1991b), 'Worker Activism: The Role of the State', in Sedaitis, J., et al. (eds), *Perestroika from Below: Social Movements in the Soviet Union*, Boulder CO, Westview Press, pp. 29-42.

Breslauer, G.W. (1984), 'On the Adaptability of Soviet Welfare-State Authoritarianism', in Hoffman, E., et al. (eds), *The Soviet Polity in the Modern Era*, New York, Aldine Publishing Company, pp. 219-245.

Britvin, B.G. (1990), 'Zabastovki na predpriyatiyakh s pozitsii trudyashchikhsya', *Sotsiologicheskie Issledovaniya* 6, pp. 42-48.

Bruszt, L. (1990), '1989: the negotiated revolution in Hungary', *Social Research*, 57, pp. 365-388.

Buketov, K. (1995a), 'Osen' 1993: profsoyuzy v period krizisa', *Rabochaya Politika* 4, pp. 15-31.

Buketov, K. (1995b), 'Russian Trade Unions in 1994', *Labour Focus on Eastern Europe* 50, pp. 24-40.

Buketov, K. and A. Nikul'nikov (1996), 'Profsoyuzy Rossii v predvybornoi kampanii 1995g.', *Rabochaya Politika* 1, pp. 5-15.

Bunce, V. (1983), 'The Political Economy of the Brezhnev Era: The Rise and Fall of Corporatism', *British Journal of Political Science*, 13, pp. 129-158.

Bunce, V. (1995), 'Should Transitologists be Grounded?', *Slavic Review*, 54(1), pp. 111-127.

Bunce, V. and J.M. Echols III (1980), 'Soviet Politics in the Brezhnev Era: "Pluralism" or "Corporatism"', in Kelley, D.R. (ed.), *Soviet Politics in the Brezhnev Era*, New York, Praeger, pp. 1-26.

Buzgalin, A.V. (1993), *Belaya Vorona (Poslednii God Zhizni TsK KPSS: Vzglyad Iznutri)*, Moscow.

Cammack, P., D. Pool and W. Tordoff (1993), *Third World Politics: A Comparative Introduction,* 2nd Edition, Basingstoke, Macmillan.

Cavarozzi, M. (1986), 'Political Cycles in Argentina since 1955', in O'Donnell, G., et al. (eds), *Transitions from Authoritarian Rule: Latin America*, Baltimore, Johns Hopkins University Press, pp. 19-48.

Chapman, J.G. (1991), 'Drastic Changes in the Soviet Social Contract', in Adam, J. (ed.), *Economic Reforms and Welfare Systems in the USSR, Poland and Hungary*, London, Macmillan, pp. 26-51.

Christensen, P.T. (1999), *Russia's Workers in Transition: Labor, Management, and the State under Gorbachev and Yeltsin*, Dekalb, Northern Illinois University Press.

Chulanov, V.A. (1980), *Sovremennye sovetskie rabochie: peredovye cherty i sotsial'naya aktivnost'*, Moscow, Mysl'.

Clarke, S. (1993), 'Trade Unions, Industrial Relations and Politics in Russia', *Journal of Communist Studies*, 9(4), pp. 133-160.

Clarke, S. (1994), 'Privatisation: The Politics of Capital and Labour', in White, S., et al. (eds), *Developments in Russian and Post-Soviet Politics*, Basingstoke, Macmillan, pp. 162-186.

Clarke, S. (1997), 'Trade unions and the non-payment of wages in Russia', Warwick University, Russian Research Programme, www.warwick.ac.uk/fac/society/complabstuds/russia/unpaid.doc.

Clarke, S. and P. Fairbrother (1993a), 'Trade Unions and the Working Class', in Clarke, S., et al., *What About the Workers? Workers and the Transition to Capitalism in Russia*, London, Verso, pp. 91-120.

Clarke, S. and P. Fairbrother (1993b), 'The Origins of the Independent Workers' Movement and the 1989 Miners' Strike', in Clarke, S., et al., *What About the Workers? Workers and the Transition to Capitalism in Russia*, London, Verso, pp. 121-144.

Clarke, S. and P. Fairbrother (1993c), 'Beyond the Mines: The Politics of the New Workers' Movement', in Clarke, S., et al., *What About the Workers? Workers and the Transition to Capitalism in Russia*, London, Verso, pp. 145-160.

Clarke, S. and P. Fairbrother (1993d), 'The Strikes of 1991 and the Collapse of the Soviet System', in Clarke, S., et al., *What About the Workers? Workers and the Transition to Capitalism in Russia*, London, Verso, pp. 161-172.

Clarke, S. and P. Fairbrother (1993e), 'After the Coup: The Workers' Movement in the Transition to a Market Economy', in Clarke, S., et al., *What About the Workers? Workers and the Transition to Capitalism in Russia*, London, Verso, pp. 173-198.

Clarke, S., P. Fairbrother and V. Borisov (1994), 'The Workers' Movement in Russia 1987-1992', *Critique* 26, pp. 55-68.

Clarke, S., P. Fairbrother and V. Borisov (1995), *The Workers' Movement in Russia*, Aldershot, Edward Elgar.

Cliff, T. (1974), *State Capitalism in Russia*, London, Pluto.

Collier, R. B. (1999), Paths Toward Democracy: The Working Class and Elites in Western Europe and South America, Cambridge, Cambridge University Press.

Collier, R. B. and D. Collier (1991), *Shaping the Political Arena: Critical Junctures, The Labor Movement and Regime Dynamics in Latin America*, Princeton, Princeton University Press.

Commander, S. and C. Mummsen (1998), *Understanding Barter in Russia*, London, European Bank for Reconstruction and Development.

Connor, W. D. (1981), 'Workers and power', in Triska, J.F., et al. (eds), *Blue Collar Workers in Eastern Europe*, London, Allen and Unwin, pp. 157-172.

Connor, W. D. (1988), *Socialism's dilemmas: state and society in the Soviet Bloc*, New York, Columbia University Press.

Connor, W. D. (1994), 'Labor politics in postcommunist Russia: a preliminary assessment', in Millar, J.R., et al. (eds), *The Social Legacy of Communism*, Cambridge, Cambridge University Press, pp. 329-353.

Connor, W. D. (1996), *Tattered Banners: Labor, Conflict, and Corporatism in Postcommunist Russia*, Boulder CO, Westview Press.

Conquest, R. (1967), *Industrial Workers in the USSR*, London, The Bodley Head.

Cook, L. J. (1993), *The Soviet Social Contract and Why It Failed: Welfare Policy and Workers' Politics from Brezhnev to Yeltsin*, Cambridge, Mass., Harvard University Press.

Cook, L. J. (1994), 'Russia's Labor Relations: Consolidation or Disintegration', in Blum, D.W. (ed.), *Russia's Future: Consolidation or Disintegration?*, Boulder CO, Westview, pp. 69-89.

Cook, L. J. and V. E. Gimpelson (1995), 'Exit and Voice in Russian Managers' Privatisation Strategies', *Communist Economies and Economic Transformation*, 7(4), pp. 465-483.

Corbridge, S. (1993a), *Debt and Development*, Oxford, Blackwell.

Corbridge, S. (1993b), 'Discipline and Punish: The New Right and the Policing of the International Debt Crisis', in Riley, S.P. (ed.), *The Politics of Global Debt*, Basingstoke, Macmillan, pp. 25-50.

Cox, R. (1987), *Production, Power, and World Order*, New York, Columbia University Press.

Crowley, S. (1995), 'Between Class and Nation: Worker Politics in the New Ukraine', *Communist and Post-Communist Studies*, 28(1), pp. 43-69.

Dabrowski, M. (1994), 'The Ukrainian Way to Hyperinflation', *Communist Economies and Economic Transformation*, 6(2), pp. 115-137.

Daniels, R.V. (1969), *The Conscience of the Revolution: Communist Opposition in Soviet Russia*, New York, Simon & Schuster.

Dawisha, K. and B. Parrott (1994), *Russia and the New States of Eurasia: The Politics of Upheaval*, Cambridge, Cambridge University Press.

Diamandouros, P.N. (1986), 'Regime Change and the Prospects for Democracy in Greece: 1974-1983', in O'Donnell, G., et al. (eds), *Transitions from Authoritarian Rule: Southern Europe*, Baltimore, Johns Hopkins University

Press, pp. 138-164.

Diamond, L. (1993), 'The Globalization of Democracy', in Slater, R.O., et al. (eds), *Global Transformation and the Third World*, Boulder CO, Lynne Rienner, pp. 31-69.

Diamond, L. (1996), 'Is the Third Wave Over?', *Journal of Democracy*, 7(3), pp. 20-37.

Diligenskii, G. (1995), 'Privatizatsiya: nekotorye sotsial'nye i sotsial'no-psikhologicheskie aspekty', *Mirovaya Ekonomika i Mezhdunarodnye Otnosheniya*, 5, pp. 68-81.

Djilas, M. (1966), *The New Class: An Analysis of the Communist System*, London, Unwin Books.

Doder, D. and L. Branson (1990), *Gorbachev: Heretic in the Kremlin*, London, Futura.

Dornbusch, R. (1989), 'The Latin American Debt Problem: Anatomy and Solutions', in Stallings, B., et al. (eds), *Debt and Democracy in Latin America*, Boulder, CO, Westview Press, pp. 7-22.

Drake, P.W. (1996), *Labor Movements and Dictatorships: The Southern Cone in Comparative Perspective*, Baltimore, Johns Hopkins University Press.

Dunlop, J.B. (1991), 'The Leadership of the Centrist Bloc', *Report on the USSR*, 3(6), pp. 4-6.

Dunlop, J.B. (1993), *The Rise of Russia and the Fall of the Soviet Empire*, Princeton, Princeton University Press.

Dyker, D. (1985), 'The New Party Program and the Future of the Soviet Economy', *Radio Liberty Research*, RL 363/85 November 4.

Erlich, A. (1960), *The Soviet Industrialization Debate: 1924-1928*, Boston, Mass., Harvard University Press.

Evangelista, M. (1996), 'Stalin's Revenge: Institutional Barriers to Internationalization in the Soviet Union', in Keohane, R.O., et al. (eds), *Internationalization and Domestic Politics*, Cambridge, Cambridge University Press, pp. 159-187.

Evstigneev, V. (1996), 'Rossiya i kreditnaya politika MVF i MBRR (I)', *Mirovaya Ekonomika i Mezhdunarodnye Otnosheniya*, 5, pp. 5-16.

Fedin, D. (1992), 'Dve redaktsii odnogo zakona o zabastovkakh: sravnitel'nyi analiz', *Gosudarstvo i pravo*, 3, pp. 49-55.

Feher, F. (1982), 'Paternalism as a Mode of Legitimation in Soviet-type Societies', in Rigby, T.H., et al. (eds), *Political Legitimation in Communist States*, Basingstoke, Macmillan, pp. 64-81.

Filatotchev, I., Y.G.V. Frausum, M. Wright, et al. (1996), 'Privatisation and Industrial Restructuring in Ukraine', *Communist Economies and Economic Transformation*, 8(2), pp. 185-203.

Filtzer, D. (1986), *Soviet workers and Stalinist industrialization: the formation of modern Soviet production relations, 1928-41*, London, Pluto Press.

Filtzer, D. (1994), *Soviet Workers and the Collapse of Perestroika: The Soviet labour process and Gorbachev's reforms, 1985-1991*, Cambridge, Cambridge

University Press.
Fishman, R.M. (1990), 'Rethinking State and Regime: Southern Europe's Transition to Democracy', *World Politics*, 42(3), pp. 422-440.
Fitzpatrick, S. (1982), *The Russian Revolution 1917-1932*, Oxford, Oxford University Press.
Foweraker, J. (1987), 'Corporatist Strategies and the Transition to Democracy in Spain', *Comparative Politics*(October), pp. 57-72.
Friedgut, T. and L. Siegelbaum (1990), 'Perestroika From Below: the Soviet Miners' Strike and its Aftermath', *New Left Review*, 181, pp. 5-32.
Füredi, F. (1986), *The Soviet Union Demystified*, London, Junius.
Garreton, M. A. (1986), 'The Political Evolution of the Chilean Military Regime and Problems in the Transition to Democracy', in O'Donnell, G., et al. (eds), *Transitions from Authoritarian Rule: Latin America*, Baltimore, Johns Hopkins University Press, pp. 95-122.
George, S. (1990), *A Fate Worse than Debt*, Harmondsworth, Penguin.
Gilbert, M. (1986), *Inflation and Social Conflict: A Sociology of Economic Life in Advanced Societies*, Brighton, Wheatsheaf.
Gill, G. (1994), *The Collapse of a Single-Party System: The Disintegration of the Communist Party of the Soviet Union*, Cambridge, Cambridge University Press.
Gillespie, C. G. (1990), 'Models of Democratic Transition in South America: Negotiated Reform versus Democratic Rupture', in Ethier, D. (ed.), *Democratic Transition and Consolidation in Southern Europe, Latin America and Southeast Asia*, Basingstoke, Macmillan, pp. 45-72.
Gills, B., J. Rocamora and R. Wilson (1993), 'Low Intensity Democracy', in Gills, B., et al. (eds), *Low Intensity Democracy: Political Power in the New World Order*, London, Pluto Press, pp. 3-34.
Gladysh, Y. (1990), 'Ot partiinogo kluba k "Demokraticheskoi Platforme"', *Narodnyi Deputat*, 6, pp. 59-62.
Gorbachev, M.S. (1986), *Political Report of the CPSU Central Committee to the 27th Party Congress*, Moscow.
Gordon, L. (1994), 'De juillet 1989 à juillet 1990: une année dans le mouvement ouvrier russe', *Le Mouvement Social*, 169, pp. 67-88.
Gordon, L.A., V.V. Komarovskii and A.K. Nazimova (1988), 'Sovetskii rabochii klass v usloviyakh rekonstruktsii, ekonomicheskoi reformy i demokratizatsii obshchestva', in Gordon, L.A., et al. (eds), *Rabochii klass v sotsialisticheskom obshchestve, tendentsii i perspektivy razvitiya v usloviyakh intensifikatsii i perestroiki ekonomiki*, Moscow, Nauka.
Gordon, L.A. and A.K. Nazimova (1985), *Rabochii klass SSSR, tendentsii i perspektivy sotsial'no- ekonomicheskogo razvitiya*, Moscow, Nauka.
Gowan, P. (1999), *The Global Gamble: Washington's Faustian Bid for World Domination*, London, Verso.
Gustafson, T. (1982), 'Soviet Energy Policy: From Big Coal to Big Gas', in Bialer, S., et al. (eds), *Russia at the Crossroads: The 26th Congress of the CPSU*, London, pp. 121-139.

Gustafson, T. (1989), *Crisis Amid Plenty: The Politics of Soviet Energy under Brezhnev and Gorbachev*, Princeton, Princeton University Press.

Haggard, S. and R.R. Kaufman (1995), *The Political Economy of Democratic Transitions*, Princeton, Princeton University Press.

Hagopian, F. (1990), ''Democracy by Undemocratic Means'? Elites, Political Pacts, and Regime Transition in Brazil', *Comparative Political Studies*, 23(2), pp. 147-170.

Halliday, F. (1983), *The Making of the Second Cold War*, London, Verso.

Hanson, P. (1985), 'A Conservative Five-Year Plan', *Radio Liberty Research*, RL 380/85 November 13.

Harding, T. and J. Petras (1988), 'Introduction: Democratization and Class Struggle', *Latin American Perspectives*, 15(3), pp. 3-17.

Hauslohner, P. (1987), 'Gorbachev's Social Contract', *Soviet Economy*, 3(1), pp. 54-89.

Hazan, B.A. (1990), *Gorbachev and his Enemies: The Struggle for Perestroika*, Boulder CO, Westview Press.

Hedlund, S. (1999), *Russia's "Market" Economy: A bad case of predatory capitalism*, London, UCL Press.

Hewett, E. and G. Zoteev (1990), 'Perestroika Ekonomiki: Beg na Meste? (II)', *Sovetskie Profsoyuzy*, 23-24, pp. 40-43.

Hoffmann, E.P. (1992), 'Perestroika and the new international economy', in Lavigne, M. (ed.), *The Soviet Union and Eastern Europe in the Global Economy*, Cambridge, Cambridge University Press, pp. 179-189.

Huntington, S.P. (1984), 'Will More Countries Become Democratic?', *Political Science Quarterly*, 99(2), pp. 193-218.

Huntington, S.P. (1991), *The Third Wave: Democratization in the Late Twentieth Century*, Norman, University of Oklahoma Press.

Igitkhanyan, E.D., I.Y. Petrushina and F.R. Filippov (1990), 'Industrial'nyi otryad trudyashchikhsya', *Sotsiologicheskie Issledovaniya*, 3, pp. 3-12.

Isaev, A. (1995), 'Interview with author', Moscow, 21 September.

Johnson, J. (1997), 'Russia's Emerging Financial-Industrial Groups', *Post-Soviet Affairs*, 13(4), pp. 333-365.

Johnstone, D. (1984), *The Politics of Euromissiles: Europe's Role in America's World*, London, Verso.

Jung, M. (1994), 'The Donbas Factor in the Ukrainian Elections', *RFE/RL Research Report*, 3(12), pp. 51-56.

Kabalina, V.I., G.A. Monusova and A.K. Nazimova (1989), 'Zabastovki sovetskikh rabochikh (1987-1989gg.)', *Rabochii klass i sovremennyi mir*, 6, pp. 74-77.

Kagarlitsky, B. (1990), *The Dialectic of Change*, London, Verso.

Kagarlitsky, B. (1991), *Farewell Perestroika*, London, Verso.

Katsva, A.M. (1990), 'Ot rabochkomov k soyuzu trudyashchikhsya Kuzbassa', *Rabochii klass i sovremennyi mir*, 1, pp. 191-194.

Katz, C.J. (1989), *From Feudalism to Capitalism: Marxian Theories of Class Struggle and Social Change*, New York, Greenwood Press.

Keohane, R.O. (1984), 'The World Political Economy and the Crisis of Embedded Liberalism', in Goldthorpe, J.H. (ed.), *Order and Conflict in Contemporary Capitalism: Studies in the Political Economy of Western European Nations*, Oxford, Oxford University Press, pp. 15-38.

Khanin, G. (1992), 'Economic growth in the 1980s', in Ellman, M., et al. (eds), *The Disintegration of the Soviet Economic System*, London, Routledge, pp. 73-85.

Kholodkovskii, K. (1995), 'Rossiiskaya privatizatsiya: stolknovenie interesov', *Mirovaya Ekonomika i Mezhdunarodnye Otnosheniya*, 1, pp. 72-86.

Kirichenko, O. A. and P. M. Kudyukin (1993), 'Pervye shagi sotsial'nogo partnerstva v Rossii', *Politicheskie issledovaniya* 1, pp. 130-135.

Kisovskaya, N. (1995), 'Rossiiskaya privatizatsiya: partiino-politicheskaya bor'ba na vauchernom etape', *Mirovaya Ekonomika i Mezhdunarodnye Otnosheniya*, 5, pp. 82-95.

Klochkov, I. (1990), 'Stanovlenie federatsii', *Sovetskie Profsoyuzy*, 19-20, pp. 18-21.

Kolganov, A. (1990), 'Doloi "Nomenklaturnyi" Kapitalizm!', *Dialog*, 17, pp. 41-48.

Konfederatsiya Truda (1992), 'Deklaratsiya osnovnykh printsipov Konfederatsii Truda', *Rabochee Dvizhenie: dokumental'nye i analiticheskie materialy*, Moscow, pp. 144-151.

Korzeniewicz, R. P. (1993), 'Contested Arenas: Recent Studies in Politics and Labor', *Latin American Research Review*, pp. 206-220.

Kostakov, V. (1987), 'Zanyatost': defitsit ili izbytok?', *Kommunist*, 2, pp. 78-89.

Kostiukovskii, V. (1990), *Kuzbass: Zharkoe Leto 89-go: Khronika, dokumenty. Vpechatleniya ochevidtsa. Razmyshleniya publitsista*, Moscow, Sovremennik.

Krawchenko, B. (1985), *Social Change and National Consciousness in Twentieth-Century Ukraine*, Basingstoke, Macmillan.

Kubas', G. V. (1990), 'Rabochie komitety Kuzbassa', *Sotsiologicheskie Issledovaniya*, 6, pp. 49-53.

Kudyukin, P. (1994), 'Labor Relations and the Choice of Models of Development', *Conference of the Aspen Institute 'Russia's Path to an Open Society'*, Berlin.

Kurashvili, B.P. (1987), 'Perestroika i predpriyatie', *Ekonomika i organizatsiya promyshlennogo proizvodstva*, 10, pp. 3-30.

Kuromiya, H. (1988), *Stalin's Industrial Revolution: Politics and Workers 1928-1932*, Cambridge, Cambridge University Press.

Kuzio, T. (1996), 'Kravchuk to Kuchma: The Ukrainian Presidential Elections of 1994', *Journal of Communist Studies and Transition Politics*, 12(2), pp. 117-144.

Ladnyi, V. (1991), 'Zabastovki', *Don*, 10, pp. 234-243.

Lane, D. (1990), *Soviet Society under Perestroika*, Boston, Unwin Hyman.

Lane, D. and F. O'Dell (1978), *The Soviet Industrial Worker: Social Class, Education and Control*, Oxford, Martin Robinson.

Lapychak, C. (1995), 'Showdown Yields Political Reform', *Transition*, 1(13), pp. 3-7.

Levine, D. H. (1988), 'Paradigm Lost: Dependence to Democracy', *World Politics*, pp. 377-394.

Lewin, M. (1988), *The Gorbachev Phenomenon: A Historical Interpretation*, London, Radius.

Lipton, D. and J. Sachs (1990), 'Privatization in Eastern Europe: The Case of Poland', *Brookings Papers on Economic Activity*, 2.

Littlejohn, G. (1984), *A Sociology of the Soviet Union*, London, Macmillan.

Logan, J. R. (1983), 'Worker Mobilization and Party Politics: Revolutionary Portugal in Perspective', in Graham, L. S., et al. (eds), *In Search of Modern Portugal*, Madison, University of Wisconsin Press, pp. 135-148.

Lopez, F. A. (1990), 'Bourgeois State and the Rise of Social Democracy in Spain', in Chilcote, R. H., et al. (eds), *Transitions from Dictatorship to Democracy: Comparative Studies of Spain, Portugal, and Greece*, New York, Crane Russak, pp. 17-72.

Löwy, M. (1981), *The Politics of Combined and Uneven Development: The Theory of Permanent Revolution*, London, Verso.

Ludlam, J. (1991), 'Reform and the Redefinition of the Social Contract under Gorbachev', *World Politics,* January, pp. 284-312.

Lukes, S. (1974), *Power: A Radical View*, London.

Lukinov, I. (1992), 'Radical Reconstruction of the Ukrainian Economy: Reasons, Reforms, Outlook', in Koropeckyj, I. S. (ed.), *The Ukrainian Economy: Achievements, Problems, Challenges*, Cambridge, Mass., Harvard Ukrainian Research Institute, pp. 21-43.

Maksimova, N. (1989), 'Zabastovka', *Eko*, 11, pp. 65-79.

Malloy, J. M. (1987), 'The Politics of Transition in Latin America', in Malloy, J. M., et al. (cds), *Authoritarians and Democrats: Regime Transition in Latin America*, Pittsburgh, University of Pittsburgh Press, pp. 235-258.

Mal'tseeva, L. L. and O. N. Pulyaeva (1990), 'Chto privelo k zabastovke', *Sotsiologicheskie Issledovaniya*, 6, pp. 38-48.

Mandel, D. (1990), 'The Rebirth of the Soviet Labor Movement: the Coalminers' Strike of July 1989', *Politics and Society*, 18(3), pp. 381-404.

Mandel, D. (1991), *Perestroika and the Soviet People*, Montreal, Black Rose Books.

Mandel, E. (1968), *Marxist Economic Theory*, London, Merlin Press.

Mandel, E. (1975), *Late Capitalism*, London, New Left Books.

Maravall, J. (1982), *The Transition to Democracy in Spain*, London, Croom Helm.

Maravall, J. M. and J. Santamaria (1986), 'Political Change in Spain and the Prospects for Democracy', in O'Donnell, G., et al. (eds), *Transitions from Authoritarian Rule: Southern Europe*, Baltimore, Johns Hopkins University Press, pp. 71-108.

Markwick, R. D. (1996), 'A Discipline in Transition?: From Sovietology to 'Transitology'', *Journal of Communist Studies and Transition Politics*, 12(3), pp. 255-276.

Marples, D. (1989), 'Why the Donbass Miners Went on Strike', *Radio Liberty*

*Report on the USSR*, September 8, pp. 30-32.

Marples, D. (1990), 'The Background of the Coal Strike on July 11', *Radio Liberty Report on the USSR*, July 27, pp. 15-17.

Marples, D. (1991), *Ukraine under Perestroika: Ecology, Economics and the Workers' Revolt*, Basingstoke, Macmillan.

Martin, A. (1994), 'Labour, the Keynesian Welfare State, and the Changing International Political Economy', in Stubbs, R., et al. (eds), *Political Economy and the Changing Global Order*, Basingstoke, Macmillan, pp. 60-74.

Marx, K. (1973 [1852]), 'The Eighteenth Brumaire of Louis Bonaparte', in Fernbach, D. (ed.), *Surveys from Exile*, Harmondsworth, Penguin, pp. 143-249.

Materialy (1992), 'Rezoliutsiya I s'ezda shakhterov po voprosam sotsial'no-ekonomicheskogo polozheniya, vypolneniya postanovleniya SM SSSR No 608 i perspektivam perekhoda k rynku', *Shakhterskoe Dvizhenie: dokumental'nye i analiticheskie materialy*, Moscow, Tsentr po Izucheniya Sotsial'no-trudovykh Otnoshenii, pp. 51-55.

Maxwell, K. (1986), 'Regime Overthrow and the Prospects for Democratic Transition in Portugal', in O'Donnell, G., et al. (eds), *Transitions from Authoritarian Rule: Southern Europe*, Baltimore, Johns Hopkins University Press, pp. 109-137.

McFaul, M. (1993), 'Russian Centrism and Revolutionary Transitions', *Post-Soviet Affairs*, 9(3), pp. 196-222.

Mihalisko, K. (1991), 'The Workers' Rebellion in Belorussia', *Radio Liberty Report on the USSR*, 17, pp. 21-25.

Milovidov, Y. (1991), 'Povtorenie proidennnogo ili s kem zhe solidarnost'', *Sovetskie Profsoyuzy*, 12, pp. 12-13.

Monusova, G. (1992a), 'Razvitie zabastovochnogo dvizheniya: ot stikhiinosti k organizovannosti', *Rabochee dvizhenie: dokumental'nye i analiticheskie materialy*, Moscow, pp. 18-29.

Monusova, G.A. (1992b), 'Khronika rabochego dvizheniya v SSSR 1987-1991gg.', *Rabochee dvizhenie: dokumental'nye i analiticheskie materialy*, Moscow, pp. 30-122.

Moore Jr, B. (1966), *Social Origins of Dictatorship and Democracy. Lord and Peasant in the Making of the Modern World*, Harmondsworth, Penguin.

Morvant, P. (1995), 'The Beleagured Coal-Mining Industry Strikes Back', *Transition*, 30 June, pp. 56-61, 70.

Moses, J.C. (1987), 'Worker Self-Management and the Reformist Alternative in Soviet Labour Policy, 1979-85', *Soviet Studies*, 39(2), pp. 205-228.

Moskoff, W. (1993), *Hard Times: Impoverishment and Protest in the Perestroika Years*, New York, M. E. Sharpe.

Mouzelis, N. (1976), 'Capitalism and Dictatorship in Post-war Greece', *New Left Review*, 96, pp. 57-80.

Munck, G.L. (1994), 'Democratic Transitions in Comparative Perspective', *Comparative Politics*(April), pp. 355-375.

Munck, R. (1989), *Latin America: The Transition to Democracy*, London, Zed

Books.

Murrell, P. (1993), 'What is Shock Therapy? What Did it Do in Poland and Russia?', *Post-Soviet Affairs*, 9(2), pp. 111-140.

Nagy, P.M. (2000), *The Meltdown of the Russian State: The deformation and collapse of the state in Russia*, Cheltenham, Edward Elgar.

Nove, A. (1969), *An Economic History of the USSR*, Harmondsworth, Penguin.

O'Brien, P. (1993), 'The Latin American Debt Crisis', in Riley, S. P. (ed.), *The Politics of Global Debt*, Basingstoke, Macmillan, pp. 85-112.

O'Donnell, G. (1979), *Modernization and Bureaucratic-Authoritarianism: Studies in South American Politics*, Berkeley, Institute of International Studies, University of California.

O'Donnell, G. (1986), 'Introduction to the Latin American Cases', in O'Donnell, G., et al. (eds), *Transitions from Authoritarian Rule: Latin America*, Baltimore, Johns Hopkins University Press, pp. 3-18.

O'Donnell, G. and P. C. Schmitter (1986), *Transitions from Authoritarian Rule: Tentative Conclusions about Uncertain Democracies*, Baltimore, Johns Hopkins University Press.

Okulov, A. (1990), 'Novye partii: ot stolbnyaka k likhoradke', *Posev*, 4, pp. 9-14.

Perez-Diaz, V. (1987), 'Economic Policies and Social Pacts in Spain during the Transition', in Scholten, I. (ed.), *Political Stability and Neo-Corporatism*, London, Sage, pp. 216-246.

Pichugin, B. (1995), 'Vneshnii dolg Rossii (Stat'ya pervaya)', *Mirovaya Ekonomika i Mezhdunarodnye Otnosheniya*, 6, pp. 21-31.

Potts, G. A. (1993), 'The Political Consequences of External Debt in Eastern Europe', in Riley, S. P. (ed.), *The Politics of Global Debt*, Basingstoke, Macmillan, pp. 151-167.

Poulantzas, N. (1976), *The Crisis of the Dictatorships: Portugal, Greece, Spain*, London, New Left Books.

Pravda, A. (1981), 'East-West interdependence and the social compact in Eastern Europe', in Bornstein, M. et al. (eds), *East-West Relations and the Future of Eastern Europe*.

Pravda, A. (1982), 'Is There a Soviet Working Class?', *Problems of Communism*, November-December, pp. 1-24.

Pridham, G. (1991), 'International Influences and Democratic Transition: Problems of Theory and Practice in Linkage Politics', in Pridham, G. (ed.), *Encouraging Democracy: The International Context of Regime Transition in Southern Europe*, Leicester & London, Leicester University Press, pp. 1-28.

Pridham, G. (1994), 'Democratic Transitions in Theory and Practice: Southern European Lessons for Eastern Europe?', in Pridham, G., et al. (eds), *Democratization in Eastern Europe: Domestic and International Perspectives*, London, Routledge, pp. 15-37.

Rau, Z. (1987), 'Some Thoughts on Civil Society in Eastern Europe and the Lockean Contractarian Approach', *Political Studies*, 35, pp. 573-592.

Rau, Z. (1991), 'The State of Enslavement: The East European Substitute for the

State of Nature', *Political Studies*, 39(2), pp. 253-269.

Redlikh, R. (1990), 'Rozhdenie svobodnykh profsoyuzov v SSSR', *Posev*, 3, pp. 59-74.

Reiman, M. (1987), *The Birth of Stalinism: The USSR on the Eve of the "Second Revolution"*, London, I. B. Tauris.

Remington, T. F. (1989), 'Gorbachev and the Strategy of Glasnost'', in Remington, T. F. (ed.), *Politics and the Soviet System: Essays in Honour of Frederick C. Barghoorn*, Basingstoke, Macmillan, pp. 56-82.

Remmer, K. L. (1991), 'New Wine or Old Bottlenecks? The Study of Latin American Democracy', *Comparative Politics*, 23(4), pp. 479-495.

Remmer, K. L. (1993), 'Democratization in Latin America', in Slater, R. O., et al. (eds), *Global Transformation and the Third World*, Boulder CO, Lynne Rienner, pp. 91-111.

Ribun, L. (1996), 'Privatizatsiya na Ukraine: illiuzii, oshibki, perspektivy', *Mirovaya Ekonomika i Mezhdunarodnye Otnosheniya*, 6, pp. 118-120.

Rigby, T. H. (1990), *Political Elites in the USSR*, Aldershot, Edward Elgar.

Riley, S. P. (1993), 'Introduction: The Politics of Debt Crises', in Riley, S. P. (ed.), *The Politics of Global Debt*, Basingstoke, Macmillan, pp. 1-22.

Robinson, N. (1994), '"Have Model, Will Travel": Russian and Western Reform Agendas', in Stanyer, J. (ed.), *Contemporary Political Studies*, pp. 595-606.

Roca, J. (1987), 'Neo-corporatism in Post-Franco Spain', in Scholten, I. (ed.), *Political Stability and Neo-Corporatism*, London, Sage, pp. 247-268.

Ruble, B. (1979), 'Factory Unions and Workers' Rights', in Kahan, A., et al. (eds), *Industrial Labor in the USSR*, Elmsford N.Y., Pergamon Press, pp. 59-84.

Ruble, B. (1981), *Soviet trade unions: their development in the 1970s*, Cambridge, Cambridge University Press.

Ruble, B. (1983), *The applicability of corporatist models to the study of Soviet politics, the case of the trade unions*, Pittsburgh PA., Carl Beck Papers in Russian and East European Studies No.303.

Rueschemeyer, D., E. H. Stephens and J. D. Stephens (1992), *Capitalist Development and Democracy*, Cambridge, Polity Press.

Rumer, B. (1986), 'Realities of Gorbachëv's Economic Program', *Problems of Communism*, May-June, pp. 20-31.

Rumer, B. (1990), 'The "Abalkanization" of Soviet Economic Reform', *Problems of Communism*, Jan-Feb, pp. 74-82.

Rutland, P. (1990), 'Labor Unrest and Movements in 1989 and 1990', *Soviet Economy*, 6(3), pp. 345-384.

Rutland, P. (1995), 'Search for Stability', *Transition*, 1, 23 June, pp. 20-23.

Rutland, P. (1997), 'The Rocky Road from Plan to Market', in White, S., et al. (eds), *Developments in Russian Politics 4*, Basingstoke, Macmillan, pp. 149-168.

Sagers, M. J. (1993), 'The Energy Industries of the Former USSR: A Mid-Year Survey', *Post-Soviet Geography*, 34(6), pp. 341-418.

Sakwa, R. (1990), *Gorbachev and his Reforms, 1985-1990*, London, Philip Allan.

Sakwa, R. (1996), *Russian Politics and Society*, 2nd Edition, London, Routledge.

Schmitter, P.C. (1986), 'An Introduction to Southern European Transitions from Authoritarian Rule: Italy, Greece, Portugal, Spain, and Turkey', in O'Donnell, G., et al. (eds), *Transitions from Authoritarian Rule: Southern Europe*, Baltimore, Johns Hopkins University Press, pp. 3-10.

Schmitter, P. C. and T. L. Karl (1994), 'The Conceptual Travels of Transitologists and Consolidologists: How Far to the East Should They Attempt to Go?', *Slavic Review*, 53(1), pp. 173-185.

Selyunin, V. and G. Khanin (1987), 'Lukavaya tsifra', *Novyi Mir*, 2, pp. 181-201.

Shabashev, V. and S. Mishenin (1999), 'Ekonomicheskie prichiny aktivizatsii rabochego dvizheniya v Kuzbasse na pubezhe 1980-1990 godov', *Conference on the Tenth Anniversary of the Birth of the Workers' Movement*, Kemerovo, http://www.center.kemsu.ru/konf/shab.htm.

Shablinskii, I. G. (1990), '"Rabochii vopros" v kontekste demokratizatsii (Razmyshleniya ob istokakh i nekotorykh perspektivakh massovogo rabochego dvizheniya v SSSR)', *Sovetskoe Gosudarstvo i Pravo*, 11, pp. 68-78.

Shevtsova, L. (1995), 'Russia's Post-Communist Politics: Revolution or Continuity?', in Lapidus, G. W. (ed.), *The New Russia: Troubled Transformation*, Boulder CO, Westview, pp. 5-36.

Shin, D. C. (1994), 'On the Third Wave of Democratization: A Synthesis and Evaluation of Recent Theory and Research', *World Politics*, 47(October), pp. 135-170.

Shmelev, N. and V. Popov (1990), *The Turning Point: Revitalizing the Soviet Economy*, London, I. B. Tauris.

Shubin, A. (1995a), ''Profsoyuzy Rossii' - lovushka ili proryv k uspekhu?', *Rabochaya Politika*, 1, pp. 32-34.

Shubin, A. (1995b), 'Traditsionnye profsoyuzy v poiskakh novykh metodov vozdeistviya na obshchestvo', *Rabochaya Politika*, 3, pp. 7-18.

Smith, A. (1993), *Russia and the World Economy: Problems of Integration*, London, Routledge.

Smith, P. H. (1991), 'Crisis and Democracy in Latin America', *World Politics*, 43(4), pp. 608-634.

Solchanyk, R. (1994), 'The Politics of State Building: Centre-Periphery Relations in Post-Soviet Ukraine', *Europe-Asia Studies*, 46(1), pp. 47-68.

Soyuz Trudyashchikhsya Kuzbassa (1992), 'Ustav Soyuza Trudyashchikhsya Kuzbassa', *Rabochee Dvizhenie: dokumental'nye i analiticheskie materialy*, Moscow, pp. 124-136.

Speranskii, A. (1990), 'Kakogo tsveta rabochie spetsovki?', *Sovetskie Profsoyuzy*, 15-16, pp. 16-19.

Steele, J. (1995), *Eternal Russia*, London, Faber and Faber.

Stent, A. (1995), 'Russia's Economic Revolution and the West', *Survival*, 37(1), pp. 121-143.

Stepan, A. (1985), 'State Power and the Strength of Civil Society in the Southern Cone of Latin America', in Evans, P. B., et al. (eds), *Bringing the State Back In*,

Cambridge, Cambridge University Press, pp. 315-343.

Stephens, J. D. (1993), 'Capitalist Development and Democracy: Empirical Research on the Social Origins of Democracy', in Copp, D., et al. (eds), *The Idea of Democracy*, Cambridge, Cambridge University Press, pp. 409-446.

Stolpovskii, B. G. (1991), 'Kakim byt' novomu proftsentru (Pervye vpechatleniya ot pervogo etapa XIX s'ezda profsoyuzov SSSR', *Politicheskie Issledovaniya*, 1, pp. 136-141.

Story, J. and B. Pollack (1991), 'Spain's Transition: Domestic and External Linkages', in Pridham, G. (ed.), *Encouraging Democracy: The International Context of Regime Transition in Southern Europe*, Leicester, Leicester University Press, pp. 125-158.

Stoyan, A. (1993), 'Interview with V. Markov', *Profsoyuzy*, 11/12, pp. 16-18.

Strange, S. (1994), *States and Markets*, 2nd Edition, London, Pinter.

Subtelny, O. (1988), *Ukraine: A History*, Toronto, University of Toronto Press.

Teague, E. (1989), 'Miners' Strike in Siberia Winds Down, Strikes in Ukraine Spread to Other Areas: A Status Report', *Radio Liberty Report on the USSR*, July 28, pp. 15-19.

Teague, E. (1993), 'Organized Labor in Russia in 1992', *RFE/RL Research Report*, 2(5), pp. 38-41.

Teague, E. and P. Hanson (1990), 'Most Soviet Strikes Politically Motivated', *Report on the USSR*, 2(34), pp. 1-2.

Tedstrom, J. (1987), 'On Perestroyka: Analyzing the "Basic Provisions"', *Problems of Communism*, July-August, pp. 93-8.

Tedstrom, J. (1989), 'The Importance of the Soviet Coal Industry', *Radio Liberty Report on the USSR*, August 4, pp. 13-14.

Temkina, A. (1990a), 'Nuzhna konsolidatsiya: zametki s pervogo s'ezda shakhterov v Donets'ke', *Leningradskii Rabochii*, Leningrad.

Temkina, A. (1990b), 'Rabochee dvizhenie: vesna 1990 goda', *mimeo*.

Therborn, G. (1977), 'The Rule of Capital and the Rise of Democracy', *New Left Review*, 103, pp. 3-41.

Ticktin, H. (1992), *Origins of the Crisis in the USSR: Essays on the Political Economy of a Disintegrating System*, Armonk, New York, M. E. Sharpe.

Tolz, V. (1994), 'The Civic Accord: Contributing to Russia's Stability?', *RFE/RL Research Report*, 3(19), pp. 1-5.

Trehub, A. (1990), 'Perestroika and Social Entitlements', in Tedstrom, J. (ed.), *Socialism, Perestroika and the Dilemmas of Soviet Economic Reform*, Boulder CO, Westview, pp. 207-231.

Trotsky, L. (1969), *The Permanent Revolution*, New York, Pathfinder Press.

Trotsky, L. (1972[1937]), *The Revolution Betrayed: What is the Soviet Union and Where is it Going?*, New York, Pathfinder Press.

Trotsky, L. (1977), *The History of the Russian Revolution*, London, Pluto Press.

Tsentr po Izucheniya Obshchestvennykh Dvizhenii (1991), *Dokumenty Politicheskikh Partii i Rabochego Dvizheniya Rossii, 1987-1991: Spravochnik*, Moscow, Moskovskoe Izdatel'stvo Nezavisimoi Pressy.

Unger, A. L. (1981), *Constitutional Development in the USSR*, London.

Valenzuela, J. S. (1989), 'Labor Movements in Transitions to Democracy: A Framework for Analysis', *Comparative Politics*, 21(4), pp. 445-472.

Vasil'enko, A. (1990), 'Vopreki privychnym traditsiyam: chto vysvetil vneocherednoi s'ezd profsoyuza rabotnikov ugol'noi promyshlennosti', *Sovetskie Profsoyuzy*, 13-14, pp. 10-13.

Verney, S. and T. Couloumbis (1991), 'State-International Systems Interaction and the Greek Transition to Democracy in the mid-1970s', in Pridham, G. (ed.), *Encouraging Democracy: The International Context of Regime Transition in Southern Europe*, Leicester, Leicester University Press, pp. 103-124.

Walker, R. (1993), *Six Years that Shook the World*, Manchester, Manchester University Press.

Walton, J. and D. Seddon (1994), *Free Markets and Food Riots*, Oxford, Blackwell.

White, S. (1986), 'Economic performance and Communist legitimacy', *World Politics*, 38(3), pp. 462-82.

White, S. (1990), *Gorbachev in Power*, Cambridge, Cambridge University Press.

White, S. (1991), 'Rethinking the CPSU', *Soviet Studies*, 43(3), pp. 405-428.

White, S. (1993), *After Gorbachev*, Cambridge, Cambridge University Press.

Whitehead, L. (1986a), 'Bolivia's Failed Democratization, 1977-1980', in O'Donnell, G., et al. (eds), *Transitions from Authoritarian Rule: Latin America*, Baltimore, Johns Hopkins University Press, pp. 49-71.

Whitehead, L. (1986b), 'International Aspects of Democratization', in O'Donnell, G., et al. (eds), *Transitions from Authoritarian Rule: Comparative Perspectives*, Baltimore, Johns Hopkins University Press, pp. 3-46.

Willerton Jr, J. P. (1997), 'Presidential Power', in White, S., et al. (eds), *Developments in Russian Politics 4*, Basingstoke, Macmillan, pp. 37-60.

Wishnevsky, J. (1991), 'Will the Conservatives Join the Liberals Against Gorbachev?', *Report on the USSR*, 3(6), pp. 1-3.

Woll, J. (1989), 'Glasnost' and Soviet Culture', *Problems of Communism*, November-December, pp. 40-50.

Wood, E. M. (1995), *Democracy Against Capitalism. Renewing Historical Materialism*, Cambridge, Cambridge University Press.

Zabastovka, (1989), *Zabastovka: vynuzhdennaya mera zashchity zakonnykh prav, no tot li eto put'?*, Moscow, Profizdat.

Zaslavsky, V. (1982), *The Neo-Stalinist State*, Armonk, N.Y., M. E. Sharpe.

# Index

For Product Safety Concerns and Information please contact our EU representative GPSR@taylorandfrancis.com Taylor & Francis Verlag GmbH, Kaufingerstraße 24, 80331 München, Germany

**Batch number: 10726009**

Printed by Printforce, the Netherlands